The Seven Deadly Sins

SAYINGS OF THE FATHERS OF THE CHURCH

The Seven Deadly Sins

Edited by Kevin M. Clarke

FOREWORD BY
MIKE AQUILINA

 The Catholic University of America Press   Washington, D.C.

In memory of Fr. Matthew L. Lamb

June 5, 1937–January 12, 2018

with deepest gratitude for his life of virtue

and his vision for Catholic higher education.

Ora pro nobis!

Copyright © 2018
The Catholic University of America Press
All rights reserved
The paper used in this publication meets the minimum requirements of American National Standards for Information Science—Permanence of Paper for Printed Library Materials, ANSI Z39.48-1984.
∞

Cataloging-in-Publication Data available from the Library of Congress
ISBN 978-0-8132-3021-4

CONTENTS

Foreword by Mike Aquilina   vii

Preface   ix

Acknowledgments   xv

List of Abbreviations   xvii

Introduction   1

1. Gluttony   23
Gluttony 23 / Self-Mastery 36

2. Lust   46
Lust 46 / Temperance and Continence 57

3. Greed   68
Greed 68 / Poverty 80

4. Anger   90
Anger 90 / Long-Suffering and Patience 102 / Almsgiving 109

5. Sloth — 115
   Sloth 115 / Work 129 / Prayer 133

6. Envy and Sadness — 140
   Envy 140 / Sadness 148 / Charity 156

7. Vainglory and Pride — 163
   Vainglory 163 / Pride 171 / Humility 179

   Conclusion — 188

   Bibliography — 199
   Scripture Index — 209
   Subject Index — 213

FOREWORD BY MIKE AQUILINA

The writings of the Church Fathers can be daunting. The books sit thick on the shelves. To open one feels a bit like taking a vow; you have got to be in it for the long haul. We know the rewards are great, because others have told us so. We know, too, because we have seen so many statues and churches dedicated to St. Augustine and St. Ambrose—and no one gets that many statues and churches without first proving their usefulness.

Still, we hesitate to make the commitment. Books of the Fathers rank with exercise equipment as possessions whose value we recognize, but whose use we avoid. I can think of no better—and more immediately helpful—way to begin to read the Fathers than in these pages, with these "sayings."

What you will find here is spiritual direction, distilled to its essence, from men whose counsel has been tested and proven by scores of generations. This is the task the Fathers relished most. "I know no other life," said Saint John Chrysostom to his congregation, "but you and the care of souls." It does not matter that these men lived so long ago. The centuries fall away in the handling of our compiler. Kevin M. Clarke has not only read the texts of the Fathers; he has breathed their air. In his introductory chapters he has produced an accessible work of intellectual history, detailing the development of a fascinating genre, the catalog of vices, in the works of both pagan and Christian authors. In subsequent chapters he helps us to understand how the church developed its understanding of each particular vice. He seems to know, however—in a more than academic way—the *kinship* of the Fathers, their counsel and direction. He knows their fatherhood. Thus, his commentary is every bit as useful as the primary sources he consults.

The saints we meet in these pages *should* be more to us than footnotes in big books. Yes, some of them were the best and brightest of their age, but they were not primarily scholars. They were pastors; they were fathers. They were daily about the business of caring for their spiritual children, raising them up in virtue, leading them away from vice. The same work remains to be done today. No advances in technology or pharmacology have eradicated the ancient sins. No new discoveries have revealed shortcuts to virtue. We stand still in need of the very practical direction the Fathers have to give.

We live in an age of unprecedented self-indulgence. So much is possible, and we want it all. The market economy—worldwide—has made it easier for more of us to enjoy more of everything, and we do. Yet we are still restless. We still desire something we cannot find even in the vast online marketplace. We still want a wisdom that we sense we will find in the tradition of our elders.

We will find what we want in the teaching of the Fathers. It is not that these men are killjoys. They argued effectively, after all, for the goodness of creation against subtle heresies that detested the things of this world. Nevertheless, the Fathers do give us pause. And we have grown unaccustomed to pausing. Kevin Clarke's book will do lasting good for us who read it.

PREFACE

> When the unclean spirit has gone out of a man, he passes through waterless places seeking rest, but he finds none. Then he says, "I will return to my house from which I came." And when he comes he finds it empty, swept, and put in order. Then he goes and brings with him seven other spirits more evil than himself, and they enter and dwell there; and the last state of that man becomes worse than the first. So shall it be also with this evil generation.[1]

Though they were first spoken of demonic possession, these words of the Savior encapsulate well, it seems to me, the teachings of the Church Fathers regarding the struggle against the vices the demons induce in the soul. It almost seems as though one can never truly conquer vice in this life. Victory over any of the capital vices leads to vainglory and pride. Humility truly is the only narrow way to perfection, as we shall see.

But why should we listen to the Fathers? Is not that very term offensive to our inclusive age? Turning to the Fathers is not to negate the profound dignity and contributions of early Christian women, of course. "Fathers" designates a select group of bishops, priests, theologians, and monks who lived at various times and in various places. Most of them are saints, but not all are recognized as such. They interpreted scripture and helped guide the church through doctrinal controversies in the first eight or nine centuries after Christ. Generally, Catholics accept that John of Damascus, who died in the mid-eighth century, is the last of the Fathers. Pope Benedict XVI said in a general audience that St. Bernard

---

[1]. Mt 12:43–45.

of Clairvaux, who lived in the twelfth century, is often considered "the last of the Fathers." Whether John marks the end of that era or whether another does, the Fathers remain an important authority. For our purposes, reading the Fathers is a sapiential activity—that is, an encounter with wisdom.

This volume aims to present short sayings (quotations) of the Fathers on the seven deadly sins, also known as the seven capital vices or the eight evil thoughts. Reading a book on vice alone would be plain drudgery. And that is not the Fathers' style either, as they often provide inspiring words concerning the development of virtues to ward off the contrary vices of the soul. Thus, the resource should become a valuable tool for homiletics and spiritual development. Most of the sayings are taken from The Fathers of the Church series published by The Catholic University of America Press. Wherever sayings are drawn from elsewhere, the source has been provided. The citations are given with each saying so that anyone looking to retrieve the context may go directly to the original source with ease.[2]

I hope this text will appeal to a wide range of audiences. Priests, deacons, and pastors of souls should find the text useful in composing homilies and ministering to the faithful. Religious and lay faithful will find many words of wisdom for instruction and meditation. Christian psychologists and counselors will discover how comprehensively the Fathers understood the human mind and the struggle with sin.[3] Academics and theologians will find a useful resource in accessing the Fathers' thought on virtue and vice. It is my hope that anyone who has never read

---

2. The nature of this volume does not often permit the full context of a particular "saying" to be given. Many of them are careful meditations or homilies on particular texts of scripture. Consider the following John Chrysostom saying that has a number of moral notes: "You see, whenever you publicize a brother's fault, you not only make him more shameless and perhaps more lethargic in his progress towards virtue, but you also render the listeners more indifferent and encourage them in their sloth—and not merely this, but also the fact that you are responsible for God being blasphemed." The text is helpful for our purposes and is cited in the chapter on sloth. It would be good for the reader who wishes to see the full scope of the context to go to the original homily, where one can see Chrysostom exhorting his faithful in light of the story of Shem and Japheth covering up rather than looking upon Noah's nakedness (cf. Gn 9:20–23).

3. Cf. George Tsakiridis, *Evagrius Ponticus and Cognitive Science: A Look at Moral Evil and the Thoughts* (Eugene, Ore.: Wipf and Stock, 2010); Dennis Okholm, *Dangerous Passions, Deadly Sins: Learning from the Psychology of Ancient Monks* (Grand Rapids, Mich.: Brazos Press, 2014).

the Church Fathers will not only find the presentation of sayings herein intriguing and accessible, but that such a one will also become emboldened to take up the writings of the Fathers. Perhaps the novice reader will have the experience shared with so many readers of the Fathers throughout the ages: the encounter with a wisdom that is as new as it is old, one that speaks to our age in a way that has not lost its relevance.

The volume, while attempting to make a modest contribution to the study of the capital vices, should also prove helpful for academic readers as well. I have tried to keep the sayings as short as possible while preserving as much as the context of the message as possible. This is a fine and challenging balance to strike, and I ask the reader's patience for longer sayings. It ought to be well noted, however, that even some of the shortest sayings import such a great wealth of theological reflection that the reader ought to take pause and reflect deeply. For example, St. Basil the Great strikes us with great spiritual force when he says plainly, "Envy is the most savage form of hatred." It is important to recognize that the Fathers were imbued with scripture, and were masters of the arts of prayer and preaching. They tend to say very much with very few words (although many said very much with very many words). They perceived some light of truth, and so words like these summon us into dialogue with them. Why is envy hatred? Why is envy savage? What is it about envy that makes it the *most* savage form of hatred? How have I myself seen envy do this?

The introductory chapter introduces and traces the development of the doctrine of the capital sins from antiquity through the era of the Fathers. The subsequent chapters will consist of brief sayings from the Fathers on each of the capital sins. The sayings have been arranged thematically within the chapters. The first part of each chapter will primarily treat the sin. Some sayings will describe the nature of the sin or the source of the disorder in the soul. The latter part of each chapter will focus on a remedy for each of the capital sins. I do not hope that this volume will fill the reader with scruples and despair. First of all, the presentation of the vices is not meant to be used as a weapon against anyone's enemies, or as a weapon to turn upon the self. Rather, knowledge of sin is key to a proper examination of conscience. As a corollary to that proposition, there also may be found substantial value in this text for confessors in helping penitents discern their own spiritual struggles. Secondly, a glimpse solely into the darkness of vice and sin can be particularly overwhelming. This is why each chapter provides some insight of the Fathers on the virtue or virtues antithetical to each vice.

The genre presented here, that of the collection of sayings (*apophthegmata*), goes back into antiquity.[4] Perhaps the most well-known examples of *apophthegmata* come to us by way of the disciples of the Desert Fathers, who produced a number of works recounting wise stories, parables, and sayings from spiritual leaders.[5] The learners would seek wisdom from an elder, literally, an "old man" (*gerōn*). These pithy wise sayings would often be recorded like this: "One of the old men used to say: 'We have found nothing written about any virtuous acts of the poor man Lazarus, except that he never murmured against the rich man, although the latter never showed him any pity; rather he bore the labor of his poverty gratefully, and for that reason was received into the bosom of Abraham.'"[6]

This volume is an effort to do a similar thing: preserving the wisdom of the elders of the former ages. That we are able to bring into a single volume the words of the Fathers on a single topic is an inevitable benefit of the work of so many gifted translators, many of whose respective translations marked the first time that these particular writings became available in English. Indeed, much remains to be done, not only in the lesser-known Fathers, but even among the "household names" of the patristic era. It makes for valuable incentive in taking up the ancient languages to know that not only are innumerable works unavailable in

---

4. Many are familiar with the *Philokalia*, which is of a similar genre, that of the *florilegium*. The difference is that while *florilegia* are collections of longer excerpts of patristic writings, *apophthegmata* are typically much shorter.

5. Cf. *The Sayings of the Desert Fathers: The Alphabetical Collection*, trans. Benedicta Ward (London: Mowbrays, 1975); *The Desert Fathers: Sayings of the Early Christian Monks*, trans. Benedicta Ward (London: Penguin Books, 2003); *The Book of the Elders: Sayings of the Desert Fathers: The Systematic Collection*, trans. John Wortley, Cistercian Studies Series [hereafter "CSS"] 240 (Trappist, Ky.: Cistercian Publications, 2012); *The Anonymous Sayings of the Desert Fathers: A Select Edition and Complete English Translation*, trans. John Wortley (Cambridge: Cambridge University Press, 2013); *Give Me a Word: The Alphabetical Sayings of the Desert Fathers*, trans. John Wortley, Popular Patristics Series [hereafter "PPS"] 52 (Yonkers, N.Y.: St. Vladimir's Seminary Press, 2014).

6. Paschasius of Dumium, *Questions and Answers of the Greek Fathers*, 4.1.

English, but others stand in great need of an update. One could spend one's whole life translating and there would remain much left to be done. Thus it is fitting to begin the quest into this topic in a spirit of gratitude for the many skilled laborers in the field who helped bring forth such a harvest of patristic literature for English speakers. May the Lord send many more.

ACKNOWLEDGMENTS

A few acknowledgments are in order, firstly to the readers of my introduction. First among them stands a dear mentor in the late Fr. Matthew Lamb, who said of this volume, "This is needed in our time when so few have any notion of the treasures of discerning wisdom in the ancients." I would also like to thank my friends and colleagues George Tsakiridis, Brandon Wanless, and Don Springer, whose critiques of my introduction immensely helped me to refine this presentation. Wanless and Springer are careful editors and themselves disciples of the Fathers; so is Tsakiridis, who wrote an excellent book on the evil thoughts, which I strongly recommend. We have a common link in the Pappas Patristic Institute, which deserves mention here as well in bringing students of the Fathers into contact under Bruce Beck's leadership, who also merits acknowledgment. I would also like to briefly acknowledge the valuable role that Logos Bible Software has played in the creation of this volume. Its interactivity and search functionality enabled helpful discoveries and encounters with ancient texts that would have only otherwise occurred only with very great strain. Having a library at one's fingertips is one of the marvels of our age. It was as though I had a dozen hired assistants helping me locate texts. I would like to thank the good people at the Catholic University of America Press, especially John Martino, who first contacted me with the idea for this text after I providentially met him at an Ave Maria University conference honoring Fr. Lamb, and Theresa Walker for her generous patience in awaiting my submission and revisions. Many thanks go also to my parents, who not only passed the faith on to me from my youth but who also have made many loving sacrifices to support my studies. Finally, and above all, I would like to acknowledge my saintly wife, Natasha, who shares the joy of rediscovering the Fathers with me and with whom I have had many delightful conversations about these sayings.

ABBREVIATIONS

ACW	Ancient Christian Writers
CCC	*Catechism of the Catholic Church*
CCSL	*Corpus Christianorum, Series Latina*
CSS	Cistercian Studies Series
CWS	Classics of Western Spirituality
FOTC	The Fathers of the Church
LF	The Library of the Fathers
LXX	*The Septuagint*
NPNF	*The Nicene and Post-Nicene Fathers*
PG	*Patrologia Graeca*
PL	*Patrologia Latina*
PPS	Popular Patristics Series
SC	Sources Chrétiennes
ST	*Summa Theologiae* (Aquinas)

The Seven Deadly Sins

Introduction

The Capital Vices

What are the capital vices? The *Catechism of the Catholic Church* identifies them as "pride, avarice, envy, wrath, lust, gluttony, and sloth or acedia."[1] But a glimpse into Christian history will show that this is perhaps too simple of an answer for our purposes. Nonetheless, this is the typical rendering of them, somewhat similar to that of Dante, who names them pride, envy, wrath, sadness, avarice, gluttony, and luxury in his *Purgatorio*.[2] The capital sins not only captured the medieval literary imagination, but also inspired artwork such as Hieronymus Bosch's ominous painting *The Seven Deadly Sins and the Four Last Things*. Bosch's list is the same as Dante's.[3] But as we shall see, there were originally eight, not seven, and even when the number went from eight to seven in the Latin West (and in a way still maintained an "eightness" in the seven), the list was slightly different from that given in the *Catechism*. Although absent

---

1. *Catechism of the Catholic Church* [hereafter "CCC"], no. 1866: "superbia, avaritia, invidia, ira, luxuria, gula, pigritia seu acedia."

2. The Italian text of Dante is similar to that of the Latin: "superbia, invidia, ira, tristizia, avarizia, gola, lussuria."

3. Indeed, the capital sins were a particular fixation in the work of Bosch, as famously illustrated by the right side of his triptych *The Garden of Earthly Delights*, wherein sinners receive their just deserts in proportion to the sins to which they were attached in this life.

from the *Catechism's* list, *vainglory* was recognized as one of the greatest evils by both East and West from the time of the Fathers through Thomas Aquinas. Instead, pride was so great a vice that it deserved to be considered on its own. Gregory the Great and Thomas Aquinas following him saw pride as the progenitrix of all the vices. Since it was of a completely higher order and most directly opposed to God, it ought not to have been counted among the capital vices.

But before pressing ahead, it ought to be observed that Dante mentioned one not found in the *Catechism* list: *sadness*. One way of understanding the vice of sadness is to describe it as sorrow over the fortune of another, thus equating it with envy (e.g., the dejection and envy of Cain), but the Fathers had a much broader notion of sadness that was far more general and referred to the dejection over sin and the unchecked passions.[4] Regardless, sadness certainly merits treatment as a vice, since Evagrius, John Cassian, Gregory, and Aquinas all include sadness as capital in their influential lists—Evagrius and Cassian his disciple did not include envy, whereas Gregory makes sloth the offshoot of sadness—but for them it seemed more properly dejection. But how could we possibly exclude envy? Indeed, this awkwardly pushes our list from the seven deadly sins, to the eight evil thoughts, to the nine naughty vices.

The vices are called "capital" (from Latin *caput*, "head") because each is as a head over similar and subordinate vices. For example, Gregory the Great writes that "from vainglory there arise disobedience, boasting, hypocrisy, contentions, obstinacies, discords, and the presumptions of novelties."[5] As such, the capital vices are the gateway drugs to countless sins (although this analogy is admittedly weak because a "gateway drug" is usually considered to be less serious than the ones that follow, whereas with the vices, it is the other way around). Because of the seriousness of the spiritual threat posed by the vices, they put before the soul a type of spiritual *fight or flight* dilemma for self-preservation. Surrender is not an option for the soul who wishes to persevere in grace. Some vices, such as envy, require the believer to engage in direct combat. With envy, one

---

4. See John Chrysostom, *Commentary on John*, hom. 75, on the envy of Cain.
5. Gregory the Great, *Morals on the Book of Job*, The Library of the Fathers [hereafter "LF"] (Oxford: John Henry Parker, 1847–50), 31.45 (88).

must tackle the temptation directly. To take flight when it comes to envy would be to only perpetuate the vice's hold over the soul. Other vices, such as lust, require the believer to take to flight. When it comes to the temptations of the flesh, the last thing the soul needs is the presence of the temptation. One who rushes into battle foolishly is not engaging in courage but is acting rashly.

Virtue and Vice among Gentiles and Jews in Antiquity

It is not as though Christianity marked the first moral reflection on virtue and vice that the world had ever seen. Knowledge of the virtues and the vices is not the same as knowledge of the new law revealed by Christ and given by the grace of the Holy Spirit to the faithful.[6] For centuries before Christ, philosophers reflected upon the good life and what it meant to truly live. Plato divided the soul into three parts, the rational, spirited (or irascible), and appetitive.[7] Each of these he corresponded to the divisions of political life in some way. His greatest student, Aristotle, identified each of the virtues as a mean between two vices, one a vice of defect, and one a vice of excess. So courage, for example, is the mean between cowardice and rashness, temperance the mean between insensibility and self-indulgence, and so on.[8] Aristotle saw clearly the difficulty of virtuous living, saying that the whole challenge of living virtuously is that of discovering and maintaining the mean of each virtue. He compares the search for the virtuous mean with finding the center of a

---

6. Cf. CCC, nos. 1965–74.

7. Plato, *Republic* IV.438a–443e. The trichotomy of the soul would become very important for Neoplatonic moral reflection in early Christianity. For example, Jerome writes concerning this passage, "We read in Plato, and it is a common dogma among the philosophers, that there are three passions in the human soul: *to logistikon*, which we can translate 'rational,' *to thymikon*, which we call 'full of anger' or 'irascible,' and *to epithymētikon*, which we call 'desirous.' That philosopher thinks that our rational part resides in the brain, anger in the gall bladder, and desire in the liver. And therefore, if we take the Gospel-leaven of the Holy Scriptures, which has been mentioned above, the three passions of the human soul are gathered into one. Thus by means of reason we possess prudence, by anger we have hatred of the vices, and by desire we have the longing for the virtues. And all this takes place through the doctrine of the Gospel, which Mother Church has presented to us" (*Commentary on Matthew*, II.13:33).

8. Cf. Aristotle, *Nicomachean Ethics* 1108b11–1109a19.

circle, navigating a ship, and straightening a crooked sapling.[9] Such endeavors would be quite challenging, as anyone who has tried to balance books on one's head can imagine, or who has attempted to correct a fishtailing car. Perhaps this is one of the reasons that our present world has such difficulty in attaining virtuous living. Virtues are no longer sought; instead, people are more inclined to seek a rule that applies in all cases. This tendency we have inherited from the Enlightenment and especially Immanuel Kant. Achieving virtue, however, really does require one to struggle between contraries. With respect to anger, it is so much easier to be irascible than to be mild. It is also much easier to be apathetic than to be mild.

Further, for the ancients the virtues and vices play an important role in the art of rhetoric, that is, oratory. Various types of speech, for example, necessitated that the speaker identify virtues and vices. Epideictic (demonstrative) discourse—award presentations, funeral orations, invectives against a political opponent, and the like—is concerned with assigning praise or blame in order to convince an audience of someone's honor or shamefulness. Thus, if a speaker wished to praise someone, he had to amplify the individual's virtues and depreciate the individual's vices. If a speaker wanted to blame or censure someone, he had to amplify vices and depreciate virtues. Aristotle lists the following virtues, and gives opposing vices for some of them: justice (injustice), courage (cowardice), self-control (lack of control), magnificence (stinginess), magnanimity (small-mindedness), liberality (illiberality), gentleness, prudence, and wisdom.[10] And if such a speaker were to be convincing, he had better be virtuous. This amounts to what is known as a speaker's ethical appeal. Such wisdom would carry into the Latin West. Similarly, the *Rhetorica ad Herennium*, attributed to Cicero, describes how to earn the goodwill of the audience by magnifying the speaker's cause and dis-

---

9. Cf. Aristotle, *Nicomachean Ethics* 1109a20–1109b7. In this volume, Didymus the Blind also demonstrates this principle at work in Christian thought: "Whereas liberality, the willingness to share, is commendable, miserliness is a veering to the left, while prodigality in wasting money is thought to be on the right when it is spent not on what is necessary and proper but on the pursuit of base pleasures" (*Commentary on Zechariah* 12:6–7). Similarly, Gregory of Nyssa calls this mean the "royal highway," from which one must not deviate either to the left by defect of virtue or to the right by excess of virtue (*Life of Moses*, II.287–90).

10. Aristotle, *Rhetoric* I.9.1366b.

paraging the adversaries. He lists the vices an orator ought to bring forth in order to disparage the opponent:

We shall force hatred upon them by adducing some base, highhanded, treacherous, cruel, impudent, malicious, or shameful act of theirs. We shall make our adversaries unpopular by setting forth their violent behavior, their dominance, factiousness, wealth, lack of self-restraint, high birth, clients, hospitality, club allegiance, or marriage alliances, and by making clear that they rely more upon these supports than upon the truth. We shall bring our adversaries into contempt by presenting their idleness, cowardice, sloth, and luxurious habits.[11]

This list is quite vast and includes both vices and non-vices such as unmerited privileges. Horace comes a bit closer to the list of capital vices. He writes:

Is your bosom fevered with avarice and sordid covetousness? There are spells and sayings whereby you may soothe the pain and cast much of the malady aside. Are you swelling with ambition? There are fixed charms which can fashion you anew, if with cleansing rites you read the booklet thrice. The slave to envy, anger, sloth, wine, lewdness—no one is so savage that he cannot be tamed, if only he lend to treatment a patient ear.[12]

Indeed, these hopeful reflections are strikingly similar to what we will see in the Fathers. One ought not to think, however, that Christian reflection is primarily indebted to Greek or Roman thought in the formation of moral theory. The closest affinity seems to be with the Testament of Reuben, part of the *Testament of the Twelve Patriarchs*, a pseudepi-

---

11. *Rhetorica ad Herennium*, I.v.8. "In odium rapiemus si quid eorum spurce, superbe, perfidiose, crudeliter, confidenter, malitiose, flagitiose factum proferemus. In invidiam trahemus si vim, si potentiam, si factionem, divitias, incontinentiam, nobilitatem, clientelas, hospitium, sodalitatem, adfinitates adversariorum proferemus, et his adiumentis magis quam veritati eos confidere aperiemus. In contemptionem adducemus si inertiam, ignaviam, desidiam, luxuriam adversariorum proferemus."

12. Horace, *Ep. 1 to Maecenas*.
"Fervet avaritia miseroque cupidine pectus:
sunt verba et voces, quibus hunc lenire dolorem
possis et magnam morbi deponere partem.
laudis amore tumes; sunt certa piacula, quae te
ter pure lecto poterunt recreare libello.
invidus, iracundus, iners, vinosus, amator,
nemo adeo ferus est, ut non mitescere possit,
si modo culturae patientem commodet aurem."

graphical work from the late second century B.C. that purports to contain the dying words of the sons of Jacob. In it the author lists seven spirits of deceit: fornication, gluttony, strife, vainglory, pride, lying, and injustice.[13] Perhaps later Christian tradition drew from this list, though there remains a fairly strong dissimilarity. Missing among these are envy, avarice, and acedia.[14] It also ought to be observed that anger is more interior than strife.

Now, this is all helpful on some level, since so many of the Fathers were educated in the wisdom of antiquity and prized whatever treasures they could from Greek and Jewish thought. Yet, the Fathers in a more particular way breathe the language of the scriptures. To that we now turn.

Scriptural Bases for the Capital Vices

The Fathers' reflections on the vices as recorded in this book are deeply scriptural.[15] While I cannot comprehensively treat the New Testament view of vice in this brief introduction, I will briefly offer some of the scriptures most pertinent to this study.[16] The New Testament does not

13. Morton W. Bloomfield, *The Seven Deadly Sins: An Introduction to the History of a Religious Concept, with Special Reference to Medieval English Literature* (Ann Arbor: Michigan State University Press, 1967), 44–45: "*porneia, gastrimargia, machē, kenodoxia, hyperphania, pseudos, adikia.*" Bloomfield also points out that the "spirits of deceit" has some parallel also in *The Shepherd of Hermas*, a Christian mystical work of the second century A.D., which speaks of an angel of luxury and deceit (49).

14. An observation that may further support knowledge of the Jewish tradition, but modification of it: it is interesting to note that there is a phonetic similarity by way of consonantal metathesis between injustice (*adikia*) and acedia (*akēdia*).

15. See, e.g., the scripture index in the back matter of this book. Some who are not familiar with the Fathers may find this dependence on the authority of the Bible strange. Contemporary thinkers tend to compartmentalize branches of the sciences into isolated units, and unfortunately this fragmentation occurs in theology too. So, for example, one finds systematic theology, moral theology, historical theology, liturgical theology, biblical theology, biblical hermeneutics, and so on. That in itself is not a problem. But the prevailing view has been that the more self-contained and independent each one is from the other, the better. This is one of the difficulties that Cardinal Ratzinger brought to the fore in his 1988 Erasmus lecture, where he lamented the chasm that had formed between biblical hermeneutics and systematic theology. Cf. his "Biblical Interpretation in Conflict," in *God's Word: Scripture, Tradition, Office* (San Francisco: Ignatius Press, 2008). But this was not so for the Fathers who approached the theological science as a unified whole. In approaching the Fathers on this topic, one does not find the type of moral reasoning we have grown accustomed to in a post-Kantian world, so filled with the language of rule and duty. Vice is most plainly identified in conversation with scripture, for it is acting or living contrary to the revealed law, to fail in the twofold charity commanded by Jesus Christ.

16. Angela Tilby in her helpful book on Evagrius and the deadly sins has given a brief treat-

attempt to group sins into a list of seven or eight from which all the rest come. Later Christian tradition came to enumerate the capital sins in their current form. Nonetheless, the New Testament writings in particular speak unambiguously concerning each of the seven, so it is not as though tradition has conjured this list out of nowhere.

Is there anywhere in the New Testament where we find a list closely resembling the capital sins? Not quite. A good starting point, however, might be taken from the Gospel of Mark, in which Jesus said, "For from within, out of the heart of man, come evil thoughts, fornication, theft, murder, adultery, coveting, wickedness, deceit, licentiousness, envy, slander, pride, foolishness. All these evil things come from within, and they defile a man."[17] Here, one finds several of the capital sins: coveting (*pleonexia*), envy (*ophthalmos ponēros*, literally, "evil eye"), and pride (*hyperēphania*). Since the "evil thoughts" would become the very paradigm for discussing the capital vices in the Greek East, the development of the capital vices tradition stems from this passage. From it we could also include fornication (*porneia*) and murders (*phonoi*), if we take this in conjunction with Christ's message about lust and anger.[18] The key point is that the vices are not demonstrated by an absence of vicious behavior, but are known by God who sees into the heart. What's more, man's composite unity—that is, his matter-form composition of body and soul—tends toward a procession from the interior (soul) to the exterior (body). Thus, one already defiled by interior thoughts of greed becomes disposed to work greedy deeds.

Paul, too, is inclined to groupings of sin.[19] He writes to Timothy, "But understand this, that in the last days there will come times of stress. For men will be lovers of self, lovers of money, proud, arrogant, abusive, disobedient to their parents, ungrateful, unholy, inhuman, implacable, slanderers, profligates, fierce, haters of good, treacherous, reckless, swollen with conceit, lovers of pleasure rather than lovers of God, holding

---

ment of the biblical background of each of the capital sins; see *The Seven Deadly Sins: Their Origin in the Spiritual Teaching of Evagrius the Hermit* (London: Society for Promoting Christian Knowledge, 2009).

17. Mk 7:21–23.
18. Cf. Mt 5:21–32.
19. Cf. Rom 1:29–31; 1 Cor 6:9–10; Gal 5:19–21; Col 3:5–8.

the form of religion but denying the power of it. Avoid such people."[20] Another similar list can be found in Galatians, where Paul says, "Now the works of the flesh are plain: fornication, impurity, licentiousness, idolatry, sorcery, enmity, strife, jealousy, anger, selfishness, dissension, party spirit, envy, drunkenness, carousing, and the like. I warn you, as I warned you before, that those who do such things shall not inherit the kingdom of God."[21] Interestingly, Paul follows this passage with the fruits of the Holy Spirit: "But the fruit of the Spirit is love, joy, peace, patience, kindness, goodness, faithfulness, gentleness, self-control."[22] This tendency to contrast darkness with light and vice with virtue would become well-explored in the patristic era.

In the Johannine writings, vice and sin could be classified in this manner: "For all that is in the world, the lust of the flesh and the lust of the eyes and the pride of life, is not of the Father but is of the world."[23] The contrast between the darkness of the world and the light of God is one of the primary themes in Johannine literature. Throughout his works, John speaks about the light overcoming the darkness, the manifestation of the Son's glory, and that the apostles have seen Jesus and so they have seen the Father.[24] Unfortunately, men loved the darkness more than the light because of their evil deeds.[25] Christ was sold at night by one who was a thief, and he would be crucified between thieves, and betrayed in the cold.[26] In the eternal city, the glory of God is light, and the Lamb is the light, and there shall be nothing in it unclean, "nor anyone who practices abomination or falsehood."[27]

So how did the Church Fathers synthesize the broad scriptural teaching into the more traditional grouping? It was a sort of natural development of biblical reflection and interpretation in the Greek East and Latin West.

---

20. 2 Tm 3:1–5.
21. Gal 5:19–21.
22. Gal 5:22–23.
23. 1 Jn 2:16.
24. Cf. Jn 1:4–5, 1:14, 14:9.
25. Cf. Jn 3:19.
26. Cf. Jn 12:6; Jn 18:25.
27. Cf. Rv 21:23; Rv 21:27.

The Eastern Church Fathers: The Evil Thoughts

Many of the Church Fathers write their works before any known articulation of the capital vices. "Known" is an important distinction, as the beginning of oral or catechetical traditions likely predate first written records, and lost written records could predate preserved written records. It could be that Evagrius is the first to conceive of the evil thoughts, but it also could be that his predecessors passed it on to him. Nonetheless, it may come to surprise Roman Catholics that the genesis of the doctrine of the capital sins seems to originate not in the Latin West, but in the Byzantine East. In the West, it is more common to refer to the deadly sins or the capital vices. In the East at its earliest expression, the tradition that developed was that of the eight evil thoughts.

Evagrius of Pontus (ca. 345–99)

Evagrius Ponticus was a much revered spiritual master of the monastic life. He is one of the first to detail the "eight thoughts" that disturb the monks and keep them from virtue. He does so in the late fourth century. His work would not only become influential over the monastic tradition, but also on John Cassian who brought the doctrine of the capital vices into the West in the early fifth century. Thus, he is a consequential figure standing at the fountainhead of the parallel traditions of both East and West. He writes, "There are eight general and basic categories of thoughts in which are included every thought. First is that of gluttony, then impurity, avarice, sadness, anger, acedia, vainglory, and last of all, pride. It is not in our power to determine whether we are disturbed by these thoughts, but it is up to us to decide if they are to linger within us or not and whether or not they are to stir up our passions."[28] Evagrius focuses on the practical life of asceticism, a sort of spiritual combat that the monk must win in order to grow in virtue. As he progresses in the spiritual life, the nature of the temptations changes. Much like Clement

---

28. Evagrius of Pontus, *Praktikos*, 6. Sayings from the *Praktikos* and the *Chapters on Prayer* in this volume are taken from *The Praktikos and the Chapters on Prayer*, trans. John Eudes Bamberger, OCSO, CSS 4 (Collegeville, Minn.: Liturgical Press, 1972). Sayings from Evagrius's *Antirrhetikos* are taken from David Brakke's translation, *Talking Back: A Monastic Handbook for Combating Demons*, CSS 229 (2009).

of Alexandria before him, Evagrius is indebted to the Stoic notion of *apatheia*, a sort of enduring detachment that, according to Evagrius, causes profound peace in an undisturbed monk who is liberated from the vicissitudes of the passions.

Evagrius's small treatise *On the Eight Thoughts* was originally attributed to Nilus of Ancyra, but Robert Sinkewicz observes that most scholars follow the evidence in the manuscript tradition and attribute this work to Evagrius.[29] One begins with gluttony, meant to be conquered by abstinence. Whereas abstinence leads invariably to chastity, gluttony leads to impurity (often referred to simply as fornication, considered as general impurity).[30] The monastic life free of possessions best remedied the vice of avarice, a vice that made the removal of other vices impossible.[31] Not only does anger make the monk unpleasant, but it makes prayer and contemplation impossible.[32] Sadness or grief is most akin to jealousy. It is born of anger and is deeply linked with the love of the world. It is often seen in the monk who longs to return to his former state of life. Perhaps in the contemporary religious or layperson, this could translate into a longing for "the glory days" (that is, days quite vainglorious before conversion). The cure for grief, according to Evagrius, is impassibility.[33] Here and elsewhere, Evagrius connects sadness with the love of pleasure in general.[34] There is another important feature to sadness for Evagrius: that of fear. One who struggles with sadness not only fears that God does not hear his prayer, but such a one is in constant torment from the fear of the demons, their manifestations, and their powers.[35] Acedia prevents the monk's stillness and leads to impa-

---

29. In some manuscripts, it is also called *On the Eight Spirits of Wickedness*. Robert E. Sinkewicz, *Evagrius of Pontus: The Greek Ascetic Corpus* (Oxford: Oxford University Press, 2003), 67. Though most of the Greek manuscripts attribute authorship to Nilus, manuscripts existing in Sahidic Coptic, Syriac, Arabic, and Ethiopic that attribute the work to Evagrius call into question this assumption.
30. Evagrius of Pontus, *Eight Evil Thoughts* (*Patrologia Graeca* [hereafter "PG"] 79:1148C–D).
31. Ibid., PG 79:1152B–C.
32. Ibid., PG 79:1153C–1156A.
33. Ibid., PG 79:1156B–1157B.
34. Cf. Evagrius of Pontus, *Praktikos*, 19: "The man who flees from all worldly pleasures is an impregnable tower before the assaults of the demon of sadness. For sadness is a deprivation of sensible pleasure, whether actually present or only hoped for" (cf. ibid., 10).
35. This theme is especially strong in Evagrius's *Antirrhetikos*.

tience with spiritual tasks such as reading and prayer. Overcoming acedia requires great perseverance.[36] Vainglory, seeking esteem from men for the virtues of the soul, is the great enemy of virtue.[37] Evagrius compares vainglory to a bag with holes in it, unable to contain the rewards of virtue. He compares it to bringing a blemished victim of sacrifice before God. Vainglory and pride are as thunder and lightning.[38] Finally, pride is the greatest threat to the soul seeking perfection; a fall from on high could destroy it. Thus, humility is the antithesis of pride. Evagrius says that while God hears the prayer of the humble person, the prayer of the proud exasperates him.[39]

Maximus the Confessor (580–662)

Maximus the Confessor was a monk who is best remembered for his engagement with the monothelite heresy of the seventh century. For our purposes, he gives a specific program for healing the vices. His spiritual teachings are in continuity with Evagrius, but are more anchored in the patristic and philosophical traditions. Maximus is a realist with regard to the difficulty in rooting out the destructive passions. One cannot do so without asceticism. His words, though spoken in reference to a monastic community, are no less true for us today. For Maximus, the soul is tripartite, comprised of rational, irascible, and concupiscible elements. He associates each of the vices with the "trichotomy of the soul." Thus, each of the vices relate to one or more of the concupiscible, irascible, or rational elements in man. For example, gluttony has to do with the concupiscible element of the soul, whereas vainglory and pride are vices of the rational element.[40] Obviously, since the body and soul are a unity, the vices affect each part of the soul in a way. For Maximus as for Evagrius, the vices have corresponding virtues, but he is not bound to strict correspon-

---

36. Evagrius of Pontus, *Eight Evil Thoughts* (PG 79:1157D–1160C).
37. More recently, Okholm has linked vainglory (and pride) with what the contemporary cultural movement he calls "self-esteemia," a movement that has undesirable manifestations via our narcissistic and aggressive tendencies; cf. *Dangerous Passions*, 160–61.
38. Evagrius of Pontus, *Eight Evil Thoughts* (PG 79:1160D–1161C). Cf. Lv 22:22.
39. Ibid., PG 79:1161C–1164D.
40. Cf. Lars Thunberg, *Man and the Cosmos: The Vision of St. Maximus the Confessor* (Crestwood, N.Y.: St. Vladimir's Seminary Press, 1997), 94.

dence, as Lars Thunberg shows. Self-mastery (*enkrateia*) and temperance (*sōphrosynē*) correspond to the bodily passions in general, but to gluttony and fornication primarily; the poverty (*aktēmosynē*) of monks contrasts with avarice; charity (*agapē*) opposes grief; long-suffering (*makrothymia*) opposes wrath; and humility (*tapeinōsis*) not only opposes pride, but all the virtues.[41]

In the *Centuries on Charity* in particular, Maximus recommends a specific ascetical program to heal the various disorders of the soul, which have self-love (*philautia*), "the mother of vices," at their source.[42] Regarding the ascetical program, he writes, "fasting, hard labor, and vigils do not allow concupiscence to grow, while solitude, contemplation, and prayer and desire for God decrease it and make it disappear. And similarly is the case with anger: for example, long-suffering, the forgetting of offenses, and meekness check it and do not allow it to grow, while love, almsgiving, kindness, and benevolence make it diminish."[43] Elsewhere, he recommends nourishing the rational part of the soul with "spiritual reading, meditation, and prayer," the irascible part with "spiritual love, which is opposed to hate," and the concupiscible with "temperance and self-mastery." Certain works especially assist in the combat of the chief vices: "A secret labor removes vainglory; attributing our upright deeds to God removes pride."[44] Not to be neglected, however, is the body, which is to be given "food and clothing and only what is necessary."[45]

Ultimately, for Maximus, the whole life of virtue is the beginning of the path of spiritual progress that leads one to pure prayer and is oriented toward deification (*theōsis*). The life of virtue enables the soul to participate in God, who is "the substance of the virtues."[46] Included with the idea of virtue (which with judgment destroys evil) is that of ascetic practice (*praxis*) coupled with dispassion (*apatheia*), which also leads

---

41. Cf. Thunberg, *Microcosm and Mediator: The Theological Anthropology of Maximus the Confessor* (Lund: C. W. K. Gleerup, 1965), 295–99.
42. Maximus the Confessor, *Centuries on Charity*, 2.57. Sayings from the *Centuries* are taken from George C. Berthold's translation in *Maximus Confessor: Selected Writings*, Classics of Western Spirituality [hereafter "CWS"] (1985).
43. Ibid., 2.47.
44. Ibid., 3.62 (editor's translation).
45. Ibid., 4.44.
46. Maximus the Confessor, *Ambiguum* 7 (PG 91:1084A).

to participation in the divine.[47] Maximus explains that "through ascetic practice coupled with dispassion, we are led up to knowledge, and with minds free of matter we are raised up from there to mystical contemplation and imitation into divine realities, and even, I make bold to add, to participation in God."[48]

The Western Fathers and the Capital Sins

Augustine of Hippo (354–430)

It may seem to be perplexing to begin with Augustine, the great "doctor of grace" who lived in northern Africa, as John Cassian is typically taken to be the source of the West's treatment of the capital vices. Nonetheless, Augustine draws our attention by his characteristic profundity. While Augustine seems to predate the articulation of the doctrine of the capital vices, in the second book of his *Confessions*, he provides a moving examination of the various vices as he examines himself after having stolen some fruit with some other youths when he was sixteen years old.[49] He stole them not because he was hungry; rather, he had an abundance of the fruit at home. He stole them simply for the sake of stealing. Afterwards, he did not enjoy them; rather, he simply cast them aside.

Presciently, Augustine manages to name (or accurately describe) the sins that would come to be recognized as the capital vices, in addition to adding others as well. He writes:

> Pride [*superbia*] mimics loftiness, whereas Thou art the one God, lifted above all things. Ambition [*ambitio*], too, what does it seek but honors and glory, whereas Thou art alone to be honored beyond all things and glorious for eternity? The cruelty [*saevitia*] of powerful men desires to be feared, but who should be feared except God alone? For, what can be snatched or withdrawn from Thy power—when, or where, or whither, or by what means can this be done? The caresses [*blanditiae*] of wanton men are desirous of a return of love, but nothing is more caressing than Thy charity, nor is anything loved more healthfully than

---

47. Maximus the Confessor, *Ambiguum* 32 (PG 91:1281D). This is not to be confused with contemporary notions of praxis.
48. Maximus the Confessor, *Ambiguum* 32 (PG 91:1285B).
49. Cf. Augustine, *Confessions*, II.6.12–14.

Thy truth, which is beautiful and bright above all things. Curiosity [*curiositas*] appears to mimic scientific study, while Thou knowest all in the highest way. Even ignorance [*ignorantia*] itself and stupidity [*stultitia*] are dressed up in the name of simplicity and innocence, but nothing can be found more simple than Thou. What is more innocent than Thou, since the things which injure evil men are their own works. Sloth [*ignavia*] inclines to a kind of rest, but what is true rest apart from the Lord? Lust [*luxuria*] craves to be called satisfaction and abundance, but Thou indeed art fullness and the unceasing plenty of incorruptible sweetness. Wasteful spending [*effusio liberalitatis*] hides under the shadow of liberality, but Thou art the most bountiful Giver of all good things. Avarice [*avaritia*] wishes to have many possessions; Thou dost possess all things. Envy [*invidentia*] quarrels over excellence; what is more excellent than Thou? Anger [*ira*] seeks revenge; who attains vindication more justly than Thou? Fear [*timor*] grows horrified at the unaccustomed and unexpected aspect of things which threaten what it loves, being concerned for its own safety.[50] But what is unusual to Thee, what is unexpected? Who takes from Thee what Thou lovest? Where is unshakeable safety, unless with Thee? Sorrow [*tristitia*] pines away at the loss of things in which passionate longing had its delight, desiring to be immune, as Thou art, from the possibility of anything being taken from it.[51]

Augustine is searching out his sin among the vices. In his retrospection, he does not attempt to trivialize his sin as he may have done in his youth. For Augustine, his action was a perverse attempt to be like God, going out and setting himself up over and against God. He sees the vices as a sort of imitation of God. For Augustine, the act of theft against the law caused pleasure simply because it was against the law. Such an examination may seem scrupulous by today's standards. One could easily suggest that stealing fruit would be a venial sin or perhaps even no sin at all. For Augustine, however, who looks beyond the object and circumstances and into his "perverse" intention, this was no small affair. It was an act of rebellion.[52]

The drama of the story aside, it is worth looking at the vices on his list, which is very skillfully arranged. Penetrating insight into individual vices appear dispersed throughout the corpus of Augustine's writings,

---

50. On vindication, cf. Rom 12:19.
51. Augustine, *Confessions*, II.6.13.
52. Cf. Augustine, *Confessions*, II.6.14.

but here he gathers his reflections into one. It is worth noting that pride is at the beginning of the list and followed immediately by *ambitio*, a vice very similar to vainglory. Further, each vice has a contrast. The vice is introduced, and the contrast is found in God himself in a highly organized arrangement:

> Avarice wishes to have many possessions;
> Thou dost possess all things.
> Envy quarrels over excellence;
> what is more excellent than Thou?

In sum, he lists fourteen vices (arguably fifteen, though it seems that *ignorantia* and *stultitia* should be taken together, since they are organized together). Among those considered to be the eight evil thoughts by his contemporaries in the East, Augustine names some explicitly by the Latin equivalent: pride (*superbia*), avarice (*avaritia*), envy (*invidentia*), and wrath (*ira*). He names both sloth (*ignavia*) and sadness (*tristitia*), which typically are considered together. His description of *ambitio* matches that of vainglory, as does his account of *blanditiae lascivientium* match that of lust. *Luxuria* could be more accurately considered gluttony according to Augustine's description. No less fascinating are the additional vices he includes in the list, such as cruelty and curiosity.[53] Thus, while Augustine is often excluded from the conversation in many volumes on the capital vices, he clearly merits careful attention. Many of his words appear throughout this volume.

---

53. For example, Augustine says that *curiositas*, which today is often (and wrongly) praised as the highest academic virtue, mimics scientific study. Who has ever attended a commencement in which curiosity has not been praised? Most speakers in doing so mean to highlight the virtue of studiousness. Cultural forces being what they are, studiousness has acquired somewhat of a pejorative aspect to it, suggesting "bookish" or "aloof." One thinks of the same phenomenon with regard to present-day culture's infatuation with "pride." Aquinas contrasts curiosity, the vice, with studiousness, the virtue. Studiousness (*studiositas*) represents the mean in the pursuit of knowledge, properly directed. Curiosity, on the other hand, represents some sort of excess. There could be evil associated with the learning, as in someone who wishes to take pride in his knowledge. Also, there could be some disorder in the pursuit of knowledge, for which Aquinas gives four reasons: pursuing knowledge that is less profitable; seeking to know from those from whom it is unlawful to learn (e.g., learning the future from demons); seeking to know creatures without directing that knowledge toward its final end, God; and seeking to know that which is beyond the individual's own capacity. Cf. *Summa Theologiae* [hereafter "ST"] II-II, qq. 166–67.

16   INTRODUCTION

John Cassian (ca. 360–ca. 435)

Columba Stewart characterizes John Cassian with the word "elusiveness." He lived concurrently with Evagrius and Augustine. Cassian says very little of himself. As Stewart says, "His humility, however virtuous, is his biographer's first challenge."[54] Fortunately, our text is not too concerned with biographical data. This much is clear: Cassian was an authority in monasticism who left his imprint throughout the ancient world.

Cassian devotes the majority of his *Institutes of the Coenobia*, a fifth-century monastic work, to a treatment of the "eight principal faults."[55] For Cassian, these are given in the same order as that of Evagrius, though it is uncertain whether Cassian takes his list directly from Evagrius or from someone else in Egypt.[56] Further, he compares the capital sins to the nations of Canaan, and he includes Egypt in order to bring the number to eight. Cassian lists gluttony (*gastrimargia*), fornication (*fornicationis*), covetousness (*philargyria*), anger (*ira*), sadness (*tristitia*), acedia (*acedia*), vainglory (*cenodoxia*), and pride (*superbia*). The only difference between the Evagrian list and the Cassian one is the ordering of anger and sadness. Further illustrating the Greek influence upon Cassian is the fact that he prefers Latin transliterations of several of the Greek terms, for example, *gastrimargia* (*gastrimargia*), *philargyria* (*philargyria*), *cenodoxia* (*kenodoxia*). Cassian's thought would have a strong influence upon those following him in the Latin West, especially Gregory the Great. According to Morton Bloomfield, Cassian's thought influenced the church in Gaul and exerted a lasting influence in Ireland and England.[57] It is important to observe that if we trace the line from

---

54. Columba Stewart, OSB, *Cassian the Monk*, Oxford Studies in Historical Theology (Oxford: Oxford University Press, 1998).

55. For this volume, most of the quotations will be drawn from the *The Nicene and Post-Nicene Fathers* [hereafter "NPNF"], vol. 11, ed. Philip Schaff and Henry Wace, trans. Edgar C. S. Gibson (New York: Christian Literature Company, 1894). Curiously, however, one finds this note in place of book VI on the spirit of fornication: "We have thought best to omit altogether the translation of this book." Fortunately, the full work has become available also through Ramsey's translation in Ancient Christian Writers [hereafter "ACW"].

56. Or Nilus (see the section on Evagrius above). Cf. Bloomfield, *The Seven Deadly Sins*, 71.

57. Bloomfield, *The Seven Deadly Sins*, 71–72.

Evagrius to Cassian, we still have eight in Cassian; the list has not yet winnowed to seven.

Gregory the Great (ca. 540–604)

With Gregory, the vices make a subtle transition from eight to seven and one. In his great commentary on Job written in the late sixth century, the *Moralia*, Gregory the Great outlines what he calls "seven principal vices" (*septem principalia vitia*).[58] While the teaching on the seven capital sins is principally contained in Book XXXI of this work, a small portion of the overall text, this work would become a focal point in the development of the doctrine of the capital sins. The *Moralia* would become the standard text for Thomas Aquinas in his questions of the *Summa Theologiae* that deal with the capital vices. Gregory lists the seven in the following order: vainglory, envy, anger, sadness, avarice, gluttony, and lust. These seven are all born from one, namely, pride.[59]

Gregory, commenting on a verse in Job—"he smelleth the battle afar off, the encouraging of the captains, and the shouting of the army"—describes the above seven principal vices as a cohort of captains each leading its own army of vices against the soul.[60] In command over the captains is their queen ruler, pride (*vitiorum regina superbia*). Gregory says that the first offspring of pride is vainglory, and the other vices follow in order.[61] As an aside, it is interesting to note that the firstborn of pride for Gregory, vainglory, is not among those that made it out of the Middle Ages.

Returning to Gregory's allegory, it is the case for the soul that per-

---

58. Gregory the Great, *Morals on the Book of Job*, XXXI.45.87–89. English translations taken from *Morals on the Book of Job*, LF 18, 21, 23, 31 (Oxford: John Henry Parker, 1844–50). Cistercian Publications is currently in the process of publishing a new English translation by Brian Kerns in six volumes from the critical edition (the first volume was published in 2014). Additionally, another complete contemporary translation of the *Moralia* may be found in French in *Sources Chrétiennes* [hereafter "SC"] 32b, 212, 221, 476, 525, and 538. Book XXXI is found in SC 525, which contains the Latin that I used in this book. The Latin may also be found in Migne's *Patrologia Latina* [hereafter "PL"] 75 and 76, and in the critical edition, *S. Gregorii Magni Moralia in Job*, in *Corpus Christianorum, Series Latina* [hereafter "CCSL"] 143, 143A, and 143B (Turnhout: Brepols, 1979–85).

59. Cf. Gregory the Great, *Morals on the Book of Job*, XXXI.45.87: "Primae autem eius soboles, septem nimirum principalia vitia, de hac virulenta radice proferuntur, scilicet inanis gloria, invidia, ira, tristitia, avaritia, ventris ingluvies, luxuria."

60. Job 39:25 [D-R].

61. Cf. Gregory the Great, *Morals on the Book of Job*, XXXI.45.89.

haps one or more of the capital vices may make its way into a "neglected mind." Then, with great furor and clamor, in come the armies. Once the howling armies of each respective vice find their way into the soul, they lay it waste with great cruelty. "The soldier of God," however, sees the battle coming from a distance and endeavors to protect himself against the vices. He sniffs the vices out in their approach, and prepares himself accordingly.

Thomas Aquinas (1225–74)

Although Thomas Aquinas is not one of the Church Fathers, he is important for our consideration. For those looking for a deeper engagement of the virtues or the vices, he is the most relevant theologian. An exposition of each of the virtues of vices found in our little book may be located in the second part (I-II and II-II) of the *Summa Theologiae*. He has more to say about the virtues and capital vices than we say in the whole of our little text.

Thomas is writing from the vantage point of scholasticism, with a great many witnesses and resources at his disposal. Thus in his work he articulated a thorough treatment of the study of sin (hamartiology), and his analysis is theological, philosophical, and thoroughly systematic. Sin and vice are often used interchangeably. But when people hear "sin," they often think of something that is quite instantiated. It does not always carry that meaning, however. Sin can refer to habitual sin, for example, where one has an enduring commitment to a particular sin. Though sin and vice are certainly related, sin is more properly understood as an act that is opposed to virtue. Vice, however, is to be understood as the opposite of the essence of virtue. Virtue is a *habitus*, or a certain mode of the perfection of a power.[62] Elsewhere, Aquinas says that virtue is a "disposition whereby the subject is well disposed according to the mode of its nature." Vice, by contrast, "seems to consist in its *not* being disposed in a way befitting its nature."[63]

---

62. ST I-II, q. 55, a. 1. The English "habit" simply does not convey the notion found in the Latin *habitus*.

63. ST I-II, q. 71, a. 1, co. (emphasis added). Cf. a. 2, that vice is contrary to nature.

For Aquinas, the primary authority on the capital vices is not Evagrius or John Cassian, but Gregory the Great. Aquinas follows Gregory consistently and closely regarding the capital sins.[64] He lists the seven as vainglory, envy, anger, avarice, sadness, gluttony, and lust.[65] Later, Aquinas counts acedia among the seven, treating it interchangeably with sorrow, as he says that "sloth is a kind of sorrow."[66] On the authority of Psalm 118:51, he says that pride is the greatest sin.[67] Like Gregory, however, he does not designate pride as one of the seven capital vices. He writes that

pride may be considered in two ways; first in itself, as being a special sin; secondly, as having a general influence towards all sins. Now the capital vices are said to be certain special sins from which many kinds of sin arise. Wherefore some, considering pride in the light of a special sin, numbered it together with the other capital vices. But Gregory, taking into consideration its general influence towards all vices, as explained above, did not place it among the capital vices, but held it to be the queen and mother of all the vices.[68]

Aquinas brings an important insight into the understanding of the seven deadly sins, saying that *they cause other sins by way of final causality*. This means that the capital vices terminate in the sins they engender. He points out that individual sinners have particular inclinations to specific ends, so they frequently move toward one of the seven. Furthermore, the ends of sins are closely related to one another, so that the capital vices can be considered causes. Man, Aquinas says, has a threefold good: the good of the soul, the good of the body, and the external goods. Each of the capital vices relates to these goods in some way or another, whether a disordered seeking of a bodily good, such as lust, or an aversion to one's own spiritual good, as in acedia. One can also have a disordered desire for the goods of another person, as in envy.

---

64. Cf. ST II-II, q. 35, a. 4, s.c. (*accidia*); q. 36, a. 4, s.c. (*invidia*); q. 118, a. 7, s.c. (*avaritia*); q. 132, a. 4, s.c. (*inanis gloria*); q. 148, a. 5, s.c. (*gula*); q. 153, a. 4, s.c. (*luxuria*); q. 158, a. 6, s.c. (*ira*).
65. Cf. ST I-II, q. 84, a. 4: "inanis gloria, invidia, ira, avaritia, tristitia, gula, luxuria."
66. ST II-II, q. 35, a. 4, co. "accidia sit tristitia quaedam."
67. ST II-II, q. 162, a. 6.
68. ST II-II, q. 162, a. 8, co.; cf. a. 2.

The Vices and the Loss of the Sense of Sin

The presentation of this volume will attempt to synthesize the tradition of both East and West on the capital sins. The text is divided into seven chapters and treats nine vices. For the most part, the text follows Evagrius's ordering: the first chapter treats gluttony, the second lust, the third avarice, the fourth anger, the fifth sloth, the sixth envy and sadness, the seventh vainglory and pride. In sum, even though there are two ways of describing the "evil thoughts" or "deadly sins," there is one and the same tradition contained in both Eastern and Western trajectories. This volume draws liberally from both and even presumes to draw theological teachings from those who preceded the development of this doctrine. On the one hand, some more historiographical readers may be disinclined to accept such a gathering of early witnesses, such as, for example, the Apostolic Fathers writing in the late first through the second centuries. The reader should naturally give pride of place to the insights of Cassian, Gregory, Maximus, and those later Fathers influenced by the Evagrian paradigm. On the other hand, theological development does not come from nowhere, but grows organically from a flourishing tradition already in place. And it is clear that the two ways are interwoven. Thus, it should prove useful for the project to consider what the earlier Fathers teach about gluttony, lust, and so forth.

Furthermore, some of the sayings are more connected to the passion rather than to the vice. So, for instance, sayings from the Fathers on the wrath of God or sadness of Christ are included in the volume not only for the edification of the reader but also for a clearer understanding of the vice by way of contrast with its proper exercise.[69] The path of the book descends through the vices, culminating with their queen ruler, pride. On the one hand, the reader will hopefully find the text to be diagnostic. The words of the Fathers will assist the reader in being more realistic about the attacks upon the soul. On the other hand, the text should

---

69. On the wrath of God, cf. Augustine of Hippo, *The City of God*, 15.25; Origen, *Homilies on Jeremiah*, hom. 20.1.1. On the sadness of Christ, cf. Augustine of Hippo, *Sermon 5.3*, *Life from Death*.

also be edifying and medicinal. Since each chapter begins with vice and ends with virtue, one's path through the chapters represents a sort of ascent out of vice and into the freedom of virtue. Yet even the Fathers' words on the vices are meant to draw their listeners from slavery into freedom. Sometimes they rebuke us, other times they put us to shame, they threaten us, or stir up our fear over the prospect of judgment, but they are always encouraging us in our struggle against the flesh.

One of the most difficult obstacles for the contemporary reader may be a particular problem keenly diagnosed by Pope Pius XII: the loss of the sense of sin. In a statement that has been echoed repeatedly by his successors, Pius famously said, "Perhaps the greatest sin in the world today is that men have begun to lose the sense of sin."[70] More recently, Pope Francis has continued in a similar vein, saying, "When you lose the sense of sin, you also lose the 'sense of the Kingdom of God' and in its place there emerges an 'anthropological vision' according to which 'I can do anything.'"[71] This is a profound additional insight by Francis. Without sin, there emerges a false utopia wherein there is no accountability. Yet, at the end of the day this Pelagian paradise of pure human potential has no answer to human misery with respect to the consequences of the Fall; there is no redemption and no kingdom of God. In this respect, the Fathers were much more realistic than our contemporaries. Sin was a problem with which the Fathers were acutely aware. To proceed requires one to wade into their dark waters, on their own terms in which they wrote, and recognize that "I can*not* do anything by myself," but "I can do all things in him who strengthens me."[72]

Often, the words of these authors are quite arresting. The Fathers sharpened their words to pierce into the heart, to convict and change the listener or reader. They were meant to heal, not to harm, to admonish, not to condemn. Today's readers may wish to proceed with a bit of holy

---

70. Pope Pius XII, *Radio Message to the U.S. National Catechetical Congress in Boston*, October 26, 1946; available at www.vatican.va.

71. Pope Francis, homily at St. Martha's House, quoted online in *La Stampa: Vatican Insider*: "Francis: 'When you lose the sense of sin, you lose the sense of the Kingdom of God'" (January 31, 2014); available at www.lastampa.it.

72. Phil 4:13.

awe, because they will find a timeless potency in these words' ability to move the soul. It is in the spirit of Paul's words that we should advance henceforth through the murky darkness of our fallen condition. "Let all things be done for edification."[73] Let us, therefore, continue to the Fathers.

---

73. 1 Cor 14:26.

1

Gluttony

Gluttony

1 The first conflict we must enter upon is that against gluttony, which we have explained as the pleasures of the palate. **John Cassian, Institutes 5.3 (ACW 58)**[1]

2 From gluttony are propagated foolish mirth, scurrility, uncleanness, babbling, dullness of sense in understanding. **Gregory the Great, Morals on the Book of Job, XXXI.45 (LF 31)**

3 There is nothing worse than gluttony, nothing more degrading. It makes the mind dull; it renders the soul carnal; it blinds [its victims] and does not permit them to see. **John Chrysostom, Commentary on John, Homily 45 (FOTC 33)**[2]

4 Gluttony is also wont to exhort the conquered heart, as if with reason, when it says, God has created all things clean, in order to be eaten, and he who refuses to fill himself with food, what else does he do but gain-

---

1. Translations from this sixth book are taken from Boniface Ramsey's translation in ACW 58 (2000). See note in introduction above.
2. FOTC = the Fathers of the Church series.

say the gift that has been granted him. **Gregory the Great, *Morals on the Book of Job*, XXXI.45 (LF 31)**

5 There is nothing wrong with eating—God forbid; the harmful thing is gluttony, stuffing yourself with food in excess of need, and ruining your stomach—something, after all, that destroys even the pleasure that comes from food. So, too, in like manner, there is nothing wrong with drinking in moderation, but rather with surrendering to drunkenness and losing control of your reasoning through excess. **John Chrysostom, *Homily 10.2 on Genesis* (FOTC 74)**

6 There are those who exult in the world, fattening their flesh on an extravagance of foods. They indulge themselves in other ways as well, yielding to unbridled impulses that lead to every form of immorality. But self-indulgence ends in punishment, bringing with it finally a cruel and inescapable penalty for love of the flesh. For "those who sow in the flesh will reap corruption from the flesh."[3] **Cyril of Alexandria, *Festal Letters*, 25.1 (FOTC 127)**

7 The Apostle also cries out: "Do not touch, nor taste, nor handle, things which must all perish"; for things which are for the body's indulgence are also for its corruption. Thus he shows us that he has found the truth—not through bodily indulgence, but through elevation of soul and humility of heart—and he continues: "But our way of life is in heaven."[4] **Ambrose of Milan, *Death as a Good*, 3.10 (FOTC 65)**

8 He who lives according to God must seek those pleasures which are both necessary and natural, while those which are natural but not necessary he must relegate to second place and only indulge in them as permitted by the suitability of time, manner, and moderation. **John Damascene, *The Orthodox Faith*, 2.13 (FOTC 37)**

---

3. Gal 6:8.
4. Col 2:21–22, Phil 3:20.

9 Question from a brother to an Old Man: "Clarify for me what the sign of gluttony is." Response by John: "When you see your thought taking pleasure in a particular food and driving you to take your food before others do, or else taking pleasure in pulling this food toward yourself, this is gluttony.... Another sign of gluttony is when one desires food before the appropriate time, which must not be done, unless there is good reason to do so." **Barsanuphius and John, *Letter* 163 (FOTC 113)**

10 The intemperance of the appetite is threefold: if you desire too avidly what is forbidden; if you seek too carefully what is not permitted, or even what is permitted, and have it prepared with special care and expense; if you do not observe the regular time for eating. **Leander of Seville, *The Training of Nuns and the Contempt of the World*, 13 (4) (FOTC 62)**

11 It is good, then, to abstain from superfluous food in due season, and to withdraw from the over-laden table, lest our self-indulgence in eating more than we need awaken the sin dormant in us. For the flesh, when it has battened upon delicacies, is irksome, and vigorously opposes the desires of the spirit. When it is weak, however, and unaided by overindulgence, it is forced to yield to the other.... Let evil, then, be idle in us, and all luxury in diet depart! Let fasting come in to us, with its temperance and hostility to all sin. **Cyril of Alexandria, *Festal Letters*, 1.3–4 (FOTC 118)**

12 Needless to say, we should not lean forward to get our helping first, under the impulse of gluttony, nor should we eagerly reach out too far, confessing lack of self-control by our fault. Neither should we, in the meantime, stand guard over our food like animals over their meat, nor indulge in too many dainties. **Clement of Alexandria, *Christ the Educator*, 2.7.55 (FOTC 23)**

13 As a sign that the flood had abated the dove is now bringing
    Back to the ark in her beak the budding green branch of an olive.

For the raven, held captive by gluttony, clung to foul bodies,
While the dove brought back the glad tidings of peace that was given.[5]

Prudentius, *Scenes from Sacred History*, 9–12 (FOTC 52)

14 Now, if abstinence is the mother of health, it is plain that eating to repletion is the mother of sickness and ill health, and brings forth diseases defying the skill of physicians themselves. And this is so, because pain in the feet, and headaches, and blindness, and pains in the hands, and trembling, and paralysis, and jaundice, and lingering burning fevers, and many others in addition to these (there is not time to run through them all), are not from abstinence and a life of self-denial, but have been caused by gluttony and satiety. **John Chrysostom, *Commentary on John*, Homily 22 (FOTC 33)**

15 Further, if you similarly wish to seek out the diseases of the soul which spring thence, you will see that greed, sloth, melancholy, laziness, licentiousness—in short, every kind of folly has its beginning from there. The souls addicted to delicate living become no better after banquets of this kind than asses that are torn asunder by wild beasts like these vices. **John Chrysostom, *Commentary on John*, Homily 22 (FOTC 33)**

16 Lust craves to be called satisfaction and abundance, but Thou indeed art fullness and the unceasing plenty of incorruptible sweetness.[6]
Augustine of Hippo, *Confessions*, 2.6.13 (FOTC 21)

17 To be sure, the necessities of life—I mean baths and banqueting—even if essential, nevertheless, if continually indulged in, make the body weak, but the soul's instruction, however much it is prolonged, makes the soul which receives it so much the stronger. **John Chrysostom, *Commentary on John*, Homily 18 (FOTC 33)**

---

5. Cf. Gn 8:7–8, 11.
6. For "lust," Augustine uses the word *luxuria*, but in a manner as to denote gluttony, as should be clear from the quote. This is also evident by his treatment of lust in this section as "wanton caresses" (*blanditiae lascivientium*). Cf. the introductory chapter above.

18 For surely it has to be feared lest perchance, once the wall of self-control has been broken down and license has been adopted, one might be sunk in the storm of gluttony and in the depths of excess and the shipwreck of chastity might follow in like manner. **Origen, *Commentary on Romans*, 10.3.5 (FOTC 104)**

19 This privilege, which Esau enjoyed by nature, he transferred to his brother, on account of his own lack of self-control. Whereas one lost even what was given him by nature, the other received as a bonus for himself what he did not get from nature. **John Chrysostom, *Homily* 51.3 on Genesis (FOTC 87)**

20 Struggle against gluttony as much as you can, and the Lord will assist you to understand and to do whatever is beneficial for you. "Be strong and bold" in the Lord.[7] **Barsanuphius and John, *Letter* 328 (FOTC 113)**

21 There are some other men going about, as they say, pretending only to devote themselves to prayer and doing no work, and making piety a pretext for cowardice and a means of gaining a living, but not thinking rightly.... If they consider it a fine thing not to touch work, since they are striving after the same thing, who is the one feeding them? Some are making their idea, that it is necessary only to devote themselves to prayer and not to touch work at all, a pretext for laziness and gluttony.[8] **Cyril of Alexandria, *Letter* 83.7–8 (FOTC 77)**

22 In general, all idolatry delights in feasting, gluttony, and the pleasures of both the belly and things that are below the belly. **Jerome, *Commentary on Galatians*, 5:19–21 (FOTC 121)**

23 Against the thoughts that stir up in us the desire to eat meat on a feast day and that advise us also to eat on account of the body's illness:

---

7. Dt 31:6.
8. The "other men" are the Euchites, the "praying ones." Regarding this sect, cf. John Damascene, *On Heresies*, 131–37. Cyril's response here is similar to Paul's, cf. 2 Thes 3:10–11.

1. GLUTTONY

"And to the people say, 'Purify yourselves for tomorrow, and you shall eat meat.... You shall not eat one day, not two, not five days, not ten days, and not twenty days. For a month of days you shall eat, until it [the meat] comes out of your nostrils. And it shall be nausea to you because you disobeyed the Lord, who is among you.'"[9] **Evagrius of Pontus, *Antirrhetikos* 1.3 (CSS 229)**

24 They enjoyed what they had longed for, he is saying, and satisfied their gluttony; yet they paid the penalty for their greed. "Food was still in their mouths when God's anger came upon them, and he slew some of their strongest and brought the elect of Israel up short": though they had great experience of the divine power and yet did not believe God could supply food, he applied chastisement to teach that he was capable of doing both, providing good things and inflicting retribution.[10]
Theodoret of Cyrus, *Commentary on Psalm 78*, 10 (FOTC 102)

25 "So when Jesus perceived that they would come to take him by force and make him king, he fled again to the mountain." Alas, how great is the tyranny of gluttony; how great the fickleness of their minds! No longer were they concerned about the breaking of the Sabbath, no longer were they consumed with zeal for the honor of God, but everything was cast to one side since their bellies had been filled. And so He was a prophet in their midst and they were going to choose Him king, but Christ fled. Why was that? To teach us to despise worldly honors and to show that He was in need of nothing belonging to earth. He who had chosen for Himself everything lowly—mother, home, city, rearing, and clothing—was not going to make a display of Himself afterwards by worldly means. **John Chrysostom, *Commentary on John*, Homily 42 (FOTC 33)**

26 Gluttony sometimes sneaks up to seize Thy servant; Thou wilt have mercy, that it may be removed far from me. For, no man can "be conti-

---

9. Nm 11:18–20.
10. Ps 78:30–31.

nent, unless Thou givest it."[11] **Augustine of Hippo, *Confessions*, 10.31.45 (FOTC 21)**

27 The devil starves while we fast since he always gorges himself on our failings. He brings our eating to the point of gluttony and extends our drinking to intoxication, so that he might make our mind mindless and render our flesh besmirched; so that our body, which is the abode of our mind, the vessel of our soul, the protection of our spirit, the school of the virtues, and the temple of God, he might reduce to a stage show of wickedness, a public spectacle of vice, and a theater of pleasure. **Peter Chrysologus, *Sermon* 12.3 (FOTC 109)**

28 With the onset of divine wrath, therefore, it is necessary to mourn, not to be carried away with fine food and drink; the fact that untimely indulgence would not escape censure and retribution is clearly stated by one of the holy prophets in reference to the people of Israel: "On that day the Lord of hosts called to weeping and mourning, to shaven heads and the wearing of sackcloth, whereas they indulged in mirth, slaughtering calves, sacrificing sheep, and saying, Let us eat and drink, for tomorrow we die."[12] There was need, therefore, with the onset of wrath, to fall to weeping and wailing, and abandon drinking. **Cyril of Alexandria, *Commentary on Joel* 2:15–17 (FOTC 115)**

29 But if we are here to gratify the pleasures of the belly and to indulge passing delights and ingest what is voided, and if we think this is a place for carousing rather than sobriety, an opportunity for transactions and trade instead of ascent or, if I may be so bold, deification, of which the martyrs are the intercessors, I do not even accept the occasion in the first place. For what has chaff to do with wheat?[13] Bodily indulgence with a martyr's struggle? The one is to be found in the theaters, the other in my congregations; the one among the pleasure-seekers, the other among men of restraint; the one among devotees of the flesh, the other

---

11. Wis 8:21.
12. Is 22:12–13.
13. Cf. Mt 3:12.

among those who free themselves from the body. **Gregory Nazianzen,** *Oration* 11.5 **(FOTC 107)**

30 Who could endure to look at him who is sunk in sensuality and gluttony or who is alarmed by fears? For, the feelings of the soul affect even the extremities of the body, just as also the traces of the beauty of the soul shine through in the state of the saint. **Basil of Caesarea,** *Homily* 12.5 **on Psalm 14 (FOTC 46)**

31 Let moderation be observed in you so that, if a weak body must be granted some relaxation from fasting, yet, at the same time, the will must not be relaxed. If a weak body deserves some indulgence, it is not the practice of eating which is at fault, but gluttony or the lack of moderation, as when you take more than you need or desire something which you could live without. **Leander of Seville,** *The Training of Nuns and the Contempt of the World,* **13 (4) (FOTC 62)**

32 Christ, then, came to this place, scorning as always to indulge in a soft and easy life, and following by preference one that was laborious and painful. He did not use beasts of burden, but traveled on foot so strenuously that He was tired out from the journey. Invariably He taught us to work with our hands, to be simple, and not to want many possessions. Therefore, He wishes us to be strangers to superfluities so that we even do without many actual necessities. For this reason He said: "The foxes have dens, and the birds of the air have nests; but the Son of Man has nowhere to lay his head."[14] And that is why He spent frequent periods in the mountains and in the deserts, not only by day, but also by night. David, indeed, foretold this when he said: "From the brook by the wayside he will drink,"[15] to show the simplicity of His way of life. **John Chrysostom,** *Commentary on John,* **Homily 31 (FOTC 33)**

33 For self-indulgence in bodies is a sort of root and origin of pleasures sharp and wild, and resists fiercely the desires for what is good, moving

---

14. Mt 18:20.
15. Ps 109:7.

as it does with licentious impulse toward what is shameful. **Cyril of Alexandria, *Festal Letters*, 22.1 (FOTC 127)**

34 How shameful it is to be a ruler of cities and conquered by indulgence at the same time; or to observe moderation in other respects, but when it comes to racetracks and theaters and arenas and hunting parties to be so addicted as to make them your life; and that she who is first among cities should be a city of pleasure-seekers when by all rights she should be a model of every virtue for the rest![16] Reject these things; be a city of God. **Gregory Nazianzen, *Oration* 36.12 (FOTC 107)**

35 Since fasting expels the hostile foes of our salvation in this manner and is so terrible to the enemies of our life, we must cherish and embrace her, not dread her. We must be afraid of drunkenness and gluttony, not of fasting. **John Chrysostom, *On Repentance and Almsgiving*, Homily 5.2 (FOTC 96)**

36 One of the fathers said: "One man is found who eats much, but is still hungry because he restrains himself; another eats little and is satisfied. He who eats much, but restrains himself while he is still hungry, has a greater reward than the one who eats little and is satisfied." **Paschasius of Dumium, *Questions and Answers of the Greek Fathers*, 1.3 (FOTC 62)**

37 To be a slave to gluttony or drunkenness, to subject one's unfortunate soul to lust or dissipation, certainly belongs to the Devil's pomps, because in such actions his will is fulfilled. **Caesarius of Arles, *Sermon* 12.4 (FOTC 31)**

38 How many men has wine wrecked, drunkenness destroyed, gluttony bloated? **Ambrose of Milan, *Letter* 25 (45), to Sabinus (FOTC 26)**[17]

---

16. Gregory is delivering this oration in Constantinople.
17. The number in parentheses corresponds to those of Ambrose's letters in LF and NPNF.

39 The drunken will not inherit the kingdom of God. The Lord said to his disciples, "Be careful that your hearts not be weighted down with drunkenness and dissipation."[18] When a man is inebriated, his sensory faculties become debilitated, his feet falter, his mind vacillates, and the fire of lust is ignited within him. This is why the Apostle warns about "wine, which leads to debauchery."[19] **Jerome, *Commentary on Galatians*, 5:19–21 (FOTC 121)**

40 A man can be drunk with anger, with unseemly desire, with greed, with vainglory, with ten thousand other passions. For drunkenness is nothing other than a loss of right reason, a derangement, and depriving the soul of its health. **John Chrysostom, *Discourses against Judaizing Christians*, 8.1.1 (FOTC 68)**

41 A terrible thing, you see, dearly beloved, a terrible thing is drunkenness, capable of dulling the senses and drowning the mind: man, rational and entrusted with responsibility for all creatures though he is, is thus shackled with unbreakable bonds and brought low like a motionless corpse. Worse in fact than a corpse: a corpse happens to be incapable of either good or evil, while the inebriate is incapable of good but more capable of evil; he lies there, an object of ridicule to all alike—wife, children, even the neighbors. **John Chrysostom, *Homily* 29.11 on Genesis (FOTC 82)**

42 "Do not err; neither fornicators, nor idolators, nor adulterers, nor the effeminate, nor sodomites, nor thieves, nor the covetous, nor drunkards, nor the evil-tongued, nor the greedy will possess the kingdom of God."[20] See what an execrable thing is drunkenness, that it even drives its devotees away from the kingdom of God. **Leander of Seville, *The Training of Nuns and the Contempt of the World*, 19 (9) (FOTC 62)**

---

18. Lk 21:34.
19. Eph 5:18.
20. 1 Cor 6:9–10.

43 Don't you daily observe thousands of disorders stemming from laden tables and immoderate eating? What is the cause of gout? of migraine? of the flood of noxious humors? of countless other ailments? Do they not spring from intemperance and from pouring ourselves more wine than we should? I mean, just as a ship that becomes waterlogged quickly sinks and slips below the water level, so, too, a person who is given over to gluttony and drunkenness goes head over heels, brings reason down to a low level, and lies for all intents and purposes like a corpse, quite capable, on the one hand, of frequently doing evil, but, on the other hand, in a condition no better than corpses for doing anything good. **John Chrysostom, *Homily* 10.5 on Genesis (FOTC 74)**

44 The cithara is our flesh when it dies to sin to live to God; it is a cithara when it receives the sevenfold Spirit in the sacrament of baptism.[21] For while the tortoise is alive, it is sunk in the mire; but when it has died, its covering is adapted to the uses of song and the gift of holy instruction, to sound forth the seven changing notes in rhythmic measures.[22] Likewise, as regards our flesh, if it lives for bodily enticements, it is living in a kind of filth and in an abyss of pleasures. But if it dies to riotous living and incontinence, then it regains true life, then it begins to produce the fine melody of good works. **Ambrose of Milan, *The Prayer of Job and David*, IV.10.36 (FOTC 65)**

45 Beware lest you be concerned for the flesh and its desires, lest you always give in to gluttony as it demands. Let not pleasure be satisfied when you eat but let weakness be supported. You should share meals with people who are not accustomed to praise the delights of the flesh but of the heart; who avidly seek the bread of angels for the interior person; who run after your spouse in the fragrance of his ointments; who taste inwardly the sweetness of God; who with pure love hunger and thirst for justice; who work for food, not that which perishes but that which remains for eternal life.[23] Let your conversations and meals

---

21. Ambrose apparently has in mind here a type of seven-stringed musical instrument made from a tortoise shell.
22. Cf. Virgil, *Aeneid* 6.646. Cf. Ambrose's *Jacob and the Happy Life*, II.9.39.
23. The "spouse" is Christ.

be held with people like these so that while you feed them with bodily foods, you may gain the merit of holy deeds and when you are fed with their spiritual words, progress in a holy life may accrue to you. Now you will not want to fill your table with such delights as you once filled it when you were the slave of carnal marriage. Hear the teacher of the nations who says of the widow: "The one who is self-indulgent," he says, "is dead while she lives."[24] **Fulgentius, Letter 2, to the Widow Galla (FOTC 95)**

46 It has been proven daily by experience, dearly beloved, that the keenness of the mind is dulled by the satisfaction of the flesh, and the vigor of the heart is blunted by a superfluity of food. The delight of eating is contrary to the health of the body unless a rational temperance resists the pleasure and withdraws from its desire what is going to be a burden. **Leo the Great, Sermon 19.1 (FOTC 93)**

47 The luxury-loving man does not say: Christ is my portion, because luxury comes and says: You are my portion; I made you my slave in that banquet, I caught you in the net of those feasts, I have you bound to payment by the surety of your gluttony. Do you not know that you valued your table more than your life? I convict you by your own judgment. Deny it if you can, but you cannot. Finally, you kept nothing for life, you spent all for your table. **Ambrose of Milan, Letter 59 (63), to the Church of Vercelli (FOTC 26)**

48 Just as I might praise a wine as good in its own way and blame a man who became drunk from this wine, nevertheless, I would set a higher value on this man, whom I reproved and who is still drunk, than I would on the wine which I praised and which made him drunk. **Augustine of Hippo, *The Free Choice of the Will*, 3.5.15 (FOTC 59)**

49 Those who give themselves up to drunkenness never have their fill; the more wine they imbibe, the more they burn with thirst, and indulgence proves to be a constant fueling of their thirst; by the time

---

24. 1 Tm 5:6. The "teacher of the nations" is Paul.

all that remains of the pleasure has disappeared, the thirst proves to be unquenchable and leads the victims of drunkenness to the very precipice. **John Chrysostom, *Homily* 29.12 on Genesis (FOTC 82)**

50 Nothing has checked intemperance like the Gospel, nor has anyone given stricter laws against gluttony than Christ, of whom one reads that He declared the poor, blessed; the hungry and the thirsty, happy.[25] He said that the wealthy are wretched because they obey the dictates of the belly and of gluttony. The mother of sensuous pleasures never abandons them and they are always in servitude to her. They consider it a proof of real happiness when they have the largest possible appetite; but the fact is that, in so doing, they succeed in obtaining less than they crave. When Christ preferred Lazarus, who was starving to death and covered with sores amid the dogs, to the rich man, He restrained with these examples the executioners of salvation, namely the belly and the gullet.[26] **Novatian, *Jewish Foods*, 6.3–4 (FOTC 67)**

51 But we must be on guard against indulgence,
Lest the bosom where faith preserves its dwelling

Be oppressed by the weight of sinful gorging.[27]
Hearts set free by sobriety and fasting
Taste the sweetness of God's life-giving presence
As the food of the soul and true refreshment.[28]

Loving Father and Guardian, Thou dost strengthen
Soul and body with food divine and earthly,
Filling us with Thy grace and holy virtue.

Prudentius, *The Book of Hymns for Every Day*, 4.28–36 (FOTC 43)

52 There are certain observers of Lent who are voluptuous rather than religious; who seek out new delights in place of doing violence to old passions; who, by the lavish and costly preparation of various fruits,

25. Cf. Mt 5:3, 6.
26. Cf. Lk 16:19–31.
27. Cf. Rom 10:10.
28. Cf. Jn 6:56.

strive to surpass the variety and taste of all other dishes.... They tax their hearts and bloat their stomachs with too many courses, and lest their appetite should become jaded by the abundance, they stimulate it by various kinds of artfully prepared and exotic condiments. In a word, when fasting, they take so much to eat that they are not able to digest it. **Augustine of Hippo,** *Sermon* **210.8 on Lent (FOTC 38)**

53 We must prudently take into account what is proper for places, circumstances, and persons, so that we may not indiscreetly convict them of sin. It is possible for a wise man to eat the most delicious food without any sin of sensuality or gluttony, while a fool is ravenous for the meanest food with a raging hunger that is most unseemly. **Augustine of Hippo,** *On Christian Instruction,* **3.12.19 (FOTC 2)**

54 We know that this command pertains more especially to us, dearly beloved, who have been forewarned of that day, which even if it is a secret is certain to be near. It is necessary for every person to be prepared for its coming, lest it should find any either given over to their stomachs or tangled up in the cares of this world. **Leo the Great,** *Sermon* **19.1 (FOTC 93)**

55 Now, if the soul had engaged alone in the contest for virtue, then it would also be crowned alone; and if it alone had indulged in pleasures, then it alone could be justly punished. However, since the soul followed neither virtue nor vice without the body, it will be just for them to receive their recompense together. **John Damascene,** *The Orthodox Faith,* **4.27 (FOTC 37)**

Self-Mastery

56 Our Lord was not hungry for the Pharisee's refreshments; He hungered for the tears of the sinful woman. Once He had been filled and refreshed by the tears He hungered for, He then chastised the one who had invited Him for food that perishes, in order to show that He had been

invited not to nourish the body but to assist the mind.²⁹ **Ephrem the Syrian, Homily on Our Lord, 15.1 (FOTC 91)**

57 Let us, O Christ, now follow as our strength permits
   The way that Thou, the Teacher of all holy truth,
   Didst show to Thy disciples by Thy word and deed,
   That when the vice of gluttony is overcome,
   The flesh may bow beneath the spirit's triumphant reign.
   Prudentius, The Book of Hymns for Every Day, 7.196–200 (FOTC 43)

58 Self-control [is defined] as a state of mind that preserves the judgments of practical wisdom in matters of choice and avoidance.
Clement of Alexandria, Stromateis, 2.18.79 (FOTC 85)

59 Indeed, in order for our body to remain calm and be soiled by none of the sins of satiety, we must provide for a life of greater self-control, by defining not only the limit and boundary of every enjoyment connected with pleasure, but the limit connected with our individual need.
Gregory of Nyssa, On Virginity, 20 (FOTC 58)

60 Against the soul that grows weary in the affliction that comes upon it from restriction of bread and water: "It is through many afflictions that we must enter the kingdom of God."³⁰ **Evagrius of Pontus, Antirrhetikos 1.51 (CSS 229)**

61 But do not let your fasts be with the hypocrites; for they fast on Monday and Thursday; but you shall fast on Wednesday and Friday.
Didache of the Twelve Apostles, 8.1 (FOTC 1)

62 For we have forty days dedicated to fasting; we have the fourth and the sixth day of the week on which we regularly fast.³¹ There is certainly freedom for the Christian to fast at all times, not by an excessive regard

---

29. Cf. Lk 7:44–47; Jn 6:27.
30. Acts 14:22.
31. In early Christianity, believers regularly fasted on Wednesdays and Fridays. Cf. *Didache* 8.1.

of an observance but by virtue of moderation. For how can chastity be preserved uncorrupted by them except sustained by the more perfect aid of continence? How can they be zealous for Scriptures; how can they be diligent in knowledge and wisdom? Is it not by the moderation of the belly and of gluttony? **Origen, *Homilies on Leviticus*, 10.2.6 (FOTC 83)**

63 Let us fast, therefore, on Wednesday and Friday. **Leo the Great, *Sermon* 19.4 (FOTC 93)**

64 This fast subdues licentiousness and gluttony,
Disgraceful sloth that springs from leaden sleep and wine,
Ignoble lust, salacious wit and pleasantry,
These manifold diseases of disordered sense,
All are restrained beneath the rod of abstinence.

For if, abandoned to excess in food and drink,
Man does not curb the body by the holy fasts,
The flame of his high spirit burning bright and pure
Will shrink and pine away, all smothered by delights,
And the soul will fall asleep within his sluggish breast.

Prudentius, *The Book of Hymns for Every Day*, 7.11–20 (FOTC 43)

65 As self-indulgence was the beginning of sins, so self-control is the source of virtue. **Leo the Great, *Sermon* 79.1 (FOTC 93)**

66 This is the most perfect goal of self-control: not to concentrate on the suffering of the body, but on the efficient working of the instruments of the soul. **Gregory of Nyssa, *On Virginity*, 22 (FOTC 58)**

67 Because the calling that is in Christ acknowledges no foods as common or unclean, but thought of self-control persuades one to abstain even from things that are lawful.[32] **Origen, *Commentary on Romans*, 9.37 (FOTC 104)**

---

32. Cf. Acts 10:28.

68 For just as it is written concerning self-control, that "no one can be self-controlled unless God grants him to be,"[33] and just as the Apostle lists it as a fruit of the Spirit,[34] so also does he list love, which "does not act falsely,"[35] because it is related to self-control. Love, through good works, "covers a multitude of sins,"[36] and through love God works in us not only so that we will turn away from evil but also so that we will do good. **Fulgentius, *The Truth about Predestination and Grace*, 1.44 (FOTC 126)**

69 Let him who is pure in the flesh be so without boasting, knowing that it is Another who grants him this continence.[37] **Clement of Rome, *First Letter*, 38.2 (FOTC 1)**

70 For the art of cooking is very properly neglected in our house, and the knives of the cooks do not come in contact with blood. Our principal foods, in which lies our abundance, consist of leafy vegetables with very coarse bread and sour wine. As a result, our faculties are not so stupefied by gluttony that they direct our actions foolishly. **Basil of Caesarea, *Letter* 41 to Julian (FOTC 13)**

71 By abstaining, therefore, from food and drink [the Israelite people] imposed the penalty of severe punishment on themselves, and to conquer their enemies, they first conquered the enticement of gluttony in themselves. In this way it happened that the fierce adversaries and harsh masters yielded to them fasting whom they had overcome when full.[38] **Leo the Great, *Sermon* 39.1 (FOTC 93)**

72 The soul is able to stop the nature of the body from becoming intoxicated and flowing like wine, and that continence makes desire

---

33. Wis 8:21.
34. Cf. Gal 5:23.
35. 1 Cor 13:4.
36. 1 Pt 4:8.
37. Here, the translator has chosen the word "continence" for *enkrateia*, when "self-mastery" or "self-control" are better suited.
38. Cf. 1 Sm 7:6–11.

its servant. **Gregory Thaumaturgus, *Metaphrase on the Ecclesiastes of Solomon*, 8 (FOTC 98)**

73 Caution, a rational process of avoidance of evil, is close to self-control. **Clement of Alexandria, *Stromateis*, 2.18.79 (FOTC 85)**

74 Whatever gluttony by excessive drinking will lose, might still better be given as an alms for the poor. Thus the body would be refreshed by drinking in a moderate fashion, and the soul's redemption might be procured through mercy to the poor. **Caesarius of Arles, *Sermon* 47.6 (FOTC 31)**

75 Teach sobriety, therefore, to all, and practice it yourselves, also. **Polycarp, *Letter to the Philippians*, 10.3 (FOTC 1)**

76 For it is agreed, it really is, that virtue is not simply accessible to just anyone; its approach is steep and difficult. It is not to be attained by the pleasure-loving and the negligent, nor by those entangled in carnal passions or wholly under their sway, driven without restraint by their impulses toward what is shameful, having let out every reef and set every sail, but rather by those distinguished by sobriety, full of boldness for what is good, lovers of good order who are nourished on virtuousness, who think nothing of labor expended on improvement, and who purchase their reputation with the efforts they put forth for it. For it would be impossible for anyone to accomplish anything admirable without acting zealously and choosing to endure the unavoidable hardship. **Cyril of Alexandria, *Festal Letters*, 16.5 (FOTC 127)**

77 That sobriety by which anyone abstains from vices does not save unless it be devout and just, i.e., that it both believe rightly in God and freely expends on the neighbor what charity demands. Justice, by which each one expends on his neighbor that which he delights to expend on himself, is not fruitful if it is not sober and devout. Devotion, by which there is right belief in God, is dead if either sobriety of morals

or charity toward the neighbor is not held. **Fulgentius, Book Concerning the Incarnation of the Son of God and the Author of Vile Animals, 38 (from Letter 10) (FOTC 95)**

78 Better genuine self-control than the sort taught by the philosophers. **Clement of Alexandria, Stromateis, 3.7.57 (FOTC 85)**

79 And the blessed apostle bids not to partake casually of the food at hand, but to render, first, what is due to the One who gave him the provisions of his life. **Gregory of Nyssa, On the Christian Mode of Life (FOTC 58)**

80 If, however, dearly beloved, you are unable to go a whole day without food because of physical weakness, no right-minded person could find fault with you in this. We have, you see, a gentle and loving Lord who demands nothing of us beyond our capabilities. In other words, it is not arbitrarily that he looks for fasting and abstinence from food to be performed by us, nor simply for the sake of our remaining without food, but rather that we may be detached from things of this life and devote all our spare time to spiritual matters. **John Chrysostom, Homily 10.2 on Genesis (FOTC 74)**

81 You do well in setting forth strict standards for us, in order that we may know not only continence but also its fruits. Now, its fruit is a participation in God. For, incorruption is a sharing in God, just as corruption is a participation in the world. In fact, continence is a denial of the body and an assent to God. It withdraws from everything mortal, having, as it were, the Spirit of God as a body. **Basil of Caesarea, Letter 366 to the Monk Urbicius (FOTC 28)**

82 Mortification of the body is a fine thing; accept the evidence of Paul who continually disciplines himself and through Israel puts fear into those who in self-conceit indulge their bodies;[39] and of Jesus himself

---

39. Cf. Rom 11:17–25; 1 Cor 9:27.

who fasted and was tempted and prevailed over the Tempter.[40] Prayer vigils are a fine thing; accept the evidence of God, who stayed sleepless praying before the Passion.[41] **Gregory Nazianzen, *Oration* 14.3 (FOTC 107)**

83 Iniquity affords a bad covering, and if anyone wishes to hold it over us, we ought to remove it; else he may begin to come into judgment with us. And if anyone tries to carry off our spiritual tunic which we have received, remove the cloak of iniquity and take up the covering of faith and of patience, with which David covered himself in fasting, so that he would not lose the garment of virtue. Fasting is itself a covering. Indeed, unless a sober fasting had served to cover the holy Joseph, he would have been stripped by the wanton adulteress.[42] Had Adam chosen to cover himself with that fasting, he would not have been made naked. But because he tasted of the tree of the knowledge of good and evil contrary to heaven's prohibition and violated the fast imposed on him by taking the food of incontinence, he knew that he was naked.[43] Had he fasted, he would have kept the clothing of faith and would not have beheld himself uncovered. **Ambrose of Milan, *The Prayer of Job and David*, III.4.10 (FOTC 65)**

84 Through this habit of continence perfect souls have so used worldly goods that are necessary for another purpose that by means of this habit they were not bound by these goods and were able not to use them when there was no need.[44] Nor does anyone use them properly unless he is able also not to use them. Many, indeed, more easily abstain from them so as not to use them at all, rather than control themselves so as to use them well. Yet, no one can use them wisely except him who through continence is able not to use them. In consequence, Paul could say of this habit: "I know how to have abundance and to suffer want."[45] **Augustine of Hippo, *The Good of Marriage*, 21.25 (FOTC 27)**

---

40. Cf. Mt 4:1–11.
41. Cf. Mt 26:36.
42. Cf. Gn 39:12.
43. Cf. Gn 3:6–11.
44. One often associates the word continence with sexuality, but here and elsewhere in this section it is clear that it refers more generally to restraint with regard to sense pleasures.
45. Phil 4:10.

85 If you love continence, cut off what is superfluous and confine your desires to narrow limits. Consider how much nature demands, not how much your own cupidity seeks. If you would be continent, you must reach the point of being satisfied with yourself, for he who is sufficient to himself was born with riches. Put a check on your desire and reject all enticements that attract the mind with secret pleasure. Eat less than you need to be filled, drink less than you need to become intoxicated. Be careful at banquets or any social affairs not to appear to condemn those whom you do not imitate. **Martin of Braga, *Rules for an Honest Life*, chap. 4 (FOTC 62)**

86 Fasting, in other words, holds the body under restraint, checks its unruly movements, and, on the other hand, renders the soul transparent, gives it wings, makes it light and raises it on high. **John Chrysostom, *Homily* 10.4 on Genesis (FOTC 74)**

87 Even with pagans themselves, there are certain meaningless fasts. Reason directs one in truth, deception the other in falsehood. With us, faith sanctifies even the one eating; with them, their unbelief mars even the one fasting. **Leo the Great, *Sermon* 79.2 (FOTC 93)**

88 Now, in my view there is also a very urgent need for those redeemed by Christ to be wanting no longer to live a heedless life; rather, they should be attentive to following the straight and narrow path of a way of life pleasing to God, and "gird their loins," that is, rise above bodily indulgence and pleasure and "make no provision for the flesh to gratify its desires," and prevail over passions and all lethargy.[46] **Cyril of Alexandria, *Commentary on Nahum* 2:1–2 (FOTC 116)**

89 There will come that time, I say, when no refreshment of food or sleep will be desired, no weariness from fasting felt, no restlessness of the flesh or temptation of the Enemy feared. With our Adversary thrust down into the depths of hell, we will first enjoy this happiness of not

---

46. Rom 13:14.

having the will or the power to commit any more sin. **Caesarius of Arles, *Sermon* 58.4 (FOTC 31)**

90 The flowing stream does not more swiftly quench the flame,
    Nor heat of broiling sun more quickly melt the snow,
    Than fasting with its cleansing power can purge away
    The foulness bred by sin and dark concupiscence,
    If joined with kindly alms and Christian charity.[47]

        Prudentius, *The Book of Hymns for Every Day*, 7.206–10 (FOTC 43)

91 Fasting is a holy oblation, a sacrifice that is pure, but without the fire of mercy it cannot ascend as a fragrant offering to God. What the soul is to the body is analogous to what mercy is to fasting. When fasting lives off mercy, then it gives life to the one who is fasting. **Peter Chrysologus, *Sermon* 41 (FOTC 109)**

92 I mean, what's the good of fasting if, on the one hand, you pass the day without food and, on the other, you abandon yourself to the dice and to brainless nonsense, and often waste the whole day in swearing and blaspheming? **John Chrysostom, *Homily* 6.22 on Genesis (FOTC 74)**

93 Temperance rightly quenches the ardor of such passions, insofar as possible. First it tempers the mind by moderation and control, it molds the mind, then tightens the reins placed on the violence of the body by its abstinence from pleasures.[48] Therefore the law curtails excess in regard to food and abundant banquets, not only to cut back on luxurious living but also to open a path for the use of reason through the consideration paid to the restricting precept.[49] Reason would then curtail the attractions of gluttony and the other excessive desires and would check the passions and emotions of the body.[50] Therefore temperance comes before correction and is the mistress of learning. **Ambrose of Milan, *Jacob and the Happy Life*, I.2.5 (FOTC 65)**

---

47. Cf. Tb 4:11, 12:9; Cyprian, *De opera et eleemosynis* 5.
48. Cf. 4 Mc 1:33–34.
49. Cf. Lv 11:4–47.
50. Cf. 4 Mc 1:35.

94 Our idea of self-control is freedom from desire. It is not a matter of having desires and holding out against them, but actually of mastering desire by self-control. It is not possible to acquire this form of self-control except by the grace of God. That is why he says, "Ask, and it shall be granted you."[51] **Clement of Alexandria, *Stromateis*, 3.7.57 (FOTC 85)**

95 Let us not be slaves, but masters, in our own house. Let us be moderate in our eating, not allowing ourselves to be carried away by gluttony. So, bridling our appetite, we shall govern also its henchman, lust. Let the soul rule the body and not be at the beck and call of animal instinct. **Cyril of Jerusalem, *Sermon on the Paralytic*, 18 (FOTC 64)**

---

51. Mt 7:7.

2

Lust

Lust

1 The thorn-bushes of lust grew above my head, and there was no hand to root them out. **Augustine of Hippo, *Confessions*, 2.3.6 (FOTC 21)**

2 My child, do not give way to evil desire, for it leads to fornication. And do not use obscene language, or let your eye wander, for from all these come adulteries. ***Didache of the Twelve Apostles*, 3.3 (FOTC 1)**

3 From lust are generated blindness of mind, inconsiderateness, inconstancy, precipitation, self-love, hatred of God, affection for this present world, but dread or despair of that which is to come. **Gregory the Great, *Morals on the Book of Job*, XXXI.45 (LF 31)**

4 For bodily fasting alone is not sufficient to procure and possess the purity of perfect chastity unless it is preceded by a contrite spirit and by persevering prayer against this most unclean spirit; then there must be constant meditation on Scripture, and to this should be added spiritual knowledge, as well as toilsome manual labor, which restrains and recalls feckless wanderings of the heart; and before all else there must have been laid a foundation of true humility, without which there can never be a victory over vice. **John Cassian, *Institutes* 6.1 (ACW 58)**

5 Lust also is wont to exhort the conquered heart, as if with reason, when it says, Why enlargest thou not thyself now in thy pleasure, when thou knowest not what may follow thee? Thou oughtest not to lose in longings the time thou hast received; because thou knowest not how speedily it may pass by. For if God had not wished man to be united in the pleasure of coition, He would not, at the first beginning of the human race, have made them male and female. **Gregory the Great, *Morals on the Book of Job*, XXXI.45 (LF 31)**

6 To indulge in intercourse without intending children is to outrage nature, whom we should take as our instructor. **Clement of Alexandria, *Christ the Educator*, 2.10.95 (FOTC 23)**

7 Licentiousness and dissipation are evil, and our bodies' vile excitability is destructive. Youth's close attendant is stupidity, and stupidity leads to destruction. **Gregory Thaumaturgus, *Metaphrase on the Ecclesiastes of Solomon*, 56 (FOTC 98)**

8 The demon of impurity impels one to lust after bodies. It attacks more strenuously those who practice continence, in the hopes that they will give up their practice of this virtue, feeling that they gain nothing by it. **Evagrius of Pontus, *Praktikos* 8 (CSS 4)**

9 The Enemy had control of the power of my will and from it he had fashioned a chain for me and had bound me in it. For, lust is the product of perverse will, and when one obeys lust habit is produced, and when one offers no resistance to habit necessity is produced. By means, as it were, of these interconnected links—whence the chain I spoke of—I was held in the grip of a harsh bondage. **Augustine of Hippo, *Confessions*, 8.5.10 (FOTC 21)**

10 A brother asked an old man: "What shall I do, father, against lustful thoughts?" He replied: "Pray God that the eyes of your soul may see the help which comes from God, which surrounds man and saves him." **Martin of Braga, *Sayings of the Egyptian Fathers*, 4 (FOTC 62)**

11 The caresses of wanton men are desirous of a return of love, but nothing is more caressing than Thy charity, nor is anything loved more healthfully than Thy truth, which is beautiful and bright above all things. **Augustine of Hippo, *Confessions*, 2.6.13 (FOTC 21)**

12 Some men, it is true, do bury their riches in the ground, but others put them away in gluttony and voluptuousness and excessive drinking, thus adding the punishment for their licentiousness to that already incurred for their greed. Some, too, make provision for parasites and flatterers; others, for gambling and prostitutes; while others take care of still other expenses of the kind, thus carving out for themselves innumerable paths leading into hell, and avoiding the straight and narrow one that leads to heaven. **John Chrysostom, *Commentary on John*, Homily 87 (FOTC 41)**

13 We should also be particularly careful of our eyes, for it is better to slip with the feet than with the eyes. The Lord offers a remedy for this weakness, indeed, with curt words: "If thy eye scandalize thee, cut in out," thereby tearing lust up by the roots.[1] Melting glances, and sly looks out of the corner of the eye, which is what is also called winking, are nothing more than adultery with the eyes, since lust operates at a distance through them. The sight sins before the rest of the body does. "The eye, seeing beautiful things, gladdens the heart," that is, when it knows how to see what is right it gives joy, "but he that winketh with the eye deceitfully, shall cause men sorrow."[2] **Clement of Alexandria, *Christ the Educator*, 3.11.69–70 (FOTC 23)**

---

1. Mt 5:29.
2. Prv 15:30.

14 The adulterer cannot say: "The Lord is my portion," because passion comes and says: I am your portion; you bound yourself to me by your love for that maiden, by a night with a harlot you came under my laws and into my power. **Ambrose of Milan, *Letter* 59 (63), to the church of Vercelli (FOTC 26)**

15 For, if a man lives with a woman for a time, until he finds another worthy either of his high station in life or his wealth, whom he can marry as his equal, in his very soul he is an adulterer, and not with the one whom he desires to find but with her with whom he now lives in such a way as not to be married to her. **Augustine of Hippo, *The Good of Marriage*, 5.5 (FOTC 27)**

16 As a youth, I was quite unhappy, unhappy in the beginning of the period of adolescence. I even begged chastity of Thee, saying: "Give me chastity and self-restraint, but not just yet." I was afraid that Thou wouldst quickly heed my prayer, that Thou wouldst quickly cure me from the disease of concupiscence, which I preferred to be appeased rather than to be abolished. **Augustine of Hippo, *Confessions*, 8.7.17 (FOTC 21)**

17 It will be a clear sign and a full proof of this purity if either no unlawful image occurs to us as we lie at rest and relaxed in slumber or at least, when one does surface, it does not arouse any movements of desire. For although a disturbance of this kind may not be accounted as fully evil and sinful, it is nonetheless the sign of an as yet imperfect mind and an indication of vice that has not been totally purified when this sort of delusion comes about by way of deceiving images. **John Cassian, *Institutes* 6.10 (ACW 58)**

18 "Neither will I condemn you."[3] What does it mean, O Lord? Do you, therefore, countenance sins? Certainly not. Mark what follows: "Go, and from now on, sin no more." Therefore, the Lord also condemned, but the sin, not the person. For if he favored sins, he would say, "Neither

---

3. Cf. Jn 8:1–11.

will I condemn you; go, live as you will. Be without anxiety as regards my liberation. However much you sin, I shall free you from all the punishment of Gehenna and the tortures of Hell." He did not say this. **Augustine of Hippo, *Tractates on the Gospel of John*, 33.6 (FOTC 88)**

19 "So to the pure, everything is pure," he says. "To the tainted minds of the faithless, nothing is pure; they are tainted in reason and conscience."[4] As to illegitimate pleasure he says, "Make no mistake. The sexually immoral, worshippers of idols, adulterers, passive perverts, homosexuals, those who pursue profit, robbers, drunkards, people who use abusive language, and swindlers will not inherit the kingdom of God." We used to be such, but "have passed through the purifying waters."[5] But they purify themselves for this licentiousness. Their baptism is out of responsible self-control into sexual immorality. Their philosophy is the gratification of their pleasures and passions. They teach a change from self-discipline to indiscipline. The hope they offer is the titillation of their genitals.[6] They make themselves excluded from the kingdom of God instead of enrolled disciples.[7] Under the name of what they falsely call knowledge[8] they have embarked on the road to outer darkness.[9] **Clement of Alexandria, *Stromateis* 3.18.109 (FOTC 85)**

20 We must entirely avoid all effeminate motions and all softness and daintiness. Daintiness of bearing in a man as he walks and, in the words of Anacreon, "walking with a sway,"[10] are positively indecent; at least it seems that way to me.[11] **Clement of Alexandria, *Christ the Educator*, 3.11.69 (FOTC 23)**

---

4. Ti 1:15.
5. 1 Cor 6:9–11.
6. Cf. Phil 3:19.
7. Cf. Rv 20:12, 15; 21:27.
8. Cf. 1 Tm 6:20.
9. Cf. Mt 8:12, 22:13, 25:30.
10. Cf. Anacreon, *Frag.* 168. Anacreon was a Greek lyric poet in the sixth and fifth centuries B.C.
11. Sometimes quotations of the Fathers are jarring, as this one is. The Fathers take scripture very seriously, and perhaps Clement has in mind Paul's censure of effeminacy (cf. 1 Cor 6:9). But perhaps what Clement means to brings forth in this one is that an outward display can betray an inward inclination toward disordered lust.

21 The prudent man "glorifies" God, the licentious man dishonors God. For he, like Nebuchadnezzar, overthrows the Temple of God and "destroys the Temple of God" and "dishonors God through transgression of the Law."[12] This is even an apostolic text. Thus the sinner adds no glory to God and asks questions about Providence, so that some doubt if there is Providence for nothing other than for evil. Take away evil and you are not offended by Providence. But those who are offended by Providence say this inside out: Why are there so many "adulterers" and so many "homosexuals," why so many atheists and so many impious?[13] And sinners are those who engender contempt for Providence, offenses to God, blasphemy on him who created the world. Thus some give glory to God, but those who do what is opposite to the glory of God through sins do not "give glory" to God. **Origen, *Homilies on Jeremiah*, 12.11.1 (FOTC 97)**

22 Because of their licentiousness, did they not show a lust beyond that of irrational animals? Hear what the prophet says of their excesses. "They are become as amorous stallions. Every one neighed after his neighbor's wife."[14] He did not say: "Everyone lusted after his neighbor's wife," but he expressed the madness which came from their licentiousness with the greatest clarity by speaking of it as the neighing of brute beasts. **John Chrysostom, *Discourses against Judaizing Christians*, 1.6.8 (FOTC 68)**

23 I think the horses, it is said, are either men who lust after women and behave like beasts, or those who had been subject to and ruled by the demons, and those that are mounted on them are their leaders.[15] **Andrew of Caesarea, *Commentary on the Apocalypse*, 9.27 (FOTC 123)**

24 "And the perfidious Judah was unafraid, and she went and prostituted herself, she also." First Israel went and prostituted herself and later Judah prostituted herself, "and her prostitution was nothing, and

---

12. Cf. Jer 52:13, 1 Cor 3:17, Rom 2:23.
13. Cf. 1 Cor 6:9.
14. Jer 5:8.
15. Cf. Rv 9:17–19.

she committed adultery with the tree and the rock."[16] Whenever we sin, with hearts of stone we do nothing other than commit adultery with the stone. Whenever we sin and prostitute ourselves "under every woody tree," we commit adultery with the wood.[17] **Origen, Homilies on Jeremiah, 4.6.1 (FOTC 97)**

25 I say further: the very barbarians are offended by our impurities. Fornication of Goths is not lawful among the Goths. Only the Romans living among them can afford to be impure by prerogative of nation and name. I ask: What hope is there for us before God? **Salvian, The Governance of God, 7.6 (FOTC 3)**

26 He who seeks only sexual pleasure turns his marriage into fornication. **Clement of Alexandria, Christ the Educator, 2.10.99 (FOTC 23)**

27 What was it that delighted me, except to love and to be loved? But, the moderate relation of mind to mind was not maintained according to the bright bond of friendship; rather, the mists of slimy concupiscence of the flesh and of the bubbling froth of puberty rose like hot breath beclouding and darkening my heart. It thus was not possible to distinguish the serenity of joy from the dark mist of lust. Both [joy and lust] seethed together in hot confusion, and swept foolish youth over the precipice of passions and engulfed it in a whirlpool of shameful actions.[18] **Augustine of Hippo, Confessions, 2.2.2 (FOTC 21)**

---

16. Jer 3:8–9.
17. Jer 3:6.
18. It is particularly important to read the Fathers of the Church in conversation with the Magisterium in order to foster a greater understanding of the mind of the church. Pope Paul VI taught in *Humanae Vitae*: "The sexual activity, in which husband and wife are intimately and chastely united with one another, through which human life is transmitted, is, as the recent Council recalled, 'noble and worthy' [*Gaudium et Spes*, no. 49]. It does not, moreover, cease to be legitimate even when, for reasons independent of their will, it is foreseen to be infertile. For its natural adaptation to the expression and strengthening of the union of husband and wife is not thereby suppressed. The fact is, as experience shows, that new life is not the result of each and every act of sexual intercourse. God has wisely ordered laws of nature and the incidence of fertility in such a way that successive births are already naturally spaced through the inherent operation of these laws. The Church, nevertheless, in urging men to the observance of the precepts of the natural law, which it interprets by its constant doctrine, teaches that each and every marital act must of necessity retain its intrinsic relationship to the procreation of human life" (par. 11).

28 In marriage, intercourse for the purpose of generation has no fault attached to it, but for the purpose of satisfying concupiscence, provided with a spouse, because of the marriage fidelity, it is a venial sin; adultery or fornication, however, is a mortal sin. **Augustine of Hippo, *The Good of Marriage*, 6.6 (FOTC 27)**

29 They who debase their sex think to be free of the charge of adultery, but justice pursues them and avenges their brazenness; inevitably they draw down upon themselves some calamity and purchase death at only small cost. Merchants of such cargo, these bedeviled fools, set sail, carrying their gross immoralities as wares like grain or wine, while others, far more pitiable, buy these pleasures as they would bread or meat. They do not take to heart the command of Moses: "Do not defile thy daughter, to commit fornication with her, and the earth shall not commit fornication, and be filled with lawlessness."[19] Those words were said long ago under divine inspiration; but their effect can be seen clearly: the whole earth has become filled with fornication and lawlessness. **Clement of Alexandria, *Christ the Educator*, 3.3.22 (FOTC 23)**

30 There are some communities that feast their eyes on the manifold spectacles of conjurors from the dim morning twilight until evening itself. Nevertheless, they never have their fill of listening to soft and dissolute melodies, which undoubtedly engender in souls great impurity. Many even pronounce such people happy, because, leaving behind their business in the market or their plans for a livelihood from the arts, they pass the time of life allotted to them in all laziness and pleasure. They do not know that a theatre, flourishing with impure sights, is a common and public school of licentiousness for those who sit there, and that the elaborate melodies of the flutes and the lewd songs, sinking into the souls of the listeners, do nothing else than move them all to unseemly behavior, as they imitate the notes of the lyre or flute players. **Basil of Caesarea, *On the Hexaemeron*, Homily 4 (FOTC 46)**

---

19. Lv 19:29.

31 When they got in and had taken their places in such seats as were available, the whole place was boiling with the most savage passions. With his eyelids tightly closed, [Alypius] forbade his mind to go out to such wicked things.[20] Would that he had been able to stop up his ears, too! For, when one man fell in the fight and an immense roar from the whole audience struck his ears with a violent shock, he was overcome by curiosity. Convinced that, whatever it was like, he could defy and overcome it, even when looking at it, he opened his eyes and was wounded more seriously in his soul than the gladiator, whom he lusted to observe, had been wounded in the body. Thus, he fell more wretchedly than that man whose fall had caused the uproar which entered through his ears and laid bare his eyes so that the means was provided by which his daring mind could be wounded and knocked down—daring rather than strong, and all the weaker for having depended on itself, when it should have depended on Thee. As he looked upon the blood, he drank in the savagery at the same time. He did not turn away his gaze, but fixed it and unconsciously imbibed the mad passions. He enjoyed the criminal contest, and became drunk with lust for bloodshed. He was no longer the man who had come in, but a member of the mob to which he had come, a true associate of those who had brought him in.
Augustine of Hippo, *Confessions*, 6.8.13 (FOTC 21)

32 If the mind finds pleasure in only thinking of unlawful things, and decides in fact that they are not to be done, but yet gladly retains and ponders over that which should have been cast aside as soon as it touched the mind, then certainly we ought not to deny that there has been no sin, but it is much less than if it had been decided to complete it in action. And, therefore, we should also ask pardon for such thoughts, and we should strike our breasts and say: "Forgive us our debts," and then do what follows and is added in the prayer: "as we also forgive our debtors."[21] **Augustine of Hippo, *The Trinity*, 12.12.18 (FOTC 45)**

---

20. Alypius was one of Augustine's close friends from Carthage; cf. *Confessions*, VI.7.11.
21. Mt 6:12.

33 There is hardly anything more deadly than being married to one who is a stranger to the faith, where the passions of lust and dissension and the evils of sacrilege are inflamed. Since the marriage ceremony ought to be sanctified by the priestly veiling and blessing, how can that be called a marriage ceremony where there is no agreement in faith? Since spouses should pray in common, how can there be love of their common wedlock between those differing in religion? Many have betrayed their faith when lured by women's charms, as did the people of the patriarchs at Baal-Peor. This is why Phineas lost his sword and killed the Hebrew and the Midianite woman, and soothed God's wrath so that all of the people would not be destroyed.[22] **Ambrose of Milan, Letter 35 (19) to Vigilius (FOTC 26)**

34 "Because I kept silence, my bones grew old from my crying aloud all day."[23] When [David] committed that awful sin, he had recourse to the remedy of repentance not at once but after Nathan's reproof.[24] Accordingly he shouts this aloud at this point. Since on receipt of the blow he did not at once show the wound to the physician but kept silence in an endeavor to conceal it, he grew old crying aloud and denouncing the sin. **Theodoret of Cyrus, *Commentary on Psalm 32* (FOTC 101)**

35 Also, what profit to Solomon were his vast store of wisdom and his great devotion toward God in his previous life, since later, because of his infatuation for women, he fell into idolatry?[25] And not even his lofty position left the blessed David blameless for his sin against the wife of Uriah.[26] **Basil of Caesarea, *Letter* 42 (FOTC 13)**

36 Since the licentious person in a figurative sense is a Canaanite, he is expelled from the holy house of the Lord almighty so as no longer

---

22. Cf. Nm 25:6–13.
23. Cf. Ps 32:3.
24. This alludes to the adultery with Bathsheba and the subsequent betrayal of her husband Uriah on the battlefield. Cf. 2 Sm 11:1–21.
25. Cf. 1 Kgs 11:1–13. For Augustine, Solomon's faithlessness and idolatry is proof that the promises made to David concerning the glories of his son (cf. 2 Sm 7:8–16) were not to be fulfilled in Solomon, but in Christ. Cf. Augustine, *City of God*, 17.8.
26. Cf. 2 Sm 11:1–21.

to occupy it. In fulfillment of this the divine apostle Paul writes to the church of the Corinthians, "It is reported that there is sexual immorality among you, and of a kind that is not found even among the nations, a man living with his father's wife. And you took pride in this! Should you not rather have mourned, so that the one guilty of this would have been removed from your midst?"[27] He was expelled from the assembly of the faithful, the purpose being that he come to a sense of the evil he had embarked on of his own free will and receive the wages of his fall. That is what happened, the result being ... seriously repentant; thus one who put aside his sinful behavior was admitted to the Church, the house of God. **Didymus the Blind, *Commentary on Zechariah*, 14:21 (FOTC 111)**

37 For [the thought of fornication] happens that while one is talking to someone, if the enemy arrives in order to attract the intellect from vigilance before God, then the intellect is found to be distracted toward the enemy and the desire of fornication; then the intellect is seized. So it does not happen through planning or pondering, but rather through inattentiveness. Such a person resembles someone who is traveling but, out of a sense of faintheartedness, leaves the straight path and finds oneself on another path.[28] Therefore, one should vigilantly recall the intellect, according to what we have said, and run toward the mercy of God. For he is compassionate and awaits us like that prodigal son. We are of course not unaware of how kindly he received him.[29] And when this war is sown in the intellect without distraction, it is necessary to be vigilant, neither taking pleasure in it nor prolonging it, but swiftly escaping toward God the Master. **Barsanuphius and John, *Letter* 660 (FOTC 114)**

38 Let us imagine that there is a certain home in which the soul dwells together with the body and the spirit, as it were with a pair of counselors. In front of the entrance of this home stands piety and all the virtues

---

27. 1 Cor 5:1–2.
28. Cf. 2 Pt 2:15.
29. Cf. Lk 15:20–24.

with her. But on the other side are ungodliness and every sort of excess and lust. They are all waiting for a nod from the soul: Which of these two troops watching before her doors does she want to have let in to herself, which does she want to repel? Suppose the soul, in compliance with the spirit and yielding to the better counselor, summons to herself the troop led by piety and modesty. Will not the other group which has been spurned and repudiated go away? But suppose the soul, yielding to the counsels of the flesh, lets into her home the ungodly lust-squad. Then that whole crowd, led by holiness and piety, over which the soul preferred the counsel of the evils, shall withdraw with righteous indignation and leave the soul to the sinful desires of her own heart. The result will be that she degrade her own bodies among herself. The soul has exchanged the truth of God for a lie and, letting into herself the servants of ungodliness and faithlessness, worships and serves the creature instead of the Creator, who is blessed forever. **Origen, Commentary on Romans, 1.18.9 (FOTC 103)**

Temperance and Continence

39 O Love, who ever burnest and art never extinguished, O Charity, my God, kindle me! Thou dost command continence; grant what Thou dost command and command what Thou wilt. **Augustine of Hippo, Confessions, 10.29.40 (FOTC 21)**

40 In every way continence sets man free, being at the same time a remedy and a power; it does not teach temperance, but provides it. **Basil of Caesarea, Letter 366 to the Monk Urbicius (FOTC 28)**

41 For, just as no one uses the body impurely except through wickedness already conceived in the spirit, so no one preserves purity of body except through chastity already rooted in the spirit. **Augustine of Hippo, Holy Virginity, 8.8 (FOTC 27)**

42 We frequently find in the Scriptures, and we have often discussed this topic, that man may be said to be spirit, body, and soul.[30] And when it is said, "The flesh desires contrary to the spirit, and the spirit desires contrary to the flesh," the soul is undoubtedly placed in the middle.[31] Either it gives assent to the desires of the spirit or it is inclined toward the lusts of the flesh. If it joins itself to the flesh it becomes one body with it in its lust and sinful desires; but if it should associate itself with the spirit it shall be one spirit with it.[32] It is after all for this reason that the Lord says in the Scriptures concerning those whose souls had been united completely with the flesh, "My Spirit shall no longer abide in these men, for they are flesh."[33] But concerning those whose soul had united with the spirit the Apostle says, "But you are not in the flesh but in the Spirit."[34] **Origen, *Commentary on Romans*, 1.18.5 (FOTC 103)**

43 The new will, which had begun to be in me, to serve Thee for Thy own sake and to desire to enjoy Thee, O God, the only sure Joyfulness, was not yet capable of overcoming the older will which was strengthened by age. Thus, my two voluntary inclinations, one old and the other new, one carnal and the other spiritual, were engaged in mutual combat and were tearing my soul apart in the conflict. Thus I came to understand by personal experience the text which I had read, how the flesh "lusts against the spirit and the spirit against the flesh."[35] **Augustine of Hippo, *Confessions*, 8.5.10–11 (FOTC 21)**

44 Suppose chastity should begin with the inner man. It will undoubtedly extend to the outer, for it is impossible for someone who does not previously commit adultery in his heart to be able to commit adultery with his body.[36] But if chastity begins in the outer man, it does not immediately pass as well into inner self control, as if the one who avoids committing adultery in the body will be free from adultery in his heart.

30. Cf. 1 Thes 5:23.
31. Gal 5:17.
32. Cf. 1 Cor 6:16–17.
33. Gn 6:3.
34. Rom 8:9.
35. Gal 5:17.
36. Cf. Mt 5:28.

In this way then circumcision of the inner and outer man should be understood according to the laws of allegorical interpretation since the inner man no longer lusts in his heart, nor does the outer man serve lustful desire in the body. So he is called circumcised in the flesh whom the Apostle says is no longer in the flesh but in the Spirit, and who puts to death the deeds of the flesh by means of the Spirit.[37] **Origen, Commentary on Romans, 2.13.35 (FOTC 103)**

45 Praise to Thee, glory to Thee, O Fount of Mercies! As I grew more unhappy, Thou didst come nearer. Thy right hand was ever ready to pluck me from the filth and cleanse me, but I did not know it.[38] Nor did anything recall me from the deeper abyss of carnal pleasures, except the fear of death and of Thy future judgment, which, despite the vagaries of my opinions, never departed from my breast. **Augustine of Hippo, Confessions, 6.16.26 (FOTC 21)**

46 The Apostle also showed how much incontinency is to be dreaded by including it among the signs of apostasy, when he said: "in the last days shall come dangerous times. Men shall be lovers of themselves." Then, after enumerating several forms of iniquity, he adds: "slanderers, incontinent."[39] ... The first disobedience befell men as a consequence of incontinency. All the saints, on the contrary, were renowned for continency. **Basil of Caesarea, *The Long Rules*, q. 16 (FOTC 9)**

47 In former times, therefore, even continence was made subordinate to marriage for the sake of propagating children. Now, the marriage bond is a remedy for the vice of incontinence, so that children are begotten by those who do not practice continence, not with a disgraceful display of unbridled lust, but through the sanctioned act of lawfully wedded spouses. **Augustine of Hippo, *Adulterous Marriages*, 2.12 (FOTC 27)**

---

37. Cf. Rom 8:9, 8:13.
38. Cf. Ps 39:3.
39. 2 Tm 3:1–3.

60 2. LUST

48 Purity and virginity are a fine thing; accept the evidence of Paul who prescribes rules for these matters and makes just provision for marriage and celibacy; and of Jesus himself, who was born of a virgin in order to honor both birth-giving and especially virginity at the same time.[40] **Gregory Nazianzen, *Oration* 14.3 (FOTC 107)**

49 Continence is a grace of God. Jesus appeared to be continence when He was made light on land and sea. For, the earth did not support Him, nor the sea, but, just as He walked on the sea, so He did not weigh down the earth. Indeed, if from corruption is death and from absence of corruption immortality, Jesus wrought divinity, not mortality. **Basil of Caesarea, *Letter* 366 to the Monk Urbicius (FOTC 28)**

50 Mary offers faithful service; pregnant, yet a virgin; a virgin, yet a mother; for it was barrenness, not purity, that she lacked. There stand at hand sanctity, sincerity, modesty, chastity, integrity, and faith, and all the virtues were present together, so that the fearless maidservant would carry her Creator in her womb, and, while being the champion of her sex, she would know no pain or groans in giving birth to the Power of heaven. Blessed is that fruitfulness which both acquired the honor of motherhood and did not lose the prize of chastity. Therefore, he does not disdain to inhabit what he deigned to fashion; he does not think that it is undignified for him to touch flesh since he had handled it in the past with his heavenly hand when it was in the form of dust.[41] **Peter Chrysologus, *Sermon* 140b.2 on the Nativity (FOTC 110)**

51 You say that Mary did not remain a virgin; as for me, I claim more emphatically that Joseph himself was also a virgin through Mary, so that a virgin son might be born of a virgin wedlock. For if fornication ill befits a holy man, and it is not written down that he had a second wife, but was the guardian rather than the husband of Mary whom he supposedly possessed as his own, the conclusion follows that he, who was deemed worthy to be called the father of the Lord, remained a virgin

---

40. On "the evidence of Paul," cf. 1 Cor 7:25–39.
41. Cf. Gn 2:7.

with Mary. **Jerome, *Against Helvidius (On the Perpetual Virginity of the Blessed Mary)*, 19 (FOTC 53)**

52 She so excelled in modesty and so surpassed all the women of her own day, not to mention those of old who were greatly famed for modesty, that in the two universal divisions of life, I mean the married and the unmarried states, of which one is more sublime and divine but more difficult and perilous, while the other is lower but safer, she avoided the disadvantages of both and chose and united the sublimity of the one with the security of the other. And she was modest without being proud, blending the virtues of the married and the unmarried states, and showing that neither of these binds us completely to or separates us from God or the world.... And she rendered marriage itself laudable by her pleasing and acceptable life in wedlock and by the fair fruit of her union. And she exhibited herself, as long as she lived, as an exemplar of every excellence to her children. **Gregory Nazianzen, *Funeral Oration for His Sister, St. Gorgonia* (FOTC 22)**

53 Because perpetual continence and, above all, virginity is a great blessing in the saints of God, it must be guarded with the utmost vigilance, lest it be corrupted by pride. **Augustine of Hippo, *Holy Virginity*, 33.33 (FOTC 27)**

54 They also make an offering of virtue who are sharers in the honorable state of marriage and an undefiled marriage bed, the condition of Joseph,[42] Susanna,[43] Anna the prophetess,[44] Elizabeth the mother of the Baptist,[45] and all other such men and women who were distinguished for purity. **Didymus the Blind, *Commentary on Zechariah*, 6:12–15 (FOTC 111)**

---

42. Here, Didymus seems to be referring to Joseph, the most beloved of Jacob's twelve sons. Cf. Gn 39:6–18.
43. Cf. Dn 13:1.
44. Cf. Lk 2:36–38.
45. Cf. Lk 1:5.

55 Finally, when Joseph went in by reason of his duty and the office entrusted to him, and the witnesses and household servants were far off, she seized him and said, "Lie with me."[46] He is absolved by the testimony of Scripture, because he was unable to abandon the service entrusted to him by his master. Indeed, it is not enough that he entered the inside of his house without concern as one who could not be seduced; the just man had an obligation to take care not to give opportunity to a woman in a state of frenzy, else she might be undone by his sin. But while he perceived that the wife of his master was his adversary, still he had to guard against giving offense to his master by neglecting his duty. At the same time, he supposed her forwardness still consisted in speech, not in laying hands on him. He is absolved for having entered in and praised for having slipped away; he did not value the clothing of his body higher than the chastity of his soul. He left the clothing, which the adulteress held back in her hands, as if it were not his, and considered foreign to him the garments that the impure woman had been able to touch and seize.[47] He was, after all, a great man; although sold, he did not know the nature of a slave; although much loved, he did not love in return; although asked, he did not acquiesce; although seized, he fled away. When he was approached by his master's wife, he could be held by his garment but not seduced in his soul. He did not endure even her words for long, either, because he judged it to be a contagion if he should delay very long; else the incentives to lust might pass over to him through the hands of the adulteress. Therefore he stripped off his garment and cast off the sin. He left behind the clothing by which he was held, and fled away, stripped to be sure, but not naked, because he was covered better by the covering of modesty. Yes, a man is not naked unless guilt has made him naked. **Ambrose of Milan, *On Joseph*, 5.24–25 (FOTC 65)**

56 Let the slothful and unmortified person, whose fancy is titillated by bodily graces, discipline his thinking and engrave on the texture of his mind the law of the Lord which says, "The man who gazes on a woman

---

46. Gn 39:12.
47. Cf. Gn 39:12.

2. LUST   63

so as to lust after her has already committed sin with her in his heart"; let him banish the passion of incontinence and practice sobriety.[48] **John Chrysostom, *Homily* 15.17 on Genesis (FOTC 74)**

57 Truly, these things seem difficult, but we are speaking about him for whom a way is being prepared to heaven by the treading under foot of earthly things. For because virtue consists in the knowledge of God, all things are burdensome while you do not know Him; when you know Him, they are easy. We who are tending toward the supreme good must go through these difficulties. **Lactantius, *The Divine Institutes*, 6.23 (FOTC 49)**

58 Putting on the weapons of chastity, show it your efforts of asceticism, and the law of sin will turn to flight, and the one you thought hard to vanquish you will suddenly see a fugitive. **Cyril of Alexandria, *Festal Letters*, 11.2 (FOTC 118)**

59 And when I examine closely, God seems to me to be continence, because He desires nothing, but has everything in Himself; and He reaches after nothing, nor does He have any lust of the eyes nor of the ears, but, being in want of naught, He is wholly satisfied. Concupiscence is a disease of the soul; continence is soundness. **Basil of Caesarea, *Letter* 366 to the Monk Urbicius (FOTC 28)**

60 That we might not fall from continence, we ought to be especially vigilant against the treachery of diabolical suggestions to presume in our own strength. **Augustine of Hippo, *On Continence*, 4.10 (FOTC 16)**

61 With God's help we should resist the other vices, but overcome lust by flight. **Caesarius of Arles, *Sermon* 41.1 (FOTC 31)**

62 If we compare the things themselves, in no way can it be doubted that the chastity of continence is better than the chastity of marriage. **Augustine of Hippo, *The Good of Marriage*, 23.28 (FOTC 27)**

---

48. Mt 5:28.

63 But, as the meals of the just are better than the fastings of the sacrilegious, so the marriage of the faithful is placed above the virginity of the unbeliever. **Augustine of Hippo, *The Good of Marriage*, 8.8 (FOTC 27)**

64 Let not those who have been married only once find fault with those who have indulged in a second marriage.[49] For, while continence is a noble and admirable thing, it is also allowable to enter upon a second marriage, that the weak may not commit fornication. **Cyril of Jerusalem, *Catechetical Lectures*, 4.26 (FOTC 61)**

65 The begetting of children which results from marriage is certainly good. Marriage, too, is good, because it does away with fornication and by licit intercourse prevents the frenzy of concupiscence from being excited to illicit actions.[50] Marriage is good for those for whom continence is impossible, but virginity is better, because it increases the fecundity of the soul and offers prayer to God as a seasonable fruit. **John Damascene, *The Orthodox Faith*, 4.24 (FOTC 37)**

66 Observe how continence has usually been pleasing to the woman, but does not please the man. The wife leaves him and begins to lead a life of continence. She obviously intends to remain chaste, but she will make an adulterer of her husband, which the Lord does not wish. For, the husband will seek another woman when it becomes impossible for him to restrain himself. What are we to say to the woman, except to repeat what the sound doctrine of the Church maintains, that is, render the debt to your husband, lest, while you seek after a source of further glory, he find the source of his damnification. **Augustine of Hippo, *Adulterous Marriages*, 1.4.4 (FOTC 27)**

---

49. Translator's note: "Apparently there was considerable prejudice against a second marriage in the early church. It was very strong among the puritan sects like the Montanists." I would also add that the question seems not to be whether it is permissible to divorce and remarry, as we might interpret this in our reading today, but whether it should be permissible to remarry after the death of a spouse. Otherwise, Cyril would not have identified the sin in question as "fornication."

50. Cf. 1 Cor 7:2.

67 I admonish the men and women who have embraced perpetual continence and sacred virginity to prefer their blessing to marriage in such a way that they may not consider marriage an evil. **Augustine of Hippo, *Holy Virginity*, 18.18 (FOTC 27)**

68 It is not possible to show endurance without courage, still less continence without self-control. **Clement of Alexandria, *Stromateis*, 2.18.80 (FOTC 85)**

69 Behold, you already not only abstain from murder, sacrifices to devils and abominations, theft, robbery, cheating, lying, drunken reveling, all extravagance and avarice, deceit, envy, irreverence, cruelty, but even those things which either are or are considered less grave are not found and do not arise in your midst: neither immodest mein, nor wandering eyes, nor unbridled tongue, nor coquettish smile, nor indecent jest, nor unbecoming dress, nor haughty or undignified carriage. Even now you do "not render evil for evil, nor abuse for abuse."[51] Finally, even now you fulfill that measure of love, that you lay down your life for your brethren.[52] ... These things, combined with virginity, display an angelic life before men, and a heavenly manner of deportment before the world. **Augustine of Hippo, *Holy Virginity*, 53.54 (FOTC 27)**

70 O Virgin, grace, and not nature, has made you a mother; God's merciful devotion wanted you to be called a "Mother," which your continence did not allow; in your conceiving, in your giving birth, purity grew, chastity increased, continence was strengthened, virginity was made firm, and all the virtues continued to thrive. O Virgin, if everything is preserved for you, what did you provide? If you are a virgin, how are you a mother? If a bride, how a mother? By the action of the One who has added to all you have and has taken nothing away. **Peter Chrysologus, *Sermon* 142.7 on the Annunciation (FOTC 110)**

---

51. 1 Pt 3:9.
52. 1 Jn 3:16; cf. Jn 15:13.

71 Mary, Mother of God, rejoices, too, the supreme example of virginity, mother of incorruption, who by her example bore you and remains pure: she bore you a living proof, yet knew not pain; she bore the Bridegroom, yet is a Virgin. Daily she bears brides, yet is a Virgin. Blessed is that womb which was able to bear without being corrupted; blessed that fertility, which in bearing filled the world and won heaven as its reward, yet did not lose the veil of virginity. **Leander of Seville, *The Training of Nuns and the Contempt of the World*, introduction (FOTC 62)**

72 To the Creator she gave that He might be created, to the Fashioner that He might be fashioned, and to the Son of God and God that He might from her innocent and undefiled flesh and blood put on flesh and become man. And thus she paid the debt for the first mother. For, as Eve was formed from Adam without carnal conjunction, so did this one bring forth the new Adam in accordance with the law of gestation but surpassing the nature of generation. Thus, He who is without a mother begotten of a father was without a father born of a woman. And because it was of a woman it was in accordance with the law of gestation; while, because it was without father, it surpassed the nature of generation. And because it was at the normal time, for having completed the nine-month period He was born at the beginning of the tenth, it was in accordance with the law of gestation; while because it was without pain, it surpassed the established order of birth—for, where pleasure had not preceded, pain did not follow, as the Prophet said: "Before she was in labor, she brought forth," and again: "before her time came to be delivered she brought forth a man child."[53] **John Damascene, *The Orthodox Faith*, 4.14 (FOTC 37)**

---

53. Is 66:7. The doctrine of Mary's perpetual virginity teaches not only that she was virginal at the time of conception, but that she remains a virgin during and after the birth of Christ. Contrary to some contemporary theologians who ascribe labor pains to Mary in the birth of Christ, John (and other Fathers before him) taught the great mystery of the miraculous birth (cf. Dionysius the Areopagite, *Letter* 4 to Gaius; Maximus the Confessor, *Ambiguum*, 5). As the Fathers and later Christian tradition has understood, pains in the childbirth of the Christ is a question of fittingness, on the one hand, for how can there be pain (*odynē*) in bearing where there was no pleasure (*hēdonē*) in generating? On the other hand, there are strong theological reasons to stop short of ascribing labor pains to Mary's childbearing. This is a consequence of her immaculate conception, being preserved from the curse of Eve. The depth of her mystery also points to God. Pope Benedict XVI says in his final *Jesus of Nazareth* book that the miraculous virgin birth is an important

73 How, then, is she not Mother of God who from herself brought forth God incarnate? Actually, she is really and truly Mother of God, Lady, and Mistress of all created things, being accounted both handmaid and mother of the Creator. And just as at His conception He had kept her who conceived Him a virgin, so also at His birth did He maintain her virginity intact, because He alone passed through her and kept her shut.[54] **John Damascene, *The Orthodox Faith*, 4.14 (FOTC 37)**

---

testament to Christ's divine origin. As the pope said, "If God does not also have power over matter, then he simply is not God," in *The Infancy Narratives: Jesus of Nazareth*, trans. Philip J. Whitmore (New York: Image, 2012), 57.

54. Cf. Ezek 44:2. This may also be likened to Christ's passing through the locked doors after his resurrection; cf. Jn 20:19, 26.

3

Greed

Greed

1 The passion of greed is revealed when one is happy in receiving but unhappy in giving. Such a person cannot be a good steward. **Maximus the Confessor, *Centuries on Charity*, 3.76 (CWS)**

2 From avarice there spring treachery, fraud, deceit, perjury, restlessness, violence, and hardnesses of heart against compassion. **Gregory the Great, *Morals on the Book of Job*, XXXI.45 (LF 31)**

3 Wealth is not an evil thing (for we can use it as we ought, when we spend it for those in need); but avarice is an evil thing and brings everlasting punishment. **John Chrysostom, *Commentary on John*, Homily 64 (FOTC 41)**

4 Avarice also is wont to exhort the conquered mind, as if with reason, when it says, It is a very blameless thing, that thou desirest some things to possess; because thou seekest not to be increased, but art afraid of being in want; and that which another retains for no good, thou thyself expendest to better purpose. **Gregory the Great, *Morals on the Book of Job*, XXXI.45 (LF 31)**

5 And so we must not only guard against the possession of money, but also must expel from our souls the desire for it. For we should not so much avoid the results of covetousness, as cut off by the roots all disposition towards it. For it will do no good not to possess money, if there exists in us the desire for getting it. **John Cassian, *Institutes* 7.21 (ACW 58)**

6 Moreover, reflect within yourself whether, when out of greed you plan and desire to lay waste to another's goods, you can say that "Christ lives in me."[1] **Origen, *Homilies on Judges*, 2.1 (FOTC 119)**

7 Against the thought of love of money that made us revile our parents because they did not give us any of their property: "The one who reviles his father or his mother shall surely die."[2] **Evagrius of Pontus, *Antirrhetikos* 3.1 (CSS 229)**

8 I say this for the desire for money is more bitter than any tyranny. Indeed, it brings no pleasure, but only cares, and envy, and scheming, and hatred, and slander, and countless hindrances to virtue: laxity, licentiousness, greed, drunkenness. These make even free men slaves and worse than slaves bought with silver; slaves, not of men but even of the most serious of the passions and of the diseases of the soul. Such a man dares to do many things displeasing both to God and to men, lest someone may deprive him of this slavery. Oh, bitter slavery and devilish tyranny, for this is the harshest one of all because, though beset by such great evils, we take pleasure in them; we cling to our bonds. Though dwelling in a prison full of darkness, we do not wish to go out into the light, but fasten the evils tightly to ourselves and revel in our disease.[3] **John Chrysostom, *Commentary on John*, Homily 59 (FOTC 41)**

9 What shall I say concerning avarice, that insatiable longing, that very lust for gold which is ever desirous of more—no matter what accumulated treasure is stored away. An object of envy to all, but to himself

---

1. Cf. Gal 2:20.
2. Ex 21:16.
3. Chrysostom's description of the slavery of greed as a dark and preferable prison has strong affinities with Plato's famous allegory of the cave (cf. *Republic* VII.514a–519e).

despicable, the avaricious man is poor in the midst of riches, slighting the fact that his bank balance is large. His desire for gain is as limitless as are his opportunities for making a profit. He is so consumed with passion that the only difference between him and an adulterer is that one has an inordinate love for physical form, the other, a desire for a farm, a rich estate. The avaricious man does violence to the elements by ploughing the earth and cleaving the sea. He importunes the very heavens with his vows. He ever gives expression to displeasure whether the skies are serene or cloudy, and is censorious no matter what his annual returns are from land or sea. **Ambrose of Milan, *Cain and Abel*, 1.5.21 (FOTC 42)**

10 Patience, not avarice, gives glory to God. If you seek to receive back double the things you have lost and for that reason praise God, you are praising Him from greediness, not from love. **Augustine of Hippo, *On the Creed*, 3.10 (FOTC 27)**

11 Riches in and of themselves are good. They offer many advantages to human society when they are in the possession of generous benefactors—but not when some extravagant person makes a show of them or some miser hides them away. When hoarded, they go to waste no less than if they had been foolishly spent. **Leo the Great, *Sermon* 10.1 (FOTC 93)**

12 If the man who brought too small an offering angered God, how will the one who offers the property of others fail to anger Him? **John Chrysostom, *Commentary on John*, Homily 73 (FOTC 41)**

13 Although gluttony and intemperance are strong passions, they are not as strong as vanity. A full table or cups in quick succession can satisfy gluttony, but those who love gold and purple and jewels would not be content with all that is upon the earth or under it, nor the whole of the Tyrrhenian sea, nor the cargo of ships from India and Ethiopia, nor even with the Pactolus overflowing with riches. **Clement of Alexandria, *Christ the Educator*, 3.2.10 (FOTC 23)**

14 Avarice is a great evil, dearly beloved; in fact, it is the source of all evils, as the Apostle says: "Covetousness is the root of all evils, and some in their eagerness to get rich have strayed from the faith."[4] You know that someone who is too stingy is dishonest when he refuses to give more than he ought of his own wealth or money to the poor, or when he envies the possessions of another. If any of you are like this, consider what you can do in God's sight if you have broken your word. **Caesarius of Arles, Sermon 71.2 (FOTC 31)**

15 Wasteful spending hides under the shadow of liberality, but Thou art the most bountiful Giver of all good things. Avarice wishes to have many possessions; Thou dost possess all things. **Augustine of Hippo, Confessions, 2.6.13 (FOTC 21)**

16 The Pharisees were zealous for this one precept, namely, the accumulation of what had been commanded. Other things that were of greater importance mattered little to them. They did not care whether anyone did them or not. And so, he accuses them of greed on this point, that they zealously exact a tithe even of common herbs, yet they neglect justice in business disputes, and mercy toward poor orphans and widows, and faithfulness to God, which are great matters. **Jerome, Commentary on Matthew, IV.23.23 (FOTC 117)**

17 Now, it is time to say what the firebrand and the burning lamp consume on the right and the left. The familiar position of impious and sinful things is on the left, while what is falsely decked out as virtue is reckoned as being on the right. To condemn both, then, the divine word says, "Keep straight the paths for your feet, and set your ways right; veer neither right nor left"; fail neither by excess or by defect, each being a vice.[5] Whereas liberality, the willingness to share, is commendable, miserliness is a veering to the left, while prodigality in wasting money is thought to be on the right when it is spent not on what is necessary and proper but on the pursuit of base pleasures. Since both the miser and

4. 1 Tm 6:10.
5. Prv 4:26–27.

the wastrel are censurable, then, the firebrand and the lamp set alight to both. **Didymus the Blind, *Commentary on Zechariah*, 12:6–7 (FOTC 111)**

18 Great lover as you are of your earthly fatherland, you should fear for your fellow citizens a life of self-indulgence, not one of want. But, if you do fear want, warn them to avoid that kind of want which abounds in the fullness of earthly goods, but leaves in them an insatiable craving, which, to quote one of your authors, "is lessened neither by plenty nor by destitution."[6] **Augustine of Hippo, *Letter* 104, to Nectarius (FOTC 18)**

19 But since other things are not loved unless they are good, let him be ashamed who is attached to them and does not love the good itself by which they are good. **Augustine of Hippo, *The Trinity*, 8.3.5 (FOTC 45)**

20 Do not make peace with avarice, and despise the rewards of unjust dealings. **Leo the Great, *Sermon* 84b (FOTC 93)**

21 Poverty like a good runner will again overtake you, and the same necessity with an increase will be present.[7] For, the loan does not provide complete deliverance, but a short delaying of your hardship. Let us suffer the difficulties from want today and not put it off until tomorrow. If you do not borrow, you will be poor today and likewise for the future; but, if you borrow, you will be more cruelly tormented, since the interest has increased your poverty still more. **Basil of Caesarea, *Homily* 12.2 on Psalm 14 (FOTC 46)**

22 Nations have often failed because of usury and this has been the cause of public calamity.[8] So it is especially up to us bishops to root out

---

6. Here, Augustine is quoting Sallust, *The Conspiracy of Catiline*, 11.3.
7. Cf. Prv 24:34.
8. Usury is the charging of interest on a loan. The Torah is fairly clear about the immorality of usury. "If you lend money to any of my people with you who is poor, you shall not be to him as a creditor, and you shall not exact interest from him" (Ex 22:25; cf. Lv 25:35–37). But it is clear that, even in the Old Testament, lending and charging interest is not intrinsically evil, "To a foreigner you may lend upon interest, but to your brother you shall not lend upon interest" (Dt 23:20). The Church Fathers seem to understand this similarly. Since it is not intrinsically evil, one can reasonably charge a modest interest on loans, but it should not be used for profiteering. Even in our time, perhaps the most obvious example is that of payday loans, which often prey upon the desperation

these vices which seem to entangle most men. **Ambrose of Milan, Letter 19 (35), to Vigilius (FOTC 26)**

23 Be a money-lender; pay out what you receive. Do not be afraid that God will judge you if you are a money-lender. By all means, by all means, be a money-lender. But God says to you: "What do you wish?" Do you wish to exact usury? What does "to exact usury" mean? To give less and receive more. Then God says to you: "Behold, give to me; I receive less and I give more. What do I say? Yes, I give a hundredfold and life everlasting." He to whom you seek to give your money so that it may increase, the man whom you thus seek, rejoices when he gets the money and weeps when he returns it; he begs to get the money, but he calumniates you to avoid repaying it. **Augustine of Hippo, Sermon 239.4 on the Resurrection (FOTC 38)**

24 If any would be benefactors to their own souls, they should entrust their goods to that one who is a suitable trustee of the poor and a most generous payer of interest. But an unjust and shameless avarice which, while deceiving, says it is offering a benefit, does not believe God who promises truly but at the same time believes human beings who bargain confusedly. While they think the present is more sure than the future, they often and deservedly run into the situation in which the desire of unjust gain is for them the cause of a not unjust loss. **Leo the Great, Sermon 17.2 (FOTC 93)**

25 Whatever the outcome, the system of usury is always evil where both to diminish the money and to increase it is a sin. Either people are unhappy in losing what they gave, or they are more unhappy in receiving what they did not give. Therefore the evil of usury must be shunned, and the profit that lacks all human kindness must be avoided. The means for unjust and grievous gain is increased, but the essence of the soul is worn down, since usury in money is the ruin of the soul. **Leo the Great, Sermon 17.3 (FOTC 93)**

---

of the poor. Charging interest on loans, therefore, is something that should be very carefully considered in light of the witness of scripture and tradition.

26 He who loves money not only will not love his enemies, but will even treat his friends as enemies.... The man who loves money will never be able to have the use of it, but will be a slave and a guard, but not its master. Since he is always striving to increase it, he will never be willing to spend it, but will restrict himself and be more poverty-stricken than any poor man, since he never has any respite from his greedy desire. Yet money exists, not for us to keep, but to use. And even if we should intend to store it away for others, what occupation could be less profitable than ours, since we labor busily in the effort to get together all we can, merely in order to hoard it up, and thus prevent its use in common? **John Chrysostom, *Commentary on John*, Homily 87 (FOTC 41)**

27 If covetousness is the root of all evils, surely he strips himself of vices who does not seek money.[9] **Ambrose of Milan, *Funeral Oration for His Brother Satyrus*, 1.55 (FOTC 22)**

28 The Spirit of the Lord, through the Apostle, has called the desire of money the root of all evils.[10] We may infer that this consists not only in the desire for that which belongs to another; even that which seems to be our own belongs to another; for nothing is our own, since all things belong to God to whom we, too, belong. **Tertullian, *On Patience*, 7.5 (FOTC 40)**

29 Not everyone, therefore, says: "The Lord is my portion." The greedy man does not say this, because greed comes and says: You are my portion; I have you under my sway, you are become my slave, you sold yourself to me in that gold of yours, you turned yourself over to me in that possession of yours. **Ambrose of Milan, *Letter* 59 (63), to the church of Vercelli (FOTC 26)**

30 Christ redeemed us when we were slaves of the wicked demons, or of our own passions, and made us servants bought with money, giving

---

9. Cf. 1 Tm 6:10.
10. Cf. 1 Tm 6:10.

in ransom for the life of all his own blood,[11] and the flesh which he bore for us. **Cyril of Alexandria, *Festal Letters*, 9.6 (FOTC 118)**

31 Having been born because of us in our situation, he did not disdain the limits of our nature, nor was he ashamed of the poverty of the form of a slave.[12] **Cyril of Alexandria, *Festal Letters*, 10.1 (FOTC 118)**

32 Listen to Paul saying that you are "worse than an unbeliever."[13] This is because, even though the unbeliever has heard nothing about almsgiving, or about the things of heaven, he has surpassed you by showing charity, whereas you who have been commanded to love your very enemies regard the members of your household as enemies and spare your money rather than their bodies. On the one hand, the money that is spent will suffer no loss, but your brother, neglected, will perish. What madness it is, therefore, to be sparing of money but unsparing of one's kindred! Whence has this passion for wealth come in upon us? Whence comes this mercilessness and cruelty? **John Chrysostom, *Commentary on John*, Homily 82 (FOTC 41)**

33 God wishes to come into your heart; are you too lazy to clean out your house for Him? He does not like to live with avarice, with an unclean and insatiable mistress whose bidding you were obeying even when you sought to see God. What have you done which God commanded? What have you not done which avarice commanded? **Augustine of Hippo, *Sermon* 261.5 on the Ascension (FOTC 38)**

34 For it is one thing to give to the needy and something else to share a disposition of mercy with the one in need; and therefore, he does not want there to be sadness in such a work. For the one who pays out his money, if he is without faith and despairs over getting it back, he inevitably is grieved like one who has lost it. But he who does this with faith

---

11. On being "bought with money": Cyril is allegorically reading the Mosaic command that slaves who were bought with money were to be circumcised and thus eat of the Passover (cf. Ex 12:43–45). On "giving in ransom," cf. Eph 1:7, 1 Tm 2:6, 1 Pt 1:19.

12. Phil 2:7.

13. Cf. Ti 1:16, 1 Tm 5:8.

3. GREED

and hope does it cheerfully and joyfully, being assured that this small amount he is spending for the sake of God's command may confer enormous wealth to him in the form of heavenly riches above, but also eternal life. **Origen, *Commentary on Romans*, 9.3.14 (FOTC 104)**

35 Therefore, I seethe with indignation because, when so many blessings lie in wait for us, we are lazy, we make little account of them, and make every effort to have splendid homes in this world. On the other hand, we are not concerned, we take no thought as to how we may possess even a little abode in heaven. **John Chrysostom, *Commentary on John*, Homily 56 (FOTC 41)**

36 "He went away sad, for he had many possessions."[14] This is the sadness that leads to death.[15] The cause of his sadness is also recorded, that he had many possessions. There are the thorns and thistles that choked the Lord's seed.[16] **Jerome, *Commentary on Matthew*, III.19.22 (FOTC 117)**

37 The Lord adds further that a camel can more easily pass through the opening of a needle than for a rich man to enter the Kingdom of heaven.[17] To possess things is not a crime; rather, the issue is about how one is supposed to preserve his possessions. How are we supposed to share, and how are we supposed to hold things in common if we do not relinquish those material things to be shared and to be held in common?[18] It is, therefore, a worse crime to possess things for their own sake than [merely] to possess things. But it is a dangerous matter to want riches when innocence is violated by the heavy burden of being occupied with accumulating wealth. On the contrary, serving God is not pursuing the things of the world without [also sharing in] the sins of this world. For this reason it is difficult for a rich man to enter the Kingdom of heaven. **Hilary of Poitiers, *Commentary on Matthew*, 19.9 (FOTC 125)**

---

14. Mt 19:22.
15. Cf. 2 Cor 7:10. Cf. Origen, *In Matth.* 15:19.
16. Cf. Mt 13:22. Augustine also makes this connection with the parable of the sower in his *Confessions*, XIII.19.24.
17. Cf. Mt 19:22–24.
18. Cf. Acts 2:44.

38 The rich should not be lazy in spending their earthly treasures if they desire to possess heavenly ones. Christ, indeed, who bestows His gifts on all men, condescends to suffer privations, hunger, and cold in the person of His poor. Therefore, no one should hesitate to give to the poor, for the hand of the poor is Christ's treasury; what he receives on earth he stores up in heaven. Thus also the Lord Himself has said: "As long as you did it for one of the least of these, you did it for me."[19] **Caesarius of Arles, *Sermon* 27.3 (FOTC 31)**

39 Let those who want Christ to spare them have compassion for the poor. Let those who desire a bond with the fellowship of the blessed be "readily disposed" toward nourishing the wretched.[20] No human being should be considered worthless by another. That nature which the Creator of the universe made his own should not be looked down upon in anyone. Is it permitted for any of the hired hands to refuse that payment which the Lord declares to have been given him? Your fellow servant receives assistance, and the Lord returns thanks. Food for someone in need is the cost of purchasing the kingdom of heaven, and the one who is generous with temporal things is made heir of the eternal. **Leo the Great, *Sermon* 9.2 (FOTC 93)**

40 For death cannot be put off with a payment of money, and the last day carries off rich and poor alike. **Ambrose of Milan, *Funeral Oration for His Brother Satyrus*, 1.5 (FOTC 22)**

41 "But when the disciples saw it, they were indignant, saying: 'Why this waste? For this could have been sold for a large sum and given to the poor.'" I know that some criticize this passage and ask why another evangelist said that Judas alone was angry, for he held the purse and was a thief from the beginning, whereas Matthew writes that all the apostles were indignant.[21] These critics are unaware of a figure of speech called *sullēpsis*, which is customarily termed "all for one and

---

19. Mt 25:40.
20. Cf. 1 Tm 6:18.
21. Cf. Jn 12:4–7.

one for many." ... We can also explain it in another way: The apostles truly are indignant for the sake of the poor, but Judas was indignant for the sake of his own profits. This is why his grumbling is recorded along with his misdeeds. For he did not care about the poor but wanted to provide for his own thievery. **Jerome, Commentary on Matthew, IV.26.8–9 (FOTC 117)**

42 O traitor Judas, you value the ointment of His Passion at three hundred pence, and you sell His Passion at thirty pence.[22] Rich in valuing, cheap in wickedness! **Ambrose of Milan, On the Holy Spirit, 3.17.128 (FOTC 44)**

43 The guards confess the miracle [of the resurrection], return agitated to the city, announce to the chief priests what they saw, the events that they had seen.[23] Those who should have converted to repentance and sought the risen Jesus persevere in their malice. They convert the money that had been given for the Temple's use into a payment for a falsehood, just as they had previously given thirty pieces of silver to Judas the betrayer.[24] Therefore, all who misappropriate the donations of the Temple and those that are given for church use for other matters by which they satisfy their own will, are like the scribes and priests who purchased a falsehood and who paid money for the Savior's blood. **Jerome, Commentary on Matthew, IV.28.12–14 (FOTC 117)**

44 Surely it was not for this that you were brought into this world, O man? Surely it was not for this that you were created a man, namely, that you might work these mines and amass gold? Not for this did He form you in His image, but that you might be pleasing to Him, that you might attain to the blessings to come, that you might take part in the chorus of the angels. **John Chrysostom, Commentary on John, Homily 59 (FOTC 41)**

---

22. Cf. Mt 26:15.
23. Cf. Origen, fragment 569 in E. Klostermann and L. Fruchtel (eds.), *Origenes Matthäuserklärung III. Fragmente und Indices* (2nd ed.), in *Origenes werke*, XII/2 (Berlin: Akademie Verlag, 1968).
24. Cf. Mt 26:15.

45 What an incredible thing! Hemmed in by his riches, he is weighed down ever more by his concern for so many things. "What shall I do?" he asks. On his wealth he bestows the sort of language suitable to poverty. Where shall I pile the good things I have? The rich man abounds in possessions. Fields thick with crops have rejoiced him, those who reap them are past counting, and perhaps he also has a vineyard laden with grapes that fills his vats to the brim with wine. So then, my dear rich friend, you have everything in abundance. Except for life.[25]
Cyril of Alexandria, *Festal Letters*, 27.3 (FOTC 127)

46 And he said to him: "Come, follow me." He did not say: "Bring to me," because he was seeking Matthew, not Matthew's purses. Come, follow me. That is, "Put down your burden, break your bonds, escape the snares, follow me; seek yourself, be done with usury, so that you can find yourself." ... See why Christ had come to Matthew: to heal the wounds of avarice, to cure the infection of usury.[26] **Peter Chrysologus, *Sermon* 28.4–5 (FOTC 109)**

47 If we cannot serve both God and mammon, can we be redeemed by mammon and by God?[27] And who is the greater servant of mammon than he who is freed by money? Finally, what example do you use to justify your redeeming yourself by money? When did the apostles, dealing with the matter, ever gain their freedom from the troubles of persecution with money? They certainly had enough money from the prices of the lands that were laid at their feet, and there were plenty of wealthy men and women among Christians who would gladly have ministered to their comfort.[28] **Tertullian, *On Flight in Time of Persecution*, 12.6 (FOTC 40)**

48 So let whoever wants to conquer avarice, to stamp out covetousness, to extinguish the burning fire of greed, give away his wealth, and not

---

25. Cf. Lk 12:16–20.
26. Cf. Mt 9:9–13.
27. Cf. Mt 6:24.
28. Cf. Acts 4:34–35. Tertullian here is reproaching Christians who would pay a ransom for themselves rather than suffer martyrdom.

store it up. Brothers, let us send our treasure chests ahead of us to heaven. The poor are the transports who in their lap can carry to the heavens what is ours. Let no one have any hesitations about the qualifications of these porters. Safe this is, safe this transportation through which our goods are carried to God with God as the guarantor. **Peter Chrysologus, *Sermon* 7.6 (FOTC 109)**

Poverty

49 Are you poor and more poverty-stricken than any man? Surely, you are not more destitute than that widow who surpassed the rich and far outdid them in generosity. Are you in want of the very necessity of food to eat? Surely, you are not in greater need than the widow of Sidon. She had fallen to the extreme depths of hunger and was expecting soon to die.[29] The throng of her children stood around her, but not even in these circumstances did she hesitate to give what little she had.[30] Yet, with her extreme poverty she bought boundless wealth. She turned her handful of meal into a threshing floor and her little jug into an oil press.[31] From a little, she made an abundance gush forth. **John Chrysostom, *On the Incomprehensible Nature of God*, 8.13 (FOTC 72)**

50 Moreover, if it is necessary to spend money elsewhere than in church, no one complains of his poverty, but when a man is smitten, he even borrows money to give. Yet, if we mention almsgiving here, they allege to us children, and wife, and home, and care of their household as excuses—and other pretexts too numerous to list. **John Chrysostom, *Commentary on John*, Homily 79 (FOTC 41)**

51 Again, someone else could plead and say: I am hindered by my poverty, my lack keeps me back, so that I cannot be hospitable. And he gets rid of this excuse with the very light command, that we should supply a

---

29. Cf. 1 Kgs 17:12.
30. Only one child is mentioned in the scriptural passage; cf. 1 Kgs 17:17–24.
31. Cf. 1 Kgs 17:16.

cup of cold water from our whole heart. He says: "of cold water," not of hot water, lest in the word "hot" people plead the pretext of poverty and lack of firewood.[32] **Jerome, *Commentary on Matthew*, I.10.42 (FOTC 117)**

52 I take it that a man of simple and frugal life, without possessions of any kind, is a subject for praise. What did [Basil] ever possess except his body and the necessary coverings for his flesh? His wealth was to have nothing, possessing the cross, which alone was his life, and which he deemed more precious than great riches. No man, even if he has the desire, can gain possession of all things, but one can know how to despise all and thereby show himself superior to all. **Gregory Nazianzen, *Funeral Oration for Basil the Great* (FOTC 22)**

53 The person attached to God, by contrast, will have sound and reliable hope, and will proclaim to God the giver of good things, "In your hands my inheritance."[33] **Cyril of Alexandria, *Commentary on Malachi* 1:2–3 (FOTC 124)**

54 For just as on the stage actors enter with the masks of kings, generals, doctors, teachers, professors, and soldiers, without themselves being anything of the sort, so in the present life poverty and wealth are only masks. **John Chrysostom, *Second Sermon on Lazarus and the Rich Man* (PPS 9)**[34]

55 We must stay alert with a restless compassion in order to "have regard" for such a one. It might then be possible to seek out those whom bashfulness conceals and shame holds back. There are some who are ashamed to ask openly for what they need. They prefer to endure the misery of poverty rather than be embarrassed by making a request in public. We must therefore "have regard for" such as these and relieve them of their hidden need.[35] This would give them all the more joy

---

32. Cf. Mt 10:42.
33. Ps 30:16 as numbered in the *Septuagint* [hereafter "LXX"].
34. Sayings from this work are taken from John Chrysostom, *On Wealth and Poverty*, trans. Catharine P. Roth, PPS 9 (Crestwood, N.Y.: St Vladimir's Seminary Press, 1981).
35. Cf. Ps 40(41):2.

since consideration would have been shown both to their poverty and to their self-respect. **Leo the Great, *Sermon* 9.3 (FOTC 93)**

56 I will say unhesitatingly that the one who manages to live in poverty prudently is the best of all. For if, when he is satisfied even with little, and earns with his sweat what is most available, so to speak, he then offers prayers of gratitude, how could he not be worthy of that epithet, and merit the highest praise? **Cyril of Alexandria, *Festal Letters*, 11.6 (FOTC 118)**

57 That whatever a man may possess over and above what is necessary for life, he is obliged to do good with, according to the command of the Lord who has bestowed on us the things we possess.[36] **Basil of Caesarea, *Rule 48*, chap. 1 (FOTC 9)**

58 Many, giving away their goods to the poor, because they did not make an effort to acquire charity, have given away their goods, but it profited them nothing, because they lost themselves by not acquiring charity which they should have acquired. By these indications, it is shown that the Holy Spirit is there where the "end of the Law" is, i.e., "love from a pure heart, and a good conscience and a sincere faith."[37] **Fulgentius, *To Monimus*, II.9.2 (FOTC 95)**

59 Truly, we are God's beggars. And, in order that He may receive His beggars, let us also take notice of ours. **Augustine of Hippo, *Sermon* 61.8 on almsgiving (FOTC 11)**

60 One of the old men used to say: "We have found nothing written about any virtuous acts of the poor man Lazarus, except that he never murmured against the rich man, although the latter never showed him any pity; rather he bore the labor of his poverty gratefully, and for that reason was received into the bosom of Abraham."[38] **Paschasius of Dumium, *Questions and Answers of the Greek Fathers*, 4.1 (FOTC 62)**

---

36. Cf. Mt 5:7; Lk 6:30; Rom 1:31–32; 1 Tm 6:18.
37. 1 Tm 1:5.
38. Cf. Lk 16:19–25.

3. GREED

61 The rich man sees Lazarus with Abraham, in order that Lazarus also may convict him of inhospitability. For that patriarch hunted out those who were going past and brought them into his own house; but this rich man overlooked the one who was lying inside his gate. Although he had such a treasure and an aid to his salvation, he passed him by every day and did not use in his need the poor man's help. **John Chrysostom, *Second Sermon on Lazarus and the Rich Man* (PPS 9)**

62 Lazarus wrestled all his days with hunger, disease, and poverty, not only for thirty-eight years but for his whole life. At any rate, he died while he was lying at the gateway of the rich man, scorned, scoffed at, famished, laid out before the dogs for food. For his body had grown too weak to scare away the dogs who came and licked his wounds.[39] Yet he did not search for a soothsayer, he did not tie tokens around his neck, and he did not resort to the charm-users, he did not call in those skilled in witchcraft, nor did he do anything he was forbidden to do. He chose to die from these troubles of his rather than betray in any small way his life of godliness. **John Chrysostom, *Discourses against Judaizing Christians*, 8.6.5 (FOTC 68)**

63 Why do you ask me to send Lazarus?[40] They have Lazarus in Moses and the prophets. Moses was Lazarus; he was a poor man; he was naked. He esteemed the poverty of Christ greater riches than the treasures of Pharaoh.[41] They also have the prophets. They have Jeremiah who is thrown into a cistern of mud[42] and who fed upon the bread of tribulation. They have all the prophets; let them hearken to them. Every day Moses and the prophets are preaching against your five brothers; let them teach them; let them instruct them. **Jerome, *Homily* 86 on the Rich Man and Lazarus (FOTC 57)**

---

39. Cf. Lk 16:19–22.
40. Cf. Lk 16:29–31.
41. Cf. Heb 11:26.
42. Cf. Jer 38:6, 9.

64 Paint this parable, you rich and you poor: the rich, on the walls of your houses; the poor, on the walls of your hearts. **John Chrysostom, *Fourth Sermon on Lazarus and the Rich Man* (PPS 9)**

65 Let us pray the Lord that we may imitate the thief and this Lazarus, the beggar; if there is persecution, the thief; if peace, Lazarus.[43] If we become martyrs, straightway we are in Paradise; if we endure the pains of poverty, instantly we are in Abraham's bosom. Blood has its own abode and so has peace. Poverty, too, has its martyrdom; need well borne is martyrdom—but need suffered for the sake of Christ and not from necessity. How many beggars there are who long to be rich men and, therefore, commit crime! Poverty of itself does not render one blessed, but poverty for the sake of Christ. Faith does not fear hunger. The lover of Christ has no fear of hunger; he who has Christ, with Him possesses all riches. **Jerome, *Homily* 86 on the Rich Man and Lazarus (FOTC 57)**

66 Abbot Moses said: "Separation from material things, that is, voluntary poverty, and endurance with patience, and understanding are the possessions of a monk. For it is written: 'Even if these three men were in it, Noah, Daniel, and Job, I live, says the Lord God, and they will be saved.'[44] Now Noah is the personification of voluntary poverty, Job the personification of endurance with patience, Daniel the personification of understanding. Accordingly, if the deeds of these three holy men are in any man, the Lord is with him, dwelling with him, receiving him, and driving away from him every temptation and every tribulation that comes from the enemy." **Martin of Braga, *Sayings of the Egyptian Fathers*, 8 (FOTC 62)**

67 As the wayfarer's step is the jauntier the lighter he travels, so in this journey of life that man is happier who lightens his needs by poverty and does not groan under the burden of riches. **Minucius Felix, *Octavius*, 36.6 (FOTC 10)**

---

43. I.e., the repentant thief, cf. Lk 23:39–43.
44. Cf. Ezek 14:14, 16.

68 He cares also for the sojourners who have abandoned idolatry and devoted themselves to the true religion, and enriches every poor and needy person by the poverty which he has accepted for our sake, according to the apostle's statement recommending thanksgiving to those lucky enough to experience it, "You know the generous act of our Lord Jesus Christ, that though he was rich, yet for our sake he became poor so that by his poverty we might become rich."[45] **Didymus the Blind, Commentary on Zechariah, 7:8–10 (FOTC 111)**

69 Frequently Abbot Agatho warned his disciple: "Never acquire anything that you would be ashamed of possessing if a brother asked you for it, lest in this you transgress the command of God: 'Give to him who asks, and from him who desires to borrow, turn not aside.'"[46] **Paschasius of Dumium, Questions and Answers of the Greek Fathers, 2.4 (FOTC 62)**

70 I have seen a piteous sight, free sons dragged to the market place to be sold because of the paternal debt. You are not able to leave money to your sons? Do not deprive them as well of their dignity. Preserve for them this one thing, the possession of their liberty, the sacred trust which you received from your parents. No one has ever been prosecuted for the poverty of his father, but a father's debt leads into prison. Do not leave a bond, a paternal curse, as it were, descending upon the sons and grandsons. **Basil of Caesarea, Homily 12.4 on Psalm 14 (FOTC 46)**

71 I have had word that you have dropped your custom of clothing the poor, a work of mercy in which I always encouraged you, when I was with you; I still do urge you not to let the pressure of worldly life overcome you and make you slothful. You see the kind of things that are happening in the world, such as our Lord and Redeemer, who cannot lie, foretold would come upon it. You ought to be so far from lessening your works of mercy that you would perform even more than you were wont to do. Those who see their home about to collapse, with crumbling

---

45. 2 Cor 8:9; cf. Ps 45:10; 68:5; 146:9.
46. Cf. Lk 6:30.

walls, move out very quickly to safer places; so should Christian hearts, the more they see the destruction of this world draw near with growing calamities, make haste to transform into heavenly treasure the riches which they were getting ready to bury in the earth. **Augustine of Hippo,** *Letter* **122 (FOTC 18)**

72 Abbot Macarius said: "If, for a monk, criticism is as praise, and poverty like riches, and hunger like a banquet, he never dies. It is impossible for one who believes in God and piously worships Him to fall into unclean passion and the error of demons." **Martin of Braga,** *Sayings of the Egyptian Fathers,* **23 (FOTC 62)**

73 Is the mind disturbed by the loss of property? In practically every passage of the holy Scriptures one is admonished to despise the world, and no greater exhortation is there to an indifference toward money than that our Lord Himself is without it. **Tertullian,** *On Patience,* **7.2 (FOTC 40)**

74 "This poor man cried, and the Lord heard him."[47] Poverty is not always praiseworthy, but only that which is practiced intentionally according to the evangelical aim. Many are poor in their resources, but very grasping in their intention; poverty does not save these; on the contrary, their intention condemns them. Accordingly, not he who is poor is by all means blessed, but he who has considered the command of Christ better than the treasures of the world. These the Lord also pronounces blessed, when He says: "Blessed are the poor in spirit," not those poor in resources, but those who from their soul have chosen poverty.[48] For, nothing that is not deliberate is to be pronounced blessed. **Basil of Caesarea,** *Homily* **16.5 on Psalm 33 (FOTC 46)**

75 You must embrace the condition of this promise and show your gratitude. Although you have nothing "except what you have received," you

---

47. Ps 33:7.
48. Mt 5:3.

cannot, nevertheless, not have what you have given.[49] Consequently, those who love money and hope to increase their wealth with immoderate growth, let them rather practice this holy investment and grow rich by this art of usury, that they should not lay hold of the necessities of laboring men or fall into the traps of impossible debts through deceitful benefits.[50] Let them instead be the creditors and the money-lenders of someone who said: "Give and it will be given to you," and "the measure with which you measure, the same will be measured back to you."[51]
Leo the Great, *Sermon* 17.2 (FOTC 93)

76 As we listen to this parable and fear the punishment it recounts, let us produce for our brothers what good we have; let us not hide it away, but let us publically share it with all men. When we share with others, then we grow all the more wealthy.[52] When we make many share as partners in our business enterprise, then will we increase our own abundance. You think that your glory is diminished when you share with many the knowledge of things which you alone know. Indeed, that is the very time when your glory and your profits will increase.
John Chrysostom, *On the Incomprehensible Nature of God*, Homily 10.4 (FOTC 72)

---

49. Cf. 1 Cor 4:7.

50. Leo the Great is here playing on a Gospel paradox, namely, that the Christian by giving away personal goods to the poor thereby enriches himself and makes a "holy investment." Leo even goes so far as to call this investment "usury" because God grows the investment and makes the Christian "rich by this art." Cf. Gary Anderson, *Charity: The Place of the Poor in the Biblical Tradition* (New Haven, Conn.: Yale University Press, 2013). If this offends our sensibilities, perhaps we are too inclined toward a Kantian altruism that emphasizes the necessity for the total removal of selfish motives in order for a deed to be considered moral. For Kant, charity has to be completely independent of any reward in order to be considered charity. This is quite at odds with the Gospel account, where Jesus promises exorbitant heavenly returns on earthly giving. Leo has no difficulty in encouraging his profiteers and usurers in the order of earthly mammon to be profiteers and usurers in the orders of grace and glory.

51. Lk 6:38.

52. What Chrysostom seems to be indicating here is that when one is generous with private goods, one gains a greater participation in the common good. In this sense, there is a sort of transaction that occurs. Distribution of private goods (e.g., bread) does cause them to diminish. Sharing private goods for the sake of Christ, however, brings about a sort of divine exchange, with a very favorable exchange rate, especially as the ultimate common good is God himself. This is at the heart of the communion (*koinōnia*) of the church. Goods that truly are common, as are those in the spiritual order, are not diminished by their sharing. Cf. Charles De Koninck's essay, "The Primacy of the Common Good Against the Personalists" in *The Writings of Charles De Koninck*, ed. and trans. Ralph McInerny (Notre Dame, Ind.: University of Notre Dame Press, 2009), 2:72–108.

77 That poverty is related to the virtues, earthly and heavenly teaching attests. The athlete goes to the contest naked, the sailor battles the waves naked, the soldier maintains his post on the battle line only if he is unencumbered. Whoever is inclined toward philosophy first scorns everything having to do with material goods. So poverty is related to the virtues. And if poverty is the parent of the virtues, and is thus considered the ally of the virtues, it will be fitting to understand why Christ thus chose the poor for the office of virtue. **Peter Chrysologus, *Sermon* 28.1 (FOTC 109)**

78 In making some modest repayment to the Savior, and gladdening our Benefactor in return with what thanks we can, let us acknowledge our poverty, saying, "What shall I render to the Lord for all the things wherein he has rewarded me? I will take the cup of salvation, and call upon the name of the Lord."[53] **Cyril of Alexandria, *Festal Letters*, 6.12 (FOTC 118)**

79 In Proverbs, Solomon also proclaims similar things about the just person when he says, "When the just person eats, he will fill his soul; but the souls of the impious will be in extreme poverty."[54] If you take it according to the literal sense that, "when the just person eats he will fill his soul but the souls of the impious will be in poverty," it will appear false. For the souls of the impious take food with eagerness and strive after "satiety"; but the just meanwhile are hungry. Finally, Paul was just and he said, "Up to this hour we are hungry, and thirsty, and naked, and we are beaten with fists."[55] And again he says, "In hunger and thirst, in many fastings."[56] And how does Solomon say, "when the just eats he will satisfy his soul"? But if you consider how "the just person" always and "without interruption" eats from "the living bread" and fills his soul and satisfies it with heavenly food which is the Word of God and his Wisdom, you will find how the just person "eats his bread in

---

53. Ps 116:12–13.
54. Prv 13:25.
55. 1 Cor 4:11.
56. 2 Cor 11:27.

abundance" from the blessing of God. **Origen, *Homilies on Leviticus*, 16.5.4 (FOTC 83)**

80 As for you, man of God, remember whose creature you are and the task to which you are called; how many things you have received and the extent of your obligation; from whom come your reason, your law, your prophets, your very knowledge of God, your absence of despair for the future. For these reasons imitate God's philanthropy. It is in this, in doing good, that man is preeminently divine. You can become God without hardship; do not forgo the opportunity for deification. **Gregory Nazianzen, *Oration* 17.9 (FOTC 107)**

4

Anger

Anger

1 Do not become angry, for anger leads to murder. Do not become jealous, or quarrelsome, or irritable, for from all these murders come. *Didache of the Twelve Apostles*, 3.2 (FOTC 1)

2 From anger are produced strifes, swelling of mind, insults, clamor, indignation, blasphemies. **Gregory the Great,** *Morals on the Book of Job,* **XXXI.45 (LF 31)**

3 Anger is also wont to exhort the conquered heart, as if with reason, when it says, "The things that are done to thee cannot be borne patiently; nay rather, patiently to endure them is a sin; because if thou dost not withstand them with great indignation, they are afterwards heaped upon thee without measure." **Gregory the Great,** *Morals on the Book of Job,* **XXXI.45 (LF 31)**

4 There are three kinds of anger; namely, wrath (which is called bile and spleen), rancor, and vindictiveness. When anger arises and starts to move, it is called wrath, bile, and spleen. Rancor is an enduring wrath, or bearing malice. It is called *mēnis* from its *menein*, or remaining, and being impressed upon the memory. Vindictiveness is wrath on the watch for an opportunity for revenge. It is called *kotos* from *keisthai*, or being laid down. **Jerome, *Commentary on Galatians*, 5:19–21 (FOTC 121)**

5 The difference between wrath and anger is this: The wrathful person is always riled, while the angry person is perturbed just for a little while. Quarrels (*rixae*) alienate us from the kingdom of God as well. The Greeks call these *eritheiai*; this word has a slightly different connotation than the Latin *rixa* (a "quarrel" is usually designated as *machē*). An *eritheia* is involved when someone is always ready to contradict, takes joy in irritating others, engages in womanish spats, and provokes the person with whom he is arguing. Among the Greeks this is known by another name, *philonikia*. **Jerome, *Commentary on Galatians*, 5:19–21 (FOTC 121)**

6 Now, in the first place, violent anger is foolish, frivolous, and silly. In the next place, bitterness arises from silliness, from silliness wrath, from wrath anger, and from anger rage. Finally, the rage that has in it such evil elements becomes a serious and incurable sin. ***The Shepherd of Hermas*, Mandate V.II.4 (FOTC 1)**

7 Whenever a harsh word opens a door, anger enters in, and on the heels of anger, injury. **Ephrem the Syrian, *Homily on Our Lord*, 22.3 (FOTC 91)**

8 Swift, indeed, is the passion of anger and swifter than any fire. Wherefore, we need to be very quick in preventing its flame and in not permitting it to mount up on high. I say this because this disease, if allowed to grow, becomes the cause of many evils. Indeed, it has upset entire households, and completely destroyed long-standing friendships, and wrought irreparable tragedies in a brief space and in a moment of time. **John Chrysostom, *Commentary on John*, Homily 4 (FOTC 41)**

9 Anger is the spearman of the reason and the avenger of desire.[1] Thus, when we desire a thing and are thwarted by someone, our reason

---

1. The Damascene's thought is quite harmonious with Plato's account of the trichotomy of the soul from *Republic* IV (cf. the introduction above).

decides that for such as would maintain their own natural position this occurrence is worthy of vexation, and we get angry at him over our having been wronged. **John Damascene, *The Orthodox Faith*, 2.16 (FOTC 37)**

10 Anger seeks revenge; who attains vindication more justly than Thou?[2] **Augustine of Hippo, *Confessions*, 2.6.13 (FOTC 21)**

11 He who avenges himself is not worthy of the vengeance of the Lord. **Jerome, *The Apology against the Books of Rufinus*, 3.1 (FOTC 53)**

12 When someone abusively insults you, do not harbor resentment against him, but against the Devil who is tempting him to do this. Vent your wrath on him, but pity the man who is tempted by him. For, if lying comes from the Devil, showing anger to no purpose is much more from that source. When you see someone making fun of you, reflect that it is the Devil who is tempting him. **John Chrysostom, *Commentary on John*, Homily 84 (FOTC 41)**

13 A person cannot accurately be called a Christian if he does not give assent to the faith with his mind, even if he conforms to it in other respects, or if his mind gives assent, but his body is not suited to his way of life, exhibiting the anger of dragons and the bestiality of serpents, or adding to his human character an equine madness for women. In such cases, a man becomes double-natured, a centaur made up of reason and passion. It is possible to see many such people: either they resemble the Minotaur, being bull-headed in their belief in idolatry, although they appear to be leading a good life; or they make themselves centaurs and dragons by combining with a Christian facade a bestial body. **Gregory of Nyssa, *On Perfection* (FOTC 58)**

14 Fierce is the passion of anger, fierce, and capable of stealing away our souls. For this reason it is necessary to shut off its approach on all sides. And this is so because it is ridiculous to be able to tame wild beasts yet

---

2. Cf. Rom 12:19.

to allow our own minds to be savagely angry. **John Chrysostom, Commentary on John, Homily 26 (FOTC 33)**

15 Against the soul that gets angry swiftly but seeks the righteousness of God: "Let everyone be quick to listen, slow to speak, slow to anger; for your anger does not produce God's righteousness."[3] **Evagrius of Pontus, Antirrhetikos 5.58 (CSS 229)**

16 There is no difference between anger and madness, but it is an evil spirit that comes and goes; rather, it is worse than demoniacal possession. For, the man possessed by a demon may even enjoy pardon, while he who indulges in anger will merit punishments without number, since he deliberately casts himself into the depths of ruin. Moreover, even before Gehenna that lies in store, he already begins to pay the penalty for his action, by introducing into his inmost thoughts a certain unceasing unrest and persistent distress all through the night and all through the day. **John Chrysostom, Commentary on John, Homily 48 (FOTC 41)**

17 How can he be consistent who is at one time aflame with anger, at another seething with fierce indignation, now with face aglow, now changed to paleness, varying and changing color every moment? But, granted that it is natural to be angry, or that there generally is good reason therefore, it is man's duty to temper wrath; not to be carried away with the fury of a lion, not knowing how to be gentle; not spreading tales, nor engendering family quarrels, for it is written: "A passionate man diggeth up sin."[4] **Ambrose of Milan, Letter 59 (63), to the church of Vercelli (FOTC 26)**

18 The flesh hates the soul and acts like an unjust aggressor, because it is forbidden to indulge in pleasures. The world hates Christians—not that they have done it wrong, but because they oppose its pleasures. The

---

3. Jas 1:19–20.
4. Prv 15:18.

soul loves the body and its members in spite of the hatred. So Christians love those who hate them. **Letter to Diognetus, 6 (FOTC 1)**

19 In the case of all who formerly indulged in hatred [of Christianity] because of their ignorance of the nature of what they hated, their hatred comes to an end as soon as their ignorance ceases. From this group come the Christians, as a result, assuredly, of their personal experience. They begin now to hate what once they were and to profess what once they hated; and the Christians are really as numerous as you allege us to be.[5] **Tertullian, *Apology* 1.6 (FOTC 10)**

20 Try harder to agree among yourselves than to find fault, for, as vinegar corrodes a vessel if it is left in it too long, so anger corrodes the heart if it goes over to the next day. **Augustine of Hippo, *Letter* 210, to Felicitas, Rusticus, and sisters (FOTC 32)**

21 Listen to what John says hate is: "Everyone who hates his brother is a murderer. And you know that no murderer has eternal life abiding in him."[6] He eliminates from eternal life the one who hates his brother as a murderer. Rather, he openly calls hatred murder. For the persons who withhold and destroy their love towards their neighbors and become an enemy instead of a friend, we would easily count as murderers, regarding the hidden hatred of one's neighbor as the hatred of murderers towards those they are plotting against. **Gregory of Nyssa, *On the Christian Mode of Life* (FOTC 58)**

---

5. Fulton Sheen made a similar statement once: "There are not over a hundred people in the United States who hate the Catholic Church. There are millions, however, who hate what they wrongly believe to be the Catholic Church—which is, of course, quite a different thing." This quotation is from Sheen's introduction to Leslie Rumble's *Radio Replies: Classic Answers to Timeless Questions about the Catholic Faith* (San Diego: Catholic Answers Press, 2014), originally published in 1938–42. Cf. Tertullian, *Apology* 1.9: "They prefer to remain ignorant because they are already filled with hatred. Consequently, they form a preconceived idea with regard to that of which they are ignorant. Yet, if they knew it, they could not hate it; because, if no ground for their hatred be found, it would certainly be best to cease their unjust hatred."

6. 1 Jn 3:15.

22 Anger is the mother of hatred. Thus the Savior wished to shut out anger lest hatred be born therefrom.[7] **Salvian, The Governance of God, 3.2 (FOTC 3)**

23 "Everyone who is angry with his brother."[8] In some codices the words are added: "without reason."[9] But in the authentic texts the judgment is definite and anger is completely taken away, since the Scripture says: "Whoever is angry with his brother." For if we are commanded to turn the other cheek to the one who strikes us, and to love our enemies, and to pray for those who persecute us, every pretext for anger is removed.[10] and to love our enemies,[11] and to pray for those who persecute us,[12] every pretext for anger is removed. Therefore, the words "without reason" should be erased. For "man's anger does not work the justice of God."[13] **Jerome, Commentary on Matthew, I.5.22 (FOTC 117)**

24 Just as exhortation and encouragement are types of discourse allied to the type called advice, so the type called encomium is allied to that of reproach and blame. This last is the art of rebuke; it indicates, not hatred, but good will. Both he who is friendly and he who is not express disapproval: the one who is hostile does so out of contempt; the friend, in good will. Therefore, it is not from hatred that the Lord reproves men, for instead of destroying him because of his personal faults, He has suffered for us. **Clement of Alexandria, Christ the Educator, 1.8.66 (FOTC 23)**

---

7. Cf. Mt 5:22.
8. Mt 5:22.
9. Other Church Fathers, such as Origen, often considered variants in the manuscript traditions to be inspired by God as well. Jerome does not take such an approach in this particular instance, unambiguously repudiating this variant. It is difficult not to agree with Jerome's point here, as the phrase seems to open the door to the justification of anger, which seems to be contrary to Jesus's intention in this verse and the following. This reading may be found in a number of contemporary Bibles, including the King James Version, the Eastern/Greek Orthodox Bible New Testament, and Young's Literal Translation.
10. Cf. Mt 5:39.
11. Cf. Mt 5:44.
12. Cf. Lk 6:27–29.
13. Jas 1:20.

25 Slander is wicked, a restless devil, never at peace, but always dwelling amid dissensions. Keep away from it and you will always be on good terms with all men. *The Shepherd of Hermas*, Mandate II.3 **(FOTC 1)**

26 Restrain yourself from anger, and do not let the desire for vengeance inflame the resentment of ill will. **Leo the Great, *Sermon* 84b (FOTC 93)**

27 What he says, "For I do not do what I want; but I do the very thing I hate,"[14] shows that even though the one who is saying these things may be of the flesh and sold into slavery under sin, he is nevertheless also attempting to resist the vices to some small extent, obviously by means of the instinct that comes from natural law; but he is conquered by the vices and, against his will, is overwhelmed. This is what frequently occurs, for example, when someone resolves patiently to endure another who is inciting him, but in the end is overcome with wrath and suffers this against his own will. Thus he becomes angry even though he does not want to become angry. The same thing regularly happens with the vice of fear, so that even contrary to one's will a person may be terrified with dread and fright. This also comes to pass quite often in connection with sudden elation or unexpected honor, resulting in one being more arrogant and haughty than one wants. The person who is not yet spiritual but fleshly is therefore conquered by each individual [vice], even contrary to his will. For that will is not yet strong and robust enough that it may determine for itself that it must struggle even to the point of death for the sake of the truth.[15] **Origen, *Commentary on Romans*, 6.9.5–6 (FOTC 104)**

28 If some time previously a camel has been struck, he saves up his wrath for a long time, but, when he finds a suitable opportunity, he repays the evil. Hear, you sullen men who pursue vengeance as though it were a virtue, who it is that you resemble when you harbor for so long a time your resentment against your neighbor like a spark hidden

---

14. Rom 7:15.
15. Cf. Sir 4:28.

in ashes, until finding material, you kindle your wrath like a flame. **Basil of Caesarea, *On the Hexaemeron*, Homily 8.1 (FOTC 46)**

29 It is an honor for a man to separate himself from quarrels; but he who is a fool meddles with such reproaches.[16] Do not love to detract lest you be destroyed. **Jerome, *The Apology against the Books of Rufinus*, 3.42 (FOTC 53)**

30 Let us put aside our hatred for one another. Let no one be an enemy to his neighbor for even a single day. He must rid himself of anger before nightfall. If he does not do this but rather goes off by himself, in his hatred, he will compile a list of all that was said and done. And this will make it harder to end the quarrel and more difficult to effect a reconciliation. **John Chrysostom, *On the Incomprehensible Nature of God*, Homily 10.58 (FOTC 72)**

31 We should not suppose that peace is limited to not quarreling with others. Rather, the peace of Christ (that is, our inheritance) is with us when the mind is at peace and undisturbed by the passions. **Jerome, *Commentary on Galatians*, 5:22–23 (FOTC 121)**

32 Anger is a strong fire, consuming all things, for it both wastes the body, and corrupts the soul, and renders a man odious and base to look upon. And if it were possible for the angry man to see himself at the time of his anger, he would not need any other admonition, for there is nothing less pleasing than an angry countenance. **John Chrysostom, *Commentary on John*, Homily 26 (FOTC 33)**

33 Return to yourself; there you find a quarrel. If you have begun to follow God, there you find a quarrel. What quarrel, you say, do I find? "Flesh lusts against spirit, and spirit against flesh."[17] Look, you are yourself. Look, you are alone. Look, you are with yourself. Look, you suffer no other man. But you see another law in your members, fighting

---

16. Cf. Prv 20:3.
17. Gal 5:17.

against the law of your mind, and imprisoning you in the law of sin which is in your members.[18] Therefore, cry out, and from your inner quarrel shout to God, that he may pacify you for yourself: "Unhappy man that I am, who will deliver me from the body of this death? The grace of God through Jesus Christ our Lord."[19] For he said "He who follows me will not walk in darkness, but will have the light of life."[20] **Augustine of Hippo, *Tractates on the Gospel of John*, 34.10.3 (FOTC 88)**

34 If, with slight forbearance, I hear some bitter or evil remark directed against me, I may return it, and then I shall inevitably be bitter myself. Either that, or I shall be tormented by unexpressed resentment. If, then, I retaliate when cursed, how shall I be found to have followed the teaching of our Lord? For it has been handed down that a man is not defiled by unclean dishes, but by the words which proceed from his mouth;[21] and, what is more, that it remains for us to render an account for every vain and idle word.[22] It follows, then, that our Lord forbids us to do certain acts, but at the same time admonishes us to endure with meekness the same treatment at the hands of another. **Tertullian, *On Patience*, 8.4–6 (FOTC 40)**

35 There are two sorts of fear, one of which is accompanied by reverence. This sort citizens feel toward their rulers if they are good, and we toward God, as well-trained children do toward their father.... The other kind of fear is mixed with hate: this is the way slaves feel toward harsh masters, and the Hebrews when they looked on God as their Master and not their Father. **Clement of Alexandria, *Christ the Educator*, 1.9.87 (FOTC 23)**

36 You know well, excellent brother, that hatred would close the door against God Himself. Anger creeps in so subtly that everyone deems his own anger just, and habitual anger becomes hatred. And the min-

---

18. Cf. Rom 7:23.
19. Cf. Rom 7:24–25.
20. Jn 8:12.
21. Cf. Mk 7:15.
22. Cf. Mt 12:36.

gled sweetness of a just resentment is like a trace of perfume in a vial, remaining too long until the whole becomes sour and the vial unfit for use. Therefore, it is better for us not to harbor even a just anger against anyone, because it is only too easy to fall unperceived from just anger into hatred. **Augustine of Hippo, *Letter* 38, to Profuturus (FOTC 12)**

37 Miserable men that we are, we cannot hold our tongue; we cannot refrain from vilifying our brothers. If anyone offends us, we put on a friendly face, but we have the venom of resentment in our heart. We are called monks, even though we are not all that we ought to be. We pray at the third hour, at the sixth, at the ninth; we say vespers at sunset; we rise in the middle of the night; then we pray again at cock-crow. How constantly we are being roused to the devout services of God: the third hour, the sixth, the ninth, vespers, midnight, dawn, early morning. We do all this, and yet it does not occur to us that if we harbor enmity against our brother, our prayer is vain. **Jerome, *Homily* 41 on Psalm 119 (120) (FOTC 48)**

38 The man who stores up injuries and resentments and yet fancies that he prays might as well draw water from a well and pour it into a cask that is full of holes. **Evagrius of Pontus, *Chapters on Prayer* 22 (CSS 4)**

39 It is of the very nature of goodness that it arouse a hatred for what is evil. **Clement of Alexandria, *Christ the Educator*, 1.8.70 (FOTC 23)**

40 God's "anger" implies no perturbation of the divine mind; it is simply the divine judgment passing sentence on sin. And when God "thinks and then has second thoughts," this merely means that changeable realities come into relation with His immutable reason. For God cannot "repent," as human beings repent, of what He has done, since in regard to everything His judgment is as fixed as His foreknowledge is clear. But it is only by the use of such human expressions that Scripture can make its many kinds of readers whom it wants to help to feel, as it were, at home. Only thus can Scripture frighten the proud and arouse the slothful, provoke enquirers and provide food for the convinced; this

is possible only when Scripture gets right down to the level of the lowliest readers. **Augustine of Hippo, *The City of God*, 15.25 (FOTC 14)**

41 Everything recorded about God, even if it may be immediately unsuitable, must be understood worthy of a good God. For who will not say that what is brought up regarding God, that he has anger, that he uses wrath, that he regrets, and that he even now sleeps, does not seem unsuitable?[23] But each of these qualities, with the knowledge to hear "dark words," will be found worthy of God.[24] For his anger is not fruitless, but just as his word instructs, so his anger instructs. He instructs with anger those who were not instructed by the word, and it is necessary that God use what is called anger as he uses what is named word. For his word is not such as the word of all others.... So indeed the anger of God is an anger ... of no one else, an anger of none whatsoever, and just as the word of God has something of a nature alien beyond every word of anyone else—and what is God and what is a "living being"[25] while being a word, what subsists in itself and what is subject to the Father, has an alien nature—so too, since once it was named as being of God, what is called anger has something alien and different from all the anger of him who is angry, so too his wrath also has something individual. For it is the wrath of the purpose of the One who reproves by wrath, who wishes to convert the one reproved through the reproof. A word also reproves as a word instructs, but a word does not reprove in the way wrath reproves. For those who are helped by the reproof from the word will not need reproof from wrath.[26] **Origen, *On Jeremiah*, Homily 20.1.1 (FOTC 97)**

---

23. Cf. Jer 38:26.
24. Cf. Prv 1:6.
25. "Living being" is from the *Acts of Paul*.
26. This challenging quotation is somewhat similar to that of Augustine's above it. The key theological idea connecting them both is that the "wrath" of God cannot be understood in the same sense as "wrath" when one speaks of man's wrath. There is a principle of analogy at work here. One of the main stumbling blocks of the new atheists is the pitfall of universally predicating anger to God and man in the same sense. For example, that they could never worship "an angry God." They make the "anger" of man the same as the "anger" of God. As Origen and Augustine point out, this is contrary to the witness of scripture. We, on the other hand, *can and should* worship "an angry God," because his anger is nothing like ours at all! It is not an outburst of passion, because he is without passion. Rather, if one is to speak of divine wrath, it is inextricable from God's perfect goodness.

42 Now I say this for anger is a wild beast, a ferocious wild beast, eager for its prey. Therefore, let us chant to ourselves incantations taken from the divine Scriptures, and let us say: "You are dust and ashes," and "Why is earth and ashes proud?"[27] Also: "The wrath of his high spirits is his ruin."[28] And: "A hot-tempered man is not seemly."[29] Indeed, nothing is more shameful than a countenance ablaze with anger, nothing more disfigured. And if this is true of the countenance much rather is it true of the soul. For, just as a noisome odor is usually given off when mud is stirred up, so when the soul is disturbed by anger great impropriety and unpleasantness will result. **John Chrysostom, *Commentary on John*, Homily 48 (FOTC 41)**

43 Let us not raise up against ourselves through anger and backbiting what has been rightly deadened for our salvation by God. This would destroy our soul and bring about an evil resurrection of what is rightly dead. But, if we have Christ, who is peace, let us also deaden hatred in ourselves in order to achieve in our life what we believe is in Him. **Gregory of Nyssa, *On Perfection* (FOTC 58)**

44 Judas does not retrace his steps, even after being rebuked for his treachery not one time but twice. Instead, the Lord's patience feeds his impudence, and he treasures up wrath for himself on the day of wrath.[30] Punishment is predicted, that the threatened penalties might correct the one whom shame did not conquer. **Jerome, *Commentary on Matthew*, IV.26.24 (FOTC 117)**

45 Therefore, let us not allow the beast to be unbridled, but let us fasten on it a muzzle that is strong in every way; namely, the fear of the judgment to come. When a friend vexes you, or some member of your household stirs you to anger, consider your transgressions against God, and that, by the clemency you exercise toward those who have offended you, you may render that judgment of His milder for yourself.

27. Cf. Gn 3:19; 18:27.
28. Sir 10:9.
29. Prv 11:25 (LXX).
30. Cf. Rom 2:5.

Scripture, in fact, says: "Forgive, and you shall be forgiven," and so your passion will quickly depart.[31] **John Chrysostom, *Commentary on John*, Homily 4 (FOTC 33)**

Long-suffering and Patience

46 Patience is a wonderful virtue. It places the soul in a calm harbor, as it were, sheltering it from the billows and winds of evil.
John Chrysostom, *Commentary on John*, Homily 84 (FOTC 41)

47 The virtue of the soul which is called patience is so great a gift of God that it is even said to belong to Him who bestows it, in that He waits for the wicked to amend. So, although God cannot suffer, and patience surely has its name from suffering [*patiendo*], we not only faithfully believe in a patient God, but also steadfastly acknowledge Him to be such. Who can explain in words the nature and the quantity of God's patience? We say He is impassible, yet not impatient; nay, rather, extremely patient. His patience is indescribable, yet it exists as does His jealousy, His wrath, and any characteristic of this kind. But, if we conceive of these qualities as they exist in us, He has none of them.[32] We do not experience these feelings without annoyance, but far be it from us to suspect an impassible God of suffering any annoyance. Just as He is jealous without any ill will, as He is angry without being emotionally upset, as He pities without grieving, as He is sorry without correcting any fault, so He is patient without suffering at all.
Augustine of Hippo, *On Patience* 1.1 (FOTC 16)

48 Long-suffering is a fine thing; once again the witness is Jesus, who not only forbore to summon the legions of angels against those who rose in rebellion against him and to rebuke Peter for raising his sword,

---

31. Lk 6:37.
32. Augustine is applying the principle of analogy to the idea of patience as a divine attribute. Analogy is a strong current of the tradition in East and West before and after Augustine. He is able to do this because God's attributes do not exist in God himself in the same way as in mankind.

but even restored the ear of the man who had been struck.[33] Stephen, too, the disciple of Christ, later acted in the same way when he prayed for those who were stoning him.[34] Meekness is a fine thing, as Moses[35] and David[36] attest—this is the quality that Scripture ascribes to them above all—and their teacher, who neither wrangles, nor cries aloud, nor lifts up his voice in the street, nor offers resistance to those who lead him off.[37] **Gregory Nazianzen, Oration 14.2 (FOTC 107)**

49 Regard the long-suffering of our Lord as salvation. **Augustine of Hippo, On Faith and Works, 14.22 (FOTC 27)**

50 "He did not maintain his wrath as testimony, because his wish is for mercy": though the wrath he bore us was just, he could not bring himself to sustain it for long, right though he was to exercise it; although he often confirmed to us what we would suffer for failing, we in no way came to our senses through the threats, yet he has overcome everything by his mercy, which he is ever concerned will overcome everything. **Theodore of Mopsuestia, *Commentary on Micah*, 7:18 (FOTC 108)**

51 He is a gentle Lord, a patient Lord, a merciful Lord, but also a just Lord and a truthful Lord. A period of time for correction is bestowed on you; but you love procrastination more than amendment. Were you evil yesterday? Be good today. And have you spent this day in wickedness? At least change tomorrow. You are always waiting, and you promise yourself very much from the mercy of God, as if he who promised you forgiveness through your repentance also promised you a longer life. How do you know what tomorrow may bring forth? **Augustine of Hippo, *Tractates on the Gospel of John*, 33.7 (FOTC 88)**

---

33. Mt 26:53; Lk 22:50–51; Jn 18:10–11.
34. Acts 7:58–60.
35. Nm 12:3.
36. Ps 132:1 (LXX 131:1).
37. Is 42:2, 53:7; Mt 12:19.

52 When subjected to the same sufferings as Christ, it seemed the more Christian thing to emulate his patience. **Gregory Nazianzen, *Concerning Himself and the Bishops*, 105 (FOTC 75)**

53 Courage is defined as the knowledge of what is to be feared, what is not, and what is intermediate between the two .... It follows that patience, sometimes called endurance, is close to courage, being the knowledge of what is to be withstood and what not. So is superiority of spirit, the science which scorns the ephemeral. **Clement of Alexandria, *Stromateis*, 2.18.79 (FOTC 85)**

54 And correct one another, not in anger but in peace, as you have it in the Gospel. ***Didache of the Twelve Apostles*, 15.3 (FOTC 1)**

55 We have reminded you that you must please Almighty God with holiness in justice and truth and long-suffering, in a life of concord. You should forget injuries in love and peace, and continue in gentleness, as our fathers aforementioned who, in their humility, were pleasing to God, the Father and Creator, and to all men. **Clement of Rome, *First Letter*, 62.2 (FOTC 1)**

56 Whenever, then, you see someone suffering patiently, do not immediately praise that patience, for true patience is recognized only through its cause. When this is good, then you have true patience. **Augustine of Hippo, *On Patience* 6.5 (FOTC 16)**

57 Since the times are evil and the Worker of evil himself holds sway, we must give heed to ourselves and search out the commandments of the Lord. The helpers of our faith are fear and patience; our allies are long-suffering and self-control. While these [virtues], then, persist in their purity in matters relating to the Lord, Wisdom, Prudence, Understanding and Knowledge rejoice with them. ***Epistle of Barnabas*, 2.1–3 (FOTC 1)**

58 "Be long-suffering," he [the angel of repentance] said, "and prudent, and you will obtain the mastery over wickedness and accomplish all justice. For, if you are long-suffering, the Holy Spirit dwelling in you will be clear, unobscured by any other spirit of evil. Dwelling in a spacious place, He will rejoice and be glad with the lodging in which He finds Himself. Thus, He will serve God with abundant cheerfulness, because He has His well-being within Himself." **The Shepherd of Hermas, Mandate V.I.1–2 (FOTC 1)**

59 Victory over anger is not to repay like for like (for this is total defeat), but for the man who has suffered wrong and heard evil of himself to bear it with equanimity. Victory consists in this: not to injure others but to bear injury. **John Chrysostom, *Commentary on John*, Homily 4 (FOTC 33)**

60 [My father] did not cherish the anger that brings ruin even to the prudent or show any mark on his body of any passion within, preserving his calmness even when he was roused. The most surprising result of all this was that while he was not the only one to deliver censure, he was the only one to be both loved and admired by those he reproved, since his goodness overcame his warmth of feeling. **Gregory Nazianzen, *Funeral Oration for His Father* (FOTC 22)**

61 Do not irritate with reproachful words a soul that is angered, to be sure, and enraged. **Jerome, *The Apology against the Books of Rufinus*, 3.39 (FOTC 53)**

62 Anger and rage and hatred should be aroused, like dogs guarding gates, only for resistance to sin, and used against the thief or enemy who enters to defile the divine treasury and comes to steal, to storm, and to destroy. Instead of a weapon in the hand, one should have courage and bravery so there would be no need to be afraid and one could withstand the onslaughts of the impious. **Gregory of Nyssa, *On Virginity*, 18 (FOTC 58)**

63 Keep away from violent anger, the most wicked spirit. Put on long-suffering and oppose violent anger as well as bitterness, and you will be found on the side of holiness, beloved by the Lord. **The Shepherd of Hermas, Mandate V.II.8 (FOTC 1)**

64 Impatience is, as it were, the original sin in the eyes of the Lord. For, to put it in a nutshell, every sin is to be traced back to impatience. Evil cannot endure good. No unchaste person but is intolerant of chastity; no scoundrel but is irked by righteousness; no negligent person but resents his obligations; no agitator but is impatient of peace. **Tertullian, On Patience, 5.21 (FOTC 40)**

65 If the Pharisee had been patient, our Lord's forgiveness of the sinful woman would have taught him everything.[38] Patience has a habit of granting everything to those who possess it. **Ephrem the Syrian, Homily on Our Lord, 45.8 (FOTC 91)**

66 Let us learn from this to overcome our anger and not to show indignation even if those who attempt to give us advice are our inferiors.[39] Christ tolerated it with mildness when the incredulous offered Him counsel, though they not only gave unseemly advice, but even gave it with evil intent. **John Chrysostom, Commentary on John, Homily 48 (FOTC 41)**

67 The Lord says: "By your patience you will win your souls."[40] He does not say: "your homes, your luxuries," but "your souls." If, then, the soul suffers so much to possess the means by which it may be lost, how much ought it to suffer that it may not be lost. Then, to mention something blameless, if the soul suffers so much for the well-being of its own flesh at the hands of doctors cutting or burning the same, how much should it bear for its own safety amid the fury of any enemies whatsoever. **Augustine of Hippo, On Patience 7.6 (FOTC 16)**

---

38. Cf. Lk 7:36–50.
39. Chrysostom here refers to the advice of the unbelieving "brothers" of Jesus who advised him to manifest his works to the world (cf. Jn 7:1–8).
40. Lk 21:19.

68 For when we also pray—and God is long-suffering in responding—he does this for the best, in order that we may learn long-suffering and not grow faint, claiming that we prayed but were not heard. **Barsanuphius and John, *Letter* 35 (FOTC 113)**

69 Gentleness, which comes after faith in the list, is the enemy of rage, quarrels, and dissensions. It is never attracted to things opposite to itself and it indeed sprouts good fruits from the good tree of the Spirit. **Jerome, *Commentary on Galatians*, 5:22–23 (FOTC 121)**

70 For, hatreds die when an injury is not pondered; anger has no power if the voice of one person is lacking in a quarrel. Consequently, a double victory awaits patience: a man has overcome the impulses of his own temper and restrained the conduct of another. **Valerian, *Homily* 12 (FOTC 17)**

71 Though patience is a virtue of the soul, the soul practices it partly in itself, and partly in its body. **Augustine of Hippo, *On Patience* 8.8 (FOTC 16)**

72 The Lord commands us to wait and to endure with a strong patience the day of future vengeance, and He also speaks in the Apocalypse, saying: "Do not seal up the words of the prophecy of this book, because now the time is close at hand and those who persevere in doing wrong, let them do wrong, and he who is filthy, let him be filthy still, but let the just man still do more just things, and likewise the holy man, holier things. Behold I come quickly! and My reward is with Me, to render to each according to his works."[41] Therefore, even the martyrs as they cry out and as they hasten to their punishment in the intensity of their suffering are still ordered to wait and to show patience until the appointed time is fulfilled and the number of martyrs is complete. **Cyprian of Carthage, *The Good of Patience*, 21 (FOTC 36)**

---

41. Rv 22:10–12.

73 Why should I mention highway robbers, all of whom spend sleepless nights lying in wait for travelers? ... Their patience is to be marveled at rather than praised; nay, neither marveled at nor praised, for it is not patience. Their endurance is to be marveled at; their patience, denied. There is nothing there rightly deserving praise, nothing profitable for imitation, and you will judge the soul more rightly deserving of severer punishment the more it subjects its instruments of vice. For, patience is the attendant of wisdom, not the handmaid of passion. Patience is the friend of a good conscience, not the enemy of innocence. **Augustine of Hippo, *On Patience* 5.4 (FOTC 16)**

74 The stronger and more vehement the lust, then, which is not from the Father but from the world, the more does each one become willing to accept all annoyances and griefs in pursuing the object of his desires. This patience, then, as we have said before, does not come from above. But the patience of the faithful, coming down from above, is from the father of lights. And so, that is earthly, this is heavenly; that animal, this spiritual; that devilish, this deifying—since the lust by which sinners suffer all things stubbornly is from the world. The charity by which the righteous bravely suffer all things is, however, from God. So the human will, without the help of God, can be sufficient and hardier for the man of false patience in that it is more lustful, and with it he sustains evils more tolerably in so far as it itself deteriorates. But, for the man with true patience, the human will does not suffice unless it is aided and inflamed from above, for the Holy Spirit is its fire, and, unless enkindled by Him, it loves impassible good, it cannot bear the evil it suffers. **Augustine of Hippo, *On Patience* 17.14 (FOTC 16)**

75 Indeed, one does not become angry with a fever patient or someone suffering from inflammation, but one pities and grieves for all such unfortunates. The soul inflamed with anger is in truth like them. **John Chrysostom, *Commentary on John*, Homily 48 (FOTC 41)**

76 "Father, forgive them, for they do not know what they are doing."[42] Was it not possible for Him to bring the sky down upon them, or to bury these insolent men in a chasm of the earth, or to throw them down from their own mountains into the sea, or to inundate the earth with the depths of ocean, or to send down upon them the Sodomitic rain of fire, or to do any other angry deed in revenge? Instead, He bore all these things in meekness and patience, legislating patience for your life through Himself. **Gregory of Nyssa, On Perfection (FOTC 58)**

77 How then will you be able to endure these things—not to swear or curse, not to seek again what has been taken away from you, on receiving a blow to offer the other cheek also to your assailant,[43] to forgive your brother who offends you not only seventy times seven times, but all his offenses without exception,[44] to love your enemies, to pray for your adversaries and persecutors,[45] if you do not have the steadfastness of patience and forbearance? We see what happened in the case of Stephen. When he was being killed by the violence and stones of the Jews, he did not ask for vengeance but forgiveness for his murderers, saying: "O Lord, do not lay this sin against them."[46] So it was most fitting that the first martyr for Christ who, in preceding by his glorious death the martyrs that were to come, was not only a preacher of the Lord's suffering but also an imitator of His most patient gentleness. **Cyprian of Carthage, The Good of Patience, 16 (FOTC 36)**

Almsgiving

78 When you can do good, do not put it off, "for almsgiving frees from death."[47] **Polycarp, Letter to the Philippians, 10.2 (FOTC 1)**

---

42. Lk 23:34.
43. Cf. Mt 5:39; Lk 6:30.
44. Cf. Mt 18:21–22.
45. Cf. Mt 5:44; Lk 6:27–28.
46. Acts 7:59.
47. Tb 4:11.

4. ANGER

79 A gift snuffs out the fire of resentment, as Jacob well knew. **Evagrius of Pontus, *Praktikos* 26 (CSS 4)**

80 The poor render us great service. Almsgiving atones for sins that we have not been able to wash away otherwise. What does Scripture say in this regard? "Water quenches a flaming fire, and alms atone for sins."[48] The effects of almsgiving are similar to those of baptism; just as baptism remits sin, even so almsgiving atones for sins. Just as water extinguishes a fire, so does almsgiving extinguish sin; the fires of hell have been kindled for sins; almsgiving quenches them. **Jerome, *Homily 46* on Psalm 133 (134) (FOTC 48)**

81 Since God is merciful, He has granted us, even after baptism, manifold means of being freed from sin, the foremost of which is that of almsgiving. For Scripture says: "Sins are purged away by almsgiving and faith."[49] **John Chrysostom, *Commentary on John*, Homily 73 (FOTC 41)**

82 Repentance without almsgiving is a corpse and is without wings. **John Chrysostom, *On Repentance and Almsgiving*, Homily 7.6.21 (FOTC 96)**

83 "Blessed are the merciful."[50] Mercy is understood not only in almsgiving but in every sin of a brother. For we are to carry the burdens of one another.[51] **Jerome, *Commentary on Matthew*, I.5.7 (FOTC 117)**

84 When you see on earth the man who has encountered the shipwreck of poverty, do not judge him, do not seek an account of his life, but free him from his misfortune. Why do you make trouble for yourself? God has excused you from all officiousness and meddlesomeness. How

---

48. Sir 3:30.
49. Cf. Sir 3:30. The Chrysostom quotation above and the preceding one by Jerome provide an interesting window into the early church notion of the forgiveness of sins after baptism, which is prior to the development of the sacramental confession of sins to a priest. Many often postponed baptism fearing they would fall into sin and be unable to attain remission of their sins. John Chrysostom here suggests that there are many ways to become forgiven after baptism, and the primary means is through almsgiving.
50. Mt 5:7.
51. Cf. Gal 6:2.

much most of us would complain, if God had bidden us first to examine each person's life exactly, to interfere with his behavior and his deeds, and only then to give alms? ... Charity is so called because we give it even to the unworthy. Paul also advises us to do this, when he says, "Do not grow weary in well-doing ... to all men, but especially to those who are of the household of faith." If we meddle and interfere with the unworthy, not even the worthy will ever willingly come to us; but if we provide also for the unworthy, undoubtedly both the worthy and those who are worth all of them together will come into our hands.[52] **John Chrysostom, *Second Sermon on Lazarus and the Rich Man* (PPS 9)**

85 You see, the magnitude of almsgiving is not calculated by the sum of money but by the eagerness of the givers. **John Chrysostom, *Homily* 55.16 *on Genesis* (FOTC 87)**

86 Concerning almsgiving, He says: "Come to Me, all ye blessed, take possession of the kingdom prepared for you from the foundation of the world; for I was hungry, and you gave Me to eat; I was thirsty, and you gave Me to drink; I was a stranger, and you gave Me shelter; naked, and you covered Me; sick, and you visited Me, in prison, and you came to Me."[53] And when did we do any of these things for the Lord? The Educator says it is a good deed, and in His charity considers the good deed done to a brother as done to Himself: "As long as you did it to these little ones, you did it for Me."[54] Such as they shall come into eternal life. **Clement of Alexandria, *Christ the Educator*, 3.12.93 (FOTC 23)**

87 Just as a stone could not produce oil, so harshness cannot produce mercy. Whenever almsgiving has such a root it is no longer almsgiving. **John Chrysostom, *Commentary on John*, Homily 13 (FOTC 33)**

88 Give to everyone who asks, and ask nothing in return; for the Father wishes that a share of His own gifts be given to all.[55] Blessed is the man

---

52. Cf. Lk 6:30: "Give to everyone who begs from you ..."
53. Cf. Mt 25:37–46.
54. Mt 25:40.
55. Cf. Lk 6:30.

who gives according to the commandment, for he is without blame. Woe to the man who takes. However, if the one who takes is in need, he is without blame. But should he not be in need, he shall give an account of the why and the wherefore of his taking it. And he will be put in prison and examined strictly about what he did, and "shall not go out from there until he has paid the last cent."[56] But in this matter the saying also holds: "Let your alms sweat in your hands until you know to whom you are giving."[57] *Didache of the Twelve Apostles*, 1.5–6 (FOTC 1)

89 It is impossible, I repeat, even if we perform countless good works, to enter the portals of the kingdom without almsgiving.
John Chrysostom, *Commentary on John*, Homily 23 (FOTC 33)

90 Therefore, not only does he give alms who gives food to the hungry, drink to the thirsty, clothing to the naked, hospitality to the pilgrim, refuge to the fugitive, visitation to the sick or shut-in, freedom to the captive, lifting-up to the weak, guidance to the blind, consolation to the sorrowful, healing to the unsound of body, a straight course to the wanderer, counsel to him who takes thought, and that which is needful to anyone who needs it, but also he who gives forgiveness to the sinner.[58] And he who corrects by a blow or restrains by any kind of discipline one over whom he has power, and at the same time forgives from the heart or prays that there may be forgiven the sin by which the other has injured or offended him, he also is a giver of alms, not only in that he forgives or prays, but also in that he rebukes and administers corrective punishment, for he shows mercy. **Augustine of Hippo, *Faith, Hope and Charity*, 19.72 (FOTC 2)**

91 It is possible for us even here to live in happiness (for nothing causes so much pleasure as almsgiving and a clear conscience), and, on departing to the next world, to be freed from all sufferings and to attain to numberless blessings. Just as evil-doing usually punishes those who

---

56. Mt 5:26.
57. The origin of this quotation is unknown.
58. Cf. Mt 25:35–36.

share in it, even before [they reach] hell, so also virtue causes those who practice it to enjoy happiness here, even before [they come to] the Kingdom, and makes them dwell amid hopes of good things to come and uninterrupted pleasure. **John Chrysostom, *Commentary on John*, Homily 40 (FOTC 33)**

92 An amount of wealth does not by its nature produce almsgiving, but the amount of good intention does. There was a time when that widow put two small coins in the collection box and she surpassed those who were proud of their wealth.[59] And the other widow entertained that lofty soul with a handful of meal and a little oil.[60] Their poverty proved to be no hindrance to either of these women. Do not, then, make idle and senseless excuses. God does not demand a large contribution but he does require a wealth of good intention. The spirit of almsgiving is not shown by the measure of what has been given but by the willingness of those who give.[61] **John Chrysostom, *On the Incomprehensible Nature of God*, Homily 8.12 (FOTC 72)**

93 You will not lose what you have given away, but you will follow what you have sent ahead. Then I give this advice: "Give to the poor, and thou shalt have treasure in heaven."[62] You will not remain without treasure, but what you possess on earth with anxiety you shall have with security in heaven. Therefore, transport your possessions. **Augustine of Hippo, *Sermon* 60.7 on almsgiving (FOTC 11)**

94 You have money? Give it away. By giving it away, you increase your justice, for "He has distributed, he has given to the poor: his justice remains for ever and ever." See what is lessened, and what is increased. Money is lessened; justice is increased. There is a lessening of that which you would have to give up, a lessening of that which you would have to leave behind; there is an increase of that which you will possess for ever and ever. **Augustine of Hippo, *Sermon* 61.3 on almsgiving (FOTC 11)**

---

59. Cf. Mk 12:41–44; Lk 21:1–4. Cf. Chrysostom, hom. 6.12, in the same collection.
60. Cf. 1 Kgs 17:8–17. This refers to the widow of Zarepheth and the prophet Elijah.
61. Cf. Lk 16:19–31.
62. Mt 19:21.

95 If we have neglected it here, let us repair our negligence when we are dying; let us lay a strict charge upon our relatives to aid us after our death by almsgiving. **John Chrysostom,** *Commentary on John,* **Homily 85 (FOTC 41)**

96 Nothing, you see, nothing else of our virtuous deeds will so succeed in quenching the fire of our sins as generosity in almsgiving: it causes the remission of our sins, proves the guarantee of confidence for us and ensures the enjoyment of those ineffable goods. **John Chrysostom,** *Homily* **34.8 on Genesis (FOTC 82)**

5

Sloth

Sloth

1 All the other passions lay hold of either the irascible or the concupiscible part of the soul only, or even of the rational part, as forgetful-ness or ignorance. But sloth, by grasping onto all the soul's powers, excites nearly all of them together. In this way, it is the most troublesome of all the passions. Well, then, did the Lord tell us in giving the remedy against it, "In your patience possess your souls."[1] **Maximus the Confessor, *Centuries on Charity*, 1.67 (CWS)**

2 The demon of acedia—also known as the noonday demon—is the one that causes the most serious trouble of all. He presses his attack upon the monk about the fourth hour and besieges the soul until the eighth hour.[2] First of all he makes it seem that the sun barely moves, if at all, and that the day is fifty hours long. Then he constrains the monk to look constantly out the windows, to walk outside the cell, to gaze carefully at the sun to determine how far it stands from the ninth hour,

---

1. Lk 21:19.
2. I.e., 10 a.m. to 2 p.m.

to look now this way and now that to see if perhaps one of the brethren appears from his cell.[3] **Evagrius of Pontus, *Praktikos* 12 (CSS 4)**

3 Mark and Luke say that Jesus "was tempted for forty days."[4] It is clear that during those days the devil first tempted him from a distance—to sleep, acedia, cowardice, and other such sins. Then, since he knew that Christ was hungry, the devil came closer to him and attacked him openly. **Origen, *Fragment 96 on Luke 4:3–4* (FOTC 94)**

4 We are weighed down in soul and body by sloth and indolence, and disinclined to make an effort because, in fact, this price of effort, even for our good, is a part of the penalty we must pay for sin. **Augustine of Hippo, *The City of God*, 22.22 (FOTC 24)**

5 Yet, dearly beloved, sloth is a terrible fault: just as it makes easy things seem hard to us, so enthusiasm and alertness render even hard things easy for us.[5] **John Chrysostom, *Homily* 14.12 *on Genesis* (FOTC 74)**

6 The good laborer receives the bread of his labor with confidence; the lazy and careless one does not look his employer in the face. **Clement of Rome, *First Letter*, 34.1 (FOTC 1)**

7 Sloth inclines to a kind of rest, but what is true rest apart from the Lord? **Augustine of Hippo, *Confessions*, 2.6.13 (FOTC 21)**

8 Do not indulge in idle curiosity—no asking "what the city has done," or the ward, or the Emperor, or the Bishop, or the priest. Lift up your eyes: now, as your hour strikes, you need Him who is above. "Be still, and know that I am God."[6] If you see the believers not recollected when they are ministering, well, they are safe; they know what they have received; they possess the grace. Your fate is still in the balance,

---

3. 3 p.m. is the hour that typically marked the end of the monastic fast and was the common dinnertime.
4. Mk 1:13; Lk 4:2.
5. Chrysostom describes sloth as *rathymia*.
6. Ps 45:11.

to be accepted or not. Instead of copying the carefree, cultivate fear. **Cyril of Jerusalem, *Prologue to the Catechetical Lectures*, 13 (FOTC 61)**

9 Restless souls are continually involved in earthly activity, and of them it is written: "The burdens of the world have made them miserable."[7] They are unable to have a sabbath, that is, repose. In reply to their restlessness, it is said that they should have, as it were, a sabbath in their heart and the sanctification of the Spirit of God: "Be swift to hear," it says, "but slow to answer."[8] **Caesarius of Arles, *Sermon* 100.4 (FOTC 47)**

10 "There is nothing in the earth without cause."[9] For on this account it often happens that even a slothful man receives ability, that he may be the more deservedly punished for his carelessness, because he scorns to acquaint himself with that which he might attain to without labor. **Gregory the Great, *Morals on the Book of Job*, IV.11 (LF 18)**

11 So, with this in mind, my brothers, let us not be slothful in pursuit of the good, but "fervent in the Spirit,"[10] lest by slow degrees we sleep "the sleep of death"[11] and the Enemy sow his evil seed upon us in our slumber,[12] for sloth is akin to sleep; and let our zeal be untainted by selfishness and folly lest we be carried away and stray from the royal road and surely stumble in one of two ways: either our slothfulness will need a whip or our fanaticism will hurl us to destruction. **Gregory Nazianzen, *Oration* 32.6 (FOTC 107)**

12 Regarding searching the meaning of the Holy Scriptures, Origen said, "If our sluggishness and complete laziness did not prevent us from even approaching to ask, since our Lord and Savior challenges us to do this,[13] we would actually turn back, considering how distant we are from the greatness of the spiritual interpretation by which the meaning

---

7. Unknown source.
8. Sir 5:13.
9. Job 5:6.
10. Acts 18:25; Rom 12:11.
11. Ps 13:3 (LXX 12:4).
12. Mt 13:25.
13. Cf. Mt 7:7.

of such great realities ought to be investigated." **Pamphilus of Caesarea, *Apology for Origen*, 5 (FOTC 120)**

13 Our own effort is roused from slothful sleep by the restlessness of heretics, forcing us to examine the Scriptures more carefully, lest they use them to harm the flock of Christ. **Augustine of Hippo, *Letter* 194 to Sixtus (FOTC 30)**

14 Anyone with a serious purpose and a little useful and salutary effort can discern the Prophet [Isaiah]'s spiritual sense; it is only a lazy and worldly person or one who is ignorant or uneducated who will rest content with the literal and superficial sense and refuse to penetrate the deeper meaning. **Augustine of Hippo, *The City of God*, 20.21 (FOTC 24)**

15 The dust of our flesh, unless it undergoes constant cultivation, from sloth and ease quickly brings forth thorns and briars, and in a worthless harvest will give fruit not to be put into the barn but to be burned by fire. **Leo the Great, *Sermon* 81.3 (FOTC 93)**

16 And just as is the case that, if an unfruitful tree is in a vineyard, while it extends its lethal shade over all the vines underneath it, it becomes hostile not only to itself, but also to vine branches that are fruitful, so too is it the case that, if a slothful and lazy human being happens to be in authority over peoples, he becomes harmful not only to himself, but to the masses, while by his example he corrupts and ruins those who follow him. **Peter Chrysologus, *Sermon* 106 (FOTC 109)**

17 Lazy and beloved one, why is your thought growing faint? Do not fear or dread like a coward, lest you fall short of God's promises.[14] Do not be terrified like an unbeliever, but give courage to your thoughts that are of little faith. Love your tribulations in all things, so that you may become an approved son of the saints. Remember "the patience of Job"[15] and those who followed him, and be zealous in following their

---

14. Cf. Heb 4:1.
15. Cf. Jas 5:11.

footsteps. Remember the dangers, tribulations, bonds, hungers, and multitude of other evils that Paul endured,[16] and say to your faintheartedness: "I am a stranger to you." **Barsanuphius and John, Letter 31 (FOTC 113)**

18 Again, a bed with silver legs stands as an accusation of extreme ostentatiousness, and couches made of "ivory, the product of a body separated from its living spirit, is not free from defilement," and is for holy men only a resting place that encourages sloth.[17] **Clement of Alexandria, Christ the Educator, 2.9.77 (FOTC 23)**

19 When [the slothful] see a lot of people displaying the same kind of unanimity, they make this a pretext and excuse for their own sloth in the words, "Why should I, tell me, take it into my head to venture something out of step with all these people by differing from such a crowd? After all, surely I don't happen to be better than all these people, do I? What would I gain from opposition of that kind? What benefit would their hatred be to me?" **John Chrysostom, Homily 22.4 on Genesis (FOTC 82)**

20 Let us neither lose hope nor be lazy, because each of these is deadly. Discouragement does not allow the one who falls to get back up, and laziness throws down the one who is upright. The latter deprives us constantly of the goods that we gain; it does not allow us to escape from the evils that are to come. Laziness throws us down even from heaven, while discouragement hurls us down even to the very abyss of wickedness. Indeed, we can quickly return from there if we do not become discouraged. **John Chrysostom, On Repentance and Almsgiving, Homily 1.2 (FOTC 96)**

21 Brother, if God has granted our requests in order that we might have our fathers lead us and in order that we might be with them inseparably, both here and there, then let us be careful not to be separated from

---

16. Cf. 2 Cor 11:24–27.
17. Plato, *Laws* XII.956A.

them by our laziness, our slackness, our indolence, or our faithlessness. For it is said: "If the unbeliever separates, then let it be so."[18] Let us remember him who said: "The one who endures to the end will be saved."[19] **Barsanuphius and John, *Letter* 187 (FOTC 113)**

22 Truly, the words of Scripture: "to make excuses to excuse sins" apply to this servant [who buried the talent] as well, as he adds the crime of arrogance to his laziness and negligence.[20] For the one who ought to have confessed his inactivity and to have pleaded with the householder speaks evil instead. He claims that he has acted by wise counsel and that he was afraid of endangering the capital while seeking to make a profit on the money. **Jerome, *Commentary on Matthew*, IV.25.24–25 (FOTC 117)**

23 We should strive with all effort not to indulge in excessive relaxation and spoil our awareness that our body has been purified. We should not be content to keep religiously only those days which our observance of fasting annually brings upon us. Even this observance is evidently distasteful to some because of their excessive sleeping and insatiable appetite. While making their way toward the day of the Holy Pasch under the urgings of their strong desire, they complain about the observance of vigils, the benefits of continence, the meager meals and the abundant fasts. They do this as if the long-desired festival made licit what the days of Lent forbid, and as if the termination of the fast gave freedom to sin. Consequently, let no one think that all things are licit for him just because he sees that the time of stricter living has passed. Careless relaxation ordinarily works deception into every state of upright living. **Valerian, *Homily* 19.1–2, on the termination of Lent (FOTC 17)**

24 Indeed, many people who gained and sealed their treasure lost everything they wanted out of neglect. Unless a person cultivates the land well, sowing the seed in expectation of rain, then all the rains, even if

18. 1 Cor 7:15.
19. Mt 10:22.
20. Ps 141:4.

abundant, will be of no use for its fruition. **Barsanuphius and John, *Letter* 573 (FOTC 114)**

25 Therefore, since we enjoy such great grace and truth, I beseech you: Let us not become more lazy on account of the greatness of the gift. The greater the dignity of which we have been deemed worthy, so much the more are we obliged to practice virtue. He who has received slight benefits will not deserve so much blame, even if he does little of value. But he who ascends to the highest peak of honor, yet produces mean and paltry results, will merit so much greater punishment.
John Chrysostom, *Commentary on John*, Homily 14 (FOTC 33)

26 Indeed, some of the fathers used to say about Abba Poemen, regarding a certain elder, that he kept his disciple in spite of his laziness. And Abba Poemen said: "If I could, I would place a pillow under his head." And they said to him: "Then, what would you say to God?" And he replied: "I would say to God: 'You are the one who said, Hypocrite, first remove the log from your own eye, and then you will see clearly to take the speck out of your brother's eye.'"[21] **Barsanuphius and John, *Letter* 654 (FOTC 114)**

27 Whereas the slothful would have no benefit if Satan did not exist, the noble would suffer great unfairness. For Satan is a kind of trainer of human beings, providing an opportunity for the contestants to receive a crown of victory. For those who love sin, who in the absence of the Devil use their own laziness as a substitute for the Devil, have not been at all unfairly treated, as I have said. **Oecumenius, *Commentary on the Apocalypse*, 11.19 (FOTC 112)**

28 If after being freed from all evil through Baptism we are willing to be slothful and idle, I fear that what is written in the Gospel may be fulfilled in us: "When the unclean spirit has gone out of a man, he roams through dry places in search of rest and finds none. If after he returns he finds his house unoccupied, he takes with him seven other spirits

---

21. Cf. Mt 7:5. See *Sayings of the Desert Fathers*, Poemen 117 and 131.

5. SLOTH

more evil than himself; and the last state of that man becomes worse than the first."[22] **Caesarius of Arles, Sermon 81.2 (FOTC 47)**

29 Hurry; run "while it is yet day," before night overtakes us—that time when the indolent mourn and the lazy repent in vain.[23] Learn that no time remains; and if the hour comes, the servant will not be ashamed. **Barsanuphius and John, Letter 790 (FOTC 114)**

30 In the past, certain people have made an auspicious beginning in their desire for [the solitary] life, but, although they have attained perfection in their intention, they have been tripped up because of their vanity. They deceived themselves, through some craziness, into thinking that that was fair towards which their own thought inclined. Among these, there are those called "the slothful" in the Book of Wisdom, who strew their path with thorns, who consider harmful to the soul a zeal for deeds in keeping with the commandments of God, the demurrers against the apostolic injunctions, who do not eat their own bread with dignity, but, fawning on others, make idleness the art of life.[24] Then, there are the dreamers who consider the deceits of dreams more trustworthy than the teachings of the Gospels, calling fantasies revelations. Apart from these, there are those who stay in their own houses, and still others who consider being unsociable and brutish a virtue without recognizing the command to love and without knowing the fruit of long-suffering and humility. **Gregory of Nyssa, On Virginity, 23 (FOTC 58)**

31 Consider, after all, how great a thrill it was to see the trees groaning under the weight of their fruit, to see the variety of the flowers, the different kinds of plants, the leaves on the branches, and all the other things you would be likely to chance upon in a garden, especially a garden planted by God. On that account, you see, Sacred Scripture had said previously that "he produced from the earth every tree fair to behold and good to eat," so that we might know that, despite his enjoyment of

---

22. Mt 12:43–45.
23. Jn 9:4.
24. Cf. Prv 15:19.

such plenty, the human being trampled underfoot the instruction given him, out of his great intemperance and sloth.²⁵ **John Chrysostom, *Homily* 14.12 on Genesis (FOTC 74)**

32 Let us say both to others and to ourselves as well: "There is a resurrection, and a fearful judgment awaits us." If we see someone puffed up and aglow because of temporal prosperity, let us say the same thing to him, to warn him that all this remains in this world. On the other hand, if we see another person downcast and afflicted with misfortune, let us address the same words to him, also, to remind him that his ill fortune will have an end. And if we see someone who is lazy and slothful, let us chant the same theme to him, to admonish him that he must render an accounting for laziness. This sentence is more potent than any remedy to cure the disease of our soul. **John Chrysostom, *Commentary on John*, Homily 45 (FOTC 33)**

33 "A slothful man is stoned with the dung of oxen."²⁶ Thus he that will not follow God is made slothful in the love of the life everlasting. And as often as he is stricken with the loss of temporal goods, he is surely troubled on the score of those things, which the righteous look down upon as "dung": what else is it with him, then, that is bruised with the buffeting of things earthly, than that he "is stoned with the dung of oxen?" **Gregory the Great, *Morals on the Book of Job*, XV.4 (LF21)**

34 Though it was possible, however, for the people of Israel now to go to work, build the divine Temple, offer sacrifices and prayers, and live life in ways corresponding to the Law, the people of Israel became slothful, doing their own thing, completely inclined to whatever suited and appealed to them, and paying extremely little attention to the glory of God. So they once again suffered hardship, with God punishing them, not with war but with famine, infertility, and loss of livestock; he wanted to bring them around, not by subjecting them to penalties commensurate with their faults, but both out of pity for their weariness and likewise

25. Gn 2:9.
26. Sir 22:2 [D-R].

from a wish to reform them out of love. This, in a nutshell, is the basis of the prophecy of Haggai. **Cyril of Alexandria, *Commentary on Haggai*, preface (FOTC 124)**

35 You see, the reason that the loving God did not allow all the contents of the Scriptures to yield themselves spontaneously clear and obvious at first glance with scant reading was that he might disturb our sloth and we might show signs of alertness and thus reap the benefit of them. It normally happens, after all, that matters discovered with effort and research are riveted more firmly in our minds, whereas what is discovered with ease soon flies away from our heart. So, far from showing indifference, I beseech you, let us stir up our thinking and make a thorough and in-depth study of the writings so as to be in a position to gain some greater benefit from them and thus go off home. **John Chrysostom, *Homily* 32.1 *on Genesis* (FOTC 82)**

36 If anyone, rejecting the grace of the present time in which the Lord has deigned to come, not to judge, but to save sinners, believes that he must remain in his iniquities, he will find no mercy in the judgment to come; because at the time of the winnowing, that winnower will not allow the chaff to be mixed with the wheat, just as the divine severity will not grant to the lazy, worthless servant the possession of a talent in the time of reckoning; but, just as he will burn the chaff with inextinguishable fire, so eternal wailing and gnashing of teeth will greet the wicked and lazy servant consigned to darkness. For what does ordering that servant bound hands and feet mean, except that in the hands is shown that the guilt of evil works and in the feet the love of an evil will are to be punished? **Fulgentius, *On the Forgiveness of Sins*, II.XIX.4 (FOTC 95)**

37 Not into the possession of those who sleep does the kingdom of heaven come, nor is the beatitude of eternity bestowed upon those who are sluggish with idleness and laziness. Instead, as the Apostle says, "if we suffer with him, we will also be glorified with him."[27] **Leo the Great, *Sermon* 35.3 (FOTC 93)**

---

27. Rom 8:17.

38 The donkey is a slothful and stupid animal, an easy prey to all mischance. What is the lesson that this animal conveys? Is it not that we should become more alert and not grow dull from physical and mental inactivity? Why not, rather, take refuge in a faith which tends to lighten our heavy burdens? **Ambrose of Milan, *Hexameron*, 6.3.11 (FOTC 42)**

39 You see, whenever you publicize a brother's fault, you not only make him more shameless and perhaps more lethargic in his progress towards virtue, but you also render the listeners more indifferent and encourage them in their sloth—and not merely this, but also the fact that you are responsible for God being blasphemed. **John Chrysostom, *Homily* 29.15 on Genesis (FOTC 82)**

40 The Canaanites are people who are restless and uneasy. When you enter into their land and notice how they are devoid of morals as a result of their levity, uneasiness, and instability, then you have an occasion to show your constancy. Do not be disturbed by any trifling argument or flightiness of speech. These are the characteristics of the Canaanite, inconsistency in language, emotional instability and restless contention. Be calm and present to them a tranquility and serenity of mind and soul. Be like one who escapes the storms of the sea by casting anchor in a safe harbor. **Ambrose of Milan, *Cain and Abel*, 1.10.42 (FOTC 42)**

41 Again, the slothful carry on low pursuits beneath the earth. And, finally, dark and shady places suit them best wherein they feel that their sins are concealed, according to the saying: "Darkness compasseth me about like walls. Whom shall I fear?"[28] Their hope of this is vain, since God sees the hidden depths of the abyss and discovers all things before they take place.[29] **Ambrose of Milan, *Letter* 80 (30), to Irenaeus (FOTC 26)**

42 The new faith of those who have been made new is strong and vigorous, seeking for itself an increase of virtue. The faith which is weak and slack—the faith which has the sluggish and slothful charac-

---

28. Sir 23:26.
29. Cf. Wis 8:8.

ter of old age—is not one that is fit for sacrifice. We need a faith which blossoms with the lush growth of wisdom and with the youthful vigor of divine knowledge, a faith, moreover, which has the sap of ancient doctrine. **Ambrose of Milan, *Cain and Abel*, 2.6.19 (FOTC 42)**

43 Out of reverence for the See [of Peter] itself over which we preside through the abundance of God's grace, we are bound to avoid as much as possible the danger of sloth. **Leo the Great, *Letter* 16 (FOTC 34)**

44 We do not believe in this life, but in the future life; nor do we believe in Him in order to escape burning here, but in order to escape passing from this fire into another fire. Go ahead, then, prepare your furnace; this heat, this fire, is our purgation. Happy he whose help is the God of Jacob! Do not miss the significance of the words, "whose help." "And because of their unbelief, he did not work many miracles there."[30] God is our helper. While we labor with determination, He delivers us and works together with us; when we are slothful, supine, irresolute, He does not set us free. **Jerome, *Homily* 55 on Psalm 145 (146) (FOTC 48)**

45 And Jacob said to his sons, "Why are you idle? Behold, I have heard that there is grain in Egypt. Go down there and buy food for us."[31] This is not something Jacob said one time; he says it daily to his sons who come to Christ's grace too late, "Why are you idle? Behold, I have heard that there is grain in Egypt." From this grain there comes the grain that rises again.[32] And so whoever suffers famine ought to attribute it to his own sloth. **Ambrose of Milan, *On Joseph*, 8.43 (FOTC 65)**

46 "The Lord says this to the prophets who deceive my people, who bite with their teeth and proclaim peace to them, and it was not put in their mouths; they provoked war against them." He severely blames the people of Israel, on the one hand, for willingly exposing themselves to ruin, involving themselves in troubles of their own making, and being

---

30. Mt 13:58.
31. Gn 42:1–2.
32. Cf. Jn 12:24–25.

firmly focused on sloth. On the other hand, he proceeds to say that they are gravely wronged by the evil and unclean spirit that misleads and deceives them. **Cyril of Alexandria, *Commentary on Micah*, 3:5 (FOTC 116)**

47 This spiritual treasure is proof against theft: when it is stored in the recesses of our mind, it is secure against every stratagem, provided we don't become slothful and give entry to the one anxious to deprive us of it. Our enemy, remember (I mean the wicked demon), when he sees spiritual wealth accumulated, grinds his teeth, and rages, and displays great vigilance so as to take advantage of the right moment to steal something of what we have within us. No such moment will suit his convenience provided we are not guilty of sloth; it behooves us therefore to remain constantly on the alert and to impede his every approach. **John Chrysostom, *Homily* 5.2 on Genesis (FOTC 74)**

48 It was not the tree [of the knowledge of good and evil] that caused the harm, but slothful will and contempt displayed for God's command. **John Chrysostom, *Homily* 16.20 on Genesis (FOTC 74)**

49 Whenever we who seem to stand firm, obliged as we are to live a good and irreproachable life, prove to be lazy and neglectful in doing so—or, rather, choose as much as the others to pay no heed to what is pleasing to God—far from simply wronging ourselves we bring others down as well and become liable for double punishment. **Cyril of Alexandria, *Commentary on Hosea*, 4:17–19 (FOTC 115)**

50 The devil is a shrewd and cruel enemy, and with the cunning of old tricks and manifold talents, by means of exceedingly evil persuasion he makes souls slothful and tepid and careless, and he even compels them to serve him through the destruction of others. Concerning such men it is written: "How I wish you were one or the other—hot or cold! But because you are lukewarm, I will begin to spew you out of my mouth!"[33] Such souls, which have been prepared for disobedience and pride, the

---

33. Rv 3:15, 16.

devil makes blind to the light of truth and charity. **Caesarius of Arles, Sermon 237.2 (FOTC 66)**

51 We exhort you in the Lord to keep your resolution and persevere to the end, and, if mother Church has need of your help, do not accede to her request with eager pride, nor refuse it with slothful complacence; rather, obey God with meek heart, and bear with submission the one who rules over you: "he who guides the mild in judgment, will teach the meek his ways."[34] **Augustine of Hippo, Letter 48 to Eudoxius (FOTC 12)**

52 Therefore, dearly beloved, though we be found weak and slothful in carrying out the duties of our office—even if we want to accomplish something devoutly and energetically, we are slowed down by the very frailty of our condition—still, we have the constant propitiation of the omnipotent and perpetual Priest. Being at once like unto us and equal with the Father, he lowered his divinity to the human state and lifted his humanity up to the divine. **Leo the Great, Sermon 3.2 (FOTC 93)**

53 Just as for those guilty of indolence in building up the Church, or in presenting themselves as a holy temple to Christ, everything takes a turn for the worse, and as well the fate befalls them of being quite overwhelmed by temptations and spiritual infertility, so too it is likewise true that to those willing to do the upbuilding and give priority to the effort of good living the gift will be given of enjoying every good, being enriched with fruitfulness of mind, and, as it were, having an interior orchard bedecked with various ornaments of virtue. **Cyril of Alexandria, Commentary on Haggai, 2:15–17 (FOTC 124)**

54 "All who wish to live in devotion to Christ Jesus suffer persecution."[35] With these words, those who are struck by no persecution are shown to be exceedingly lukewarm and lazy. None can have peace in this world unless they love the world. **Leo the Great, Sermon 70.5 (FOTC 93)**

---

34. Cf. Ps 24:9.
35. 2 Tm 3:12.

55 Unproductive sloth and undisciplined passion are equally useless things; the one, because it does not draw nigh to the good, the other, because it overshoots the mark and produces something that is righter than right, as the divine Solomon well understood: "Do not swerve," he says, "to the right or to the left," and do not fall from opposite extremes into an equal evil, namely, sin.[36] **Gregory Nazianzen, *Oration* 32.6 (FOTC 107)**

56 He does not allow people who are wrongfully slothful about divine things to pursue their own goals successfully and to give more earthly things priority over what redounds to his glory. Rather, he urges them to consider that unless what is incomparably superior is given proper ranking, neither would what is of less importance or of interest to them succeed. **Cyril of Alexandria, *Commentary on Haggai*, 1:9–11 (FOTC 124)**

57 Turn your mind to the recovery of courage. And even if the carnal nature makes itself heard to you, that nature whose concern is so much with pleasure, do not fail to resist it. The slightest efforts are enough to subdue it, and even if you see it moved, and incited against the will of the spirit, put aside indolence as quickly as you can, and, in imitation of the best athletes, prepare yourself the more ardently. **Cyril of Alexandria, *Festal Letters*, 11.2 (FOTC 118)**

Work

58 Whatever is affected suffers a change and whatever suffers a change is mutable. Hence, one can no more think of God in His leisure suffering from indolence, inactivity, or inertia any more than we can think of Him suffering from labor, effort, or eagerness in His work. For He knows how to rest while He acts and to act while He rests. To every new work whatsoever He applies not a new but an eternal design. Nor does regret for any former inactivity prompt Him to create what had not been created before. **Augustine of Hippo, *The City of God*, 12.18 (FOTC 14)**

---

36. Prv 4:27.

59 "Shake off the sleep of laziness," he says, "and strengthen your members, who are about to die completely through unbelief."[37] For it is not the beginning of good works that crowns the worker, but the completion. **Andrew of Caesarea, *Commentary on the Apocalypse*, 3.7 (FOTC 123)**

60 He warns us: "Behold the Lord comes, and his reward is before his face, to pay each man according to his work."[38] He therefore urges us who believe in Him with all our heart not to be lazy or careless in any good work.[39] **Clement of Rome, *First Letter*, 34.3–4 (FOTC 1)**

61 The Passion of Christ discloses the miseries of this life; the Resurrection of Christ points to the happiness of the life to come. At present, let us labor; let us hope for the future. Now is the time for work; then, for reward. He who is lazy in doing his work here is shameless if he demands recompense. **Augustine of Hippo, *Sermon* 233.1 on the Resurrection (FOTC 38)**

62 In the field of the Lord, whose workers we are, dearly beloved, we ought to practice cultivation of the soul with untiring prudence. That way, attending with constant exertion to what the law requires at this time, we might take delight in the fruit of holy works. If we neglect these works as a result of slothful leisure and lazy inactivity, our soil will not bear generous seed. On the contrary, laden with brambles and thistles, it will not produce things to be stored away in the barns, but things that will have to be burned with flames. **Leo the Great, *Sermon* 14.1 (FOTC 93)**

63 If they [i.e., those who say that God is anthropomorphic] consider it a fine thing not to touch work, since they are striving after the same thing, who is the one feeding them? Some are making their idea, that it is necessary only to devote themselves to prayer and not to touch work

---

37. Cf. Rv 3:2.
38. Cf. Is 40:10, 62:11; Prv 24:12; Rv 22:12.
39. Cf. Ti 3:1.

at all, a pretext for laziness and gluttony. **Cyril of Alexandria, Letter 83.8 (FOTC 77)**

64 To whom was it said, "Sail that you may not die," and he put it off? To whom was it said, "Work that you may not die," and he was lazy? God orders slight things that we may live forever, and we neglect to obey. **Augustine of Hippo, Tractates on the Gospel of John, 49.2.2 (FOTC 88)**

65 Manichaeans, those scions of sloth, who will not work themselves yet eat up the fruits of those who do, receive with smiling countenances those who bring them food, and repay them with curses instead of blessings. **Cyril of Jerusalem, Catechetical Lectures, 6.32 (FOTC 61)**

66 If you are slothful in the work, why do you hasten to the reward? **Caesarius of Arles, Sermon 153.1 (FOTC 47)**

67 Although these things [i.e., those associated with leisure and wealth] contain, indeed, the highest and most pleasant luxuries of life, they do not seem to differ much from the pleasures of animals, that are free from work and are sated with food, as they roam about in the forests or in the rich pastures. **Hilary of Poitiers, The Trinity, 1.1 (FOTC 25)**

68 Since all this is well known, it is obviously quite shameful, and fully abhorrent, if we err in the reckoning that matters, and find ourselves ridiculous in God's sight. And quite rightly so, if we do not eagerly seize the time which is already upon us, and which offers a chance to distinguish themselves in the virtues to those who drive for them at the gallop. For if we shrink back, and continually neglect the opportunity to stir ourselves to search for what is better, and foolishly bring upon ourselves the loss of what is good, we may rightly find spoken to us the words which apply to the indolent: "The slothful come to want."[40] **Cyril of Alexandria, Festal Letters, 8.1 (FOTC 118)**

---

40. Prv 11:16 (LXX).

69 A certain brother said to an old man: "My thoughts say to me: 'I am good.'" The old man answered: "He who does not see his sins always thinks he is good; but he who sees his sins can never be persuaded by his thoughts that he is good, for he knows what he sees. Therefore, one needs to work hard to reflect upon himself, for negligence, sloth, and idleness cause the eyes of the mind to be blind." **Paschasius of Dumium, Questions and Answers of the Greek Fathers, 15.4 (FOTC 62)**

70 The reward is not obtained by laziness or sleep. The sleeper does no work, leisure has no profit, but loss instead. Esau, by taking leisure, lost the primacy of blessing, because he preferred to have food given him rather than to go in search of it.[41] **Ambrose of Milan, Letter 59 (63), to the church of Vercelli (FOTC 26)**

71 The Lord couples sloth with wickedness, saying: "Wicked and slothful servant."[42] Wise Solomon, also, praises the laborer not only in the words already quoted, but also, in rebuking the sluggard, associating him by contrast with the tiniest of insects: "Go to the ant, O sluggard."[43] We have reason to fear, therefore, lest, perchance, on the day of judgment this fault also may be alleged against us, since He who has endowed us with the ability to work demands that our labor be proportioned to our capacity; for He says: "To whom they have committed much, of him they will demand the more."[44] **Basil of Caesarea, The Long Rules, q. 37 (FOTC 9)**

72 "You who dwell in the shelter of the Most High." It is ours to begin a work, it is God's part to further it, for He does not give a crown to the slothful, but to those who toil.[45] **Jerome, Homily 68 on Psalm 90 (91) (FOTC 57)**

---

41. Cf. Gn 27:35.
42. Mt 25:26.
43. Prv 6:6.
44. Lk 12:48.
45. Cf. hom. 63 on Ps 83; hom. 2 on Ps 5; hom. 34 on Ps 107; hom. 61 on Ps 15; *Against the Pelagians* 1.5 and 3.1; *Letter* 130.12.

73 Let us not remain in our present state of negligence and passivity and, by ever postponing to the morrow and the future the beginning of the work, fritter away the time at hand by our continued sloth. Then, being taken unprepared, with our hands empty of good works, by Him who demands our souls from us, we shall not be admitted to the joy of the nuptial chamber and we shall then bewail and lament the time of our life wasted in evil doing, when penance is no longer possible. "Now is the acceptable time," says the Apostle, "now is the day of salvation."[46] **Basil of Caesarea, *The Long Rules*, preface (FOTC 9)**

Prayer

74 When God watches His contestants, He helps those who invoke Him, for the voice of the athlete says in the Psalm: "When I say, 'My foot is slipping,' your kindness, O Lord, sustains me."[47] Therefore, let us not be slothful, my brethren. Let us seek, and ask, and knock.[48] **Caesarius of Arles, *Sermon* 114.6 (FOTC 47)**

75 But you say: "Granted that I can ask; how shall I be able to knock at heaven in its hidden mystery?" How? By repeating your prayers, and by waiting to see what judgment the Benefactor makes; by very patiently putting up with the delays of the Giver; because the one who, as soon as he knocks, becomes angry if he is not given an immediate hearing, is not a humble suppliant but an overbearing bully. Listen to the prophet as he says: "Wait for the Lord, act courageously, and let your heart be strengthened."[49] Even if he continues to delay into the future, patiently wait for your Lord. **Peter Chrysologus, *Sermon* 39 (FOTC 109)**

76 We, of course, in our helplessness shall pray for those things that we need, and shall apply ourselves with tireless zeal to the study of all the words of Your Prophets and Apostles and shall knock at all the doors of

---

46. 2 Cor 6:2.
47. Ps 93:18.
48. Cf. Mt 7:7–8.
49. Ps 26:14.

wisdom that are closed to us, but it is for You to grant our prayer, to be present when we seek, to open when we knock. Because of the laziness and dullness of our nature, we are, as it were, in a trance, and in regard to the understanding of Your attributes we are restricted within the confines of ignorance by the weakness of our intellect. **Hilary of Poitiers, The Trinity, 1.37 (FOTC 25)**

77   The Word does not want the man of faith to be indifferent to truth, and in fact lazy. For he says, "Seek and you shall find" but sets a limiting point to the search—discovery.[50] He banishes idle chatter and approves only the sort of investigation that strengthens our faith. **Clement of Alexandria, *Stromateis*, 1.11.51 (FOTC 85)**

78   Since Paul thus cries, "Run so as to win the prize,"[51] and since our holy feast is rising over us like the sun, let us cast far away our fruitless laziness, overcome the heavy darkness of our idleness, and with brave and luminous hearts set ourselves to seek every virtue, repeating to each other the words, "Come, let us go up to the mountain of the Lord, and to the house of the God of Jacob, and he will announce his way to us, and we will walk in it."[52] **Cyril of Alexandria, *Festal Letters*, 1.1 (FOTC 118)**

79   Whenever Christ is asleep in our boat, and he is asleep in the body with the slumber of our sloth, the storm with whirling winds in full besets us, threatening waters surge, and while they repeatedly rise and fall with their waves of foam, they produce in the sailors a heightened fear of shipwrecks ... let us approach him in faith rather than in body, and let us rouse him by a work of mercy rather than by a touch in desperation; let us wake him, not by excessive noise, but by the sound of spiritual canticles, not by restless grumbling, but by vigilant supplication. Let us give to God some time out of our life, so that this unprofitable sadness and miserable anxiety may not consume the whole day; so

50. Mt 7:7.
51. 1 Cor 9:24.
52. Is 2:3.

that ill-spent sleep and useless slumber may not waste away the entire night, but rather that a portion of the day and a portion of the night may be given over to the very Creator of time. **Peter Chrysologus, *Sermon* 21.1 and 21.5, on Christ's slumber in the boat (FOTC 109)**

80 Let us believe that we walk always in the light; let us not be hindered by the darkness which we have escaped; let there be no loss of prayers in the hours of the night, no slothful or neglectful waste of opportunities for prayer.[53] **Cyprian of Carthage, *The Lord's Prayer*, 36 (FOTC 36)**

81 Question: "Father, pray for me and tell me what it means that, when I want to chant Psalms during the night, I feel lazy, especially if it is cold. So I chant most of them sitting down and supposedly praying. Now since I am afraid that I suffer these things out of negligence, deem it worthy to illumine me, father, and pray that I may do whatever I am told." Response: "We have all been commanded to pray for one another.[54] Now, as for what you asked me, wanting to know what it is all about, part of it is mingled with the seed of the demons, and part of it comes from the weakness of the body.[55] Therefore, chanting the Psalms or praying while sitting down with compunction does not prevent us from pleasing God through our service. For if one stands in prayer and yet is distracted, then one's labor is in vain.[56] May the Lord help you, brother. Amen." **Barsanuphius and John, *Letter* 509 (FOTC 114)**

82 Scripture helps to kindle the fire in our soul, it directs our natural sight to contemplation, it is swift to implant something new (like a farmer grafting), it rouses to new life our natural endowment. In the divine Apostle's words: "There are many weak and without strength" among us, "and some have fallen asleep. But if we judged ourselves properly, we should not be judged."[57] **Clement of Alexandria, *Stromateis*, 1.1.10 (FOTC 85)**

---

53. Cf. 1 Jn 1:7.
54. Jas 5:16.
55. Cf. Mt 13:39.
56. Cf. 1 Thes 3:5.
57. 1 Cor 11:30–31.

83 Even the three children after attaining the summit of virtue and garlanded with the victor's crown prayed in the furnace, "We sinned, we broke the law, we did wrong, we departed from your commandments and did not keep your ordinances."[58] Likewise remarkable Daniel, likewise the divinely inspired Jeremiah, likewise the divine Isaiah, likewise the eminently wise Paul: "Christ Jesus came into the world to save sinners, of whom I am the foremost,"[59] and again, "I am not worthy to be called an apostle."[60] Likewise therefore the Church of God, buffeted by billows from the godless, in its struggles is not carried away, but attributes developments to sins and failings, and begs to enjoy assistance from the Savior. In a particular way, the Church of God is not composed completely of perfect people; instead, it numbers also those addicted to sloth and inclined to the careless life, who choose to serve pleasure. Since it is one body, both features are displayed as in the case of one person. **Theodoret of Cyrus, *Commentary on Psalm 40* (FOTC 101)**

84 Imitators of God as you are, with hearts warmed in the blood of God, you have done perfectly the work that fell to you to do; for you were eager to visit me when you heard that I was on my way from Syria, in chains because of our common name and hope, and longing, with the help of your prayers, to face the wild beasts in Rome and not to fail and so become a disciple. **Ignatius of Antioch, *Letter to the Ephesians*, 1.1–2 (FOTC 1)**

85 Now, if a person visits a perfume factory or remains near those engaged in this business, he is scented by the fragrant smell, even though he does not wish to be. Much more is this the case with a man as he departs from the church. For, just as sloth is the fruit of laziness, so also zeal develops from activity. Even if you are full of evil traits without number, even if you are impure, do not avoid spending time in this place. **John Chrysostom, *Commentary on John*, Homily 53 (FOTC 41)**

---

58. Cf. Dn 3:29 (LXX).
59. 1 Tm 1:15.
60. 1 Cor 15:9.

86 What slothfulness it is to be drawn away and to be captured by foolish and profane thoughts, when you are praying to the Lord, as if there were anything that you should ponder more than what you speak with God. How do you ask that you be heard by God, when you do not hear your very self? **Cyprian of Carthage, *The Lord's Prayer*, 31 (FOTC 36)**

87 Question: "If a person argues with another about something relating to God and they find no solution, how long should one persist?" Response: "If the argument gives rise to harm for the soul, then one should not persist at all. If it is not harmful, then one should become neither faint-hearted nor indifferent; otherwise, one will be condemned for indolence. For it is written: 'Accursed is the one who is neglectful in the work of the Lord.'[61] One should, however, entreat God to contribute to a beneficial solution." **Barsanuphius and John, *Letter* 748 (FOTC 114)**

88 God aiding our efforts, we must ward off the inclinations to be slothful in serving our neighbors, to allow pagan calumnies to wear down our Christian conscience, to permit our own rash judgments to mislead us in regard to others, to suffer others' lies to break our spirit. **Augustine of Hippo, *The City of God*, 22.23 (FOTC 24)**

89 Pray every minute of the day, and be neither fainthearted nor lazy in asking for God's love toward mankind. When you stand fast, He will not turn away from you, but will forgive your sins and grant your requests. If you are heard praying, continue to give thanks in the prayer; if you are not heard, remain praying so that you may be heard. **John Chrysostom, *On Repentance and Almsgiving*, Homily 3.4 (FOTC 96)**

90 So, too, from the heart's blood of my mother, through her tears, sacrifice was offered to Thee for me every day and night, and Thou didst work with me in wondrous ways. **Augustine of Hippo, *Confessions*, 5.7.13 (FOTC 21)**

---

61. Cf. Jer 31:10.

91 I have no doubt that some who are taking part in the warfare which wins heaven experience a feeling of despair. It arises from this, that the very entrance to the laborious journey of the celestial warfare is distressingly narrow. True, indeed, dearly beloved, for those who tend toward the heights, that journey is not merely laborious, but also difficult and more toilsome. On the other hand, those who are unwilling and lazy, and those who are busy but negligent—they also certainly find that their need of effort grows greater even when they travel through level regions. Lofty destinations are indeed vexatiously hard to attain, but, without doubt, travelers who refuse to despair do at length reach an open field. **Valerian, *Homily* 3, on the "Narrow Way" (FOTC 17)**

92 Although this exercise [i.e., Lenten fasting], dearly beloved, may be undertaken profitably at any time in order to overcome with constant zeal the ever-watchful enemy, nevertheless, we ought to pursue it more carefully and more eagerly now when those very cunning adversaries are lying in wait with shrewder craftiness. For they know that the holy days of Lent are pressing on us in the observance of which all past sloth is chastened and all negligence repaired. **Leo the Great, *Sermon* 39.2 (FOTC 93)**

93 Accordingly, among those who know how to hear willingly and humbly and who lead a quiet life in sweet and healthful pursuits, let Holy Church be delighted, and let her say, "I am sleeping, and my heart keeps vigil." What does it mean, "I am sleeping, and my heart keeps vigil," except, "I so rest that I may hear"? My leisure is not devoted to nurturing laziness but to gaining wisdom. "I am sleeping, and my heart keeps vigil." I am at leisure, and I see that you are the Lord because "the wisdom of the scribe [comes] in the time of leisure, and he who is less in action shall gain it."[62] "I am sleeping, and my heart keeps vigil." I rest from busied activities, and my mind directs its efforts at affections pertaining to God. **Augustine of Hippo, *Tractates on the Gospel of John*, 57.3.2 (FOTC 90)**

---

62. Sir 38:25 [D-R].

94 There are some among ourselves who take offense at the practice of salutary vigils. I can only hope that they are suffering from nothing worse than laziness or sleepiness or, what is much the same, old age or infirmity. If it is laziness, they should be ashamed of themselves, and listen to the words of Solomon: "Go to the ant, O sluggard, and consider her ways."[63] If the trouble is drowsiness, let them be wakened with the words of Scripture: "How long wilt thou sleep, O sluggard? When wilt thou rise out of thy sleep? Thou wilt sleep a little, thou wilt slumber a little, thou wilt fold thy hands a little to sleep. And want shall come upon thee, as a traveler, and poverty as a man armed."[64] If you are an old man, no one will force you to keep awake—although, for that matter, your years should be enough to keep you awake. If, finally, you are too weak to stand, and think you are unable, you have no right to recruit to your own torpor those who are young and strong. You must remember youth has many temptations and should mortify itself with appropriate vigils.... Certainly, it is foolish and strange to hold back those who run merely because we are unable to run ourselves. Unable as we are we should congratulate rather than envy those who can.
Niceta of Remesiana, *The Vigils of the Saints***, 2 (FOTC 7)**

95 Stay awake, man, stay awake! You have an example—offer to your Creator what service the cock devotes to you his host, especially since he crows for your benefit, he rouses you for work, and announces that day draws near; how much more appropriate then is it for you with celestial hymns to rouse God to use his heavenly power for your salvation. **Peter Chrysologus,** *Sermon* **21.6, on Christ's slumber in the boat (FOTC 109)**

96 Thou hast made us for Thee and our heart is unquiet till it finds its rest in Thee. **Augustine of Hippo,** *Confessions***, 1.1.1 (FOTC 21)**

63. Prv 6:6.
64. Prv 6:9–11.

6

Envy and Sadness

Envy

1 Envy is the most savage form of hatred. **Basil of Caesarea, *Concerning Envy*, Homily 11 (FOTC 9)**

2 Jealousy and quarreling have destroyed great cities and uprooted mighty nations. **Clement of Rome, *First Letter*, 6.4 (FOTC 1)**

3 From envy there spring hatred, whispering, detraction, exultation at the misfortunes of a neighbor, and affliction at his prosperity. **Gregory the Great, *Morals on the Book of Job*, XXXI.45 (LF 31)**

4 Envy is also wont to exhort the conquered heart, as if with reason, when it says, In what art thou inferior to this or that person? Why then art thou not either equal or superior to them? What great things art thou able to do, which they are not able to do! They ought not then to be either superior, or even equal, to thyself. **Gregory the Great, *Morals on the Book of Job*, XXXI.45 (LF 31)**

5 There are four kinds of pain; namely, grief, distress, envy, and compassion. Grief is a pain which makes one speechless; distress is one which oppresses; envy is one arising from another's good fortune; and compassion is one arising from another's misfortune. **John Damascene, The Orthodox Faith, 2.14 (FOTC 37)**

6 We should not imagine that envy is the same as zeal. Zeal can be for a good cause when someone makes a point of emulating better things, but envy is tormented by another person's good fortune and is torn by a twofold passion either when one is in a position in which he does not want another person to be, or when he sees another person better than himself and is pained that he is not like him. **Jerome, Commentary on Galatians, 5:19–21 (FOTC 121)**

7 Envy quarrels over excellence; what is more excellent than Thou? **Augustine of Hippo, Confessions, 2.6.13 (FOTC 21)**

8 Jealousy has no terminus; it is a continually abiding evil and a sin without end, and as he who is envied proceeds with greater success, to this extent does the envious one burn to a greater heat with the fires of envy. **Cyprian of Carthage, Jealousy and Envy, 7 (FOTC 36)**

9 Are you unwilling to rejoice with one who has been glorified? The heavenly Physician sees in you the disease of envy, and He will cut you off from the body, so do not envy. What should you do? Rejoice. **Caesarius of Arles, Sermon 24.2 (FOTC 31)**

10 The manifold and fruitful destruction of jealousy is widely spread. It is the root of all evils, the source of disasters, the nursery of sins, the substance of transgressions. From it hatred arises; animosity proceeds from it. Jealousy inflames avarice, when one cannot be content with its own on seeing another richer. Jealousy incites ambition when one sees another more exalted in honors. **Cyprian of Carthage, Jealousy and Envy, 6 (FOTC 36)**

11 As rust wears away iron, so envy corrodes the soul it inhabits. More than this, it consumes the soul that gives it birth, like the vipers which are said to be born by eating their way through the womb that conceived them. **Basil of Caesarea, *Concerning Envy*, Homily 11 (FOTC 9)**

12 We have often stated, dearly beloved, that drunkenness and covetousness are sources of vices. From them rushing torrents of sins well forth, and drag along to the depths a great part of the human race. Drunkenness stirs the whirlpool of gluttony, and covetousness enkindles a frenzy for odious thefts. Covetousness is the mother of pride; drunkenness, of impurity. The one is the companion of lying, the other, of ugly deformity. Both impel men to commit murders, to plan deeds of adultery, and to destroy the bases of friendship. **Valerian, *Homily* 6 (FOTC 17)**

13 For the sanctuary I had reverence, but from a good distance, the effect being that of sunlight upon weak eyes. In all the ups and downs of life I had hoped for any other dignity than this.[1] In sum, one can say nothing ambitious when one is mere man: envy always goes with elevation. And one need seek no other evidence than my own experience. **Gregory Nazianzen, *Concerning His Own Life*, 330–36 (FOTC 75)**

14 For this reason the devil at the very beginnings of the world was both the first to perish and to ruin [others]. He supported by his angelic majesty, acceptable and dear to God, after he had seen man made to the image of God, with malevolent envy plunged into jealousy, not casting down another by the instinct of jealousy before he himself was cast down by jealousy, a captive before capturing, ruined before ruining; when at the instigation of envy he deprived man of the grace of immortality which had been given him, he himself lost that which he had been before. Of such a nature is the evil, most beloved brethren, by which an angel fell, by which that high and glorious sublimity could have been circumvented, and overturned, by which he who deceived was deceived. Therefore, envy rages on earth, when he who is about to perish from

---

1. Gregory's veiled language indicates that he would have preferred to have reverence for the sanctuary from among the people, not as one serving, a vocation for which he himself felt most unworthy.

jealousy obeys the master of perdition, when he who becomes jealous imitates the devil, just as it is written: "But by the envy of the devil, death came into world."[2] So they who are on his side imitate him. **Cyprian of Carthage, *Jealousy and Envy*, 4 (FOTC 36)**

15 I mean, tell me: if he had not fallen before the creation of the human being, how could he have envied the human being while retaining his former status? After all, what sense does it make for an angel to envy a human being, the incorporeal being enjoying such great dignity to envy a creature encumbered with a body? Since, however, he had fallen from heavenly glory into utter disrepute, and though incorporeal himself he saw the newly created human being enjoying such great esteem despite its bodily condition through the love of the Creator, his burning rage led him into envy, and by means of the deceit he practiced through the serpent he caused the human being to be liable to punishment of death. This, you see, is what wickedness is like; it cannot take kindly to the prosperity of others. **John Chrysostom, *Homily* 22.7 on Genesis (FOTC 82)**

16 Rightly is the devil called calumniator: he both directed calumny against God, claiming it was out of envy that God had prevented the taking from the tree, and also against Job he employed the same lies, saying, "Surely Job does not fear God without reason? Touch all that he has," he says, "and surely he will curse you to your face."[3] **Theodoret of Cyrus, *Commentary on Psalm* 72, 3 (FOTC 101)**

17 And so it was that man was overcome by the envy of the Devil. For that envious and hateful demon, having himself been brought low by his conceit, would not suffer us to attain the higher things. So the liar tempted that wretched man with the very hope of divinity, and, having raised him up to his own heights of conceit, dragged him down to the same abyss of ruin. **John Damascene, *The Orthodox Faith*, 2.30 (FOTC 37)**

---

2. Wis 2:24.
3. Cf. Gn 3:5; Job 1:9, 11.

18 From where, then, did death come? By the envy of the Devil death came into the world. If, then, there is something excellent in our regard, God has made it, but we have created evil and sins for ourselves.[4] **Origen, *On Jeremiah*, Homily 2 (FOTC 97)**

19 And as freedom from envy is consistent with the good, so envy relates to the Devil. Therefore, brethren, let us shun the vice of envy. **Basil of Caesarea, *Concerning Envy*, Homily 11 (FOTC 9)**

20 He [Satan] pursued the woman [Mary], since he knew that the one who was born of her was too powerful to be captured. He was moved with envy against human beings because of their salvation by the Lord. He could not bear such a great reversal, by which he himself had been thrown out of heaven, and human beings by their virtue had gone up from earth to heaven. **Oecumenius, *Commentary on the Apocalypse*, 12:13–17 (FOTC 112)**

21 It is this sin of regret because someone else—in this case, his brother—is good that God, in a special way, held against Cain. It was this that God accused him of in asking: "Why art thou angry? And why is thy countenance fallen?" What God saw was the envy toward his brother and it is for this envy that God reproaches Cain. **Augustine of Hippo, *The City of God*, 15.7 (FOTC 14)**

22 Cain killed his brother Abel because envy subdued him; thus the murder was a consequence of envy. **John Chrysostom, *On Repentance and Almsgiving*, Homily 2 (FOTC 96)**

23 What drove the Devil, that author of evils, to wage furious war upon mankind? Was it not envy? Because of envy, too, he was guilty even of open conflict with God. Filled with bitterness against God because of His liberality toward man, he wreaked vengeance upon man, since he was unable to avenge himself upon God. Cain also attempted this maneuver—Cain, that first disciple of the Devil, who learned from him

---

4. Cf. Wis 2:24.

envy and murder, crimes of brother against brother. This combination of vices Paul also presents to us when he says, "full of envy, murder."[5] What, then, did Cain do? He saw the honor conferred by God and was inflamed with jealousy. He slew the recipient of the honor in an effort to reach Him who had bestowed it. Since he could not contend with God, he followed the next best course and slew his brother.[6] Let us flee, brethren, from this disease that would teach us to wage war upon God. It is mother to homicide, does violence to nature, causes us to disregard the closest ties of kinship, and brings upon us an unhappiness based upon irrational motives. **Basil of Caesarea, *Concerning Envy*, Homily 11 (FOTC 9)**

24 Jealousy was the cause of Esau having been hostile to his brother Jacob, for because Jacob had received the blessing of his father, Esau burned with the firebrands of envy into a persecuting hatred.[7] As for Joseph's having been sold by his brothers, the cause for the selling came from jealousy.[8] ... What other than the stimulus of jealousy provoked Saul the king also to hate David, to desire to kill that innocent, merciful man, patient with a gentle mildness, by often repeated persecutions?[9] **Cyprian of Carthage, *Jealousy and Envy*, 5 (FOTC 36)**

25 It was envy that dimmed the light of Lucifer, brought down through his pride[10] for, being in origin divine, he found it intolerable not to be considered a god as well; envy too tricked Adam with a woman's charms and drove him from paradise, for he was led to believe that it was through denial of access to the tree of knowledge up to then that his claim to be a god was begrudged him.[11] Envy it was that made a fratricide of Cain because he could not endure his brother's more acceptable sacrifice.[12] Envy it was that wiped out the failure of the world

---

5. Rom 1:29.
6. Gn 4:8.
7. Cf. Gn 27:41.
8. Cf. Gn 37:17–28.
9. Cf. 1 Sm 18:6–16, 28–29; 19:1–17; 24:1–15; 26:1–16.
10. Cf. Is 14:12.
11. Cf. Gn 2:16–17; 3.
12. Cf. Gn 4:1–16.

with a deluge[13] and destroyed the people of Sodom with a cataclysm of fire.[14] Envy it was that swallowed up Dathan and Abiram for their mad challenge of Moses[15] and made a leper of Miriam for grumbling about her brother.[16] Envy it was that stained the ground with the blood of prophets[17] and used women to bring down Solomon the most wise.[18] Envy it was that turned Judas, tricked by a few pieces of silver, into a traitor deserving to hang,[19] and made Herod a killer of children[20] and Pilate a killer of Christ.[21] Envy it was that winnowed and scattered Israel like chaff, a sin from which they have yet even now to emerge. Envy it was that provoked the Apostate to be our oppressor, one whose embers, although we have come safely through the flames, continue to scorch us still to this very day. Envy it was that sliced and split the beautiful body of the Church into hostile and opposing camps. **Gregory Nazianzen, Oration 36.5 (FOTC 107)**

26 We have rejoiced over the younger son's return and safety; with tearful grief we now take up the elder son's envy.[22] Through his excessive sin of envious jealousy he spoiled the great virtue of his thriftiness.... O cancer of jealousy! A spacious house does not contain two brothers! And what is strange about this, brethren? Envy has wrought this. Envy has made the whole breadth of the world too narrow for two brothers. For it goaded Cain to kill his younger brother.[23] Thus, the law of nature made Cain the first-born son, but envious jealousy made him an only son. **Peter Chrysologus, Sermon 4 on the elder brother's jealousy (FOTC 17)**

---

13. Cf. Gn 6:5–8:22.
14. Cf. Gn 19:24.
15. Cf. Nm 16:31–33.
16. Cf. Nm 12:10.
17. Cf. 2 Kgs 9:7.
18. Cf. 1 Kgs 11:1–5.
19. Cf. Mt 26:14–16; 27:3–5.
20. Cf. Mt 2:16.
21. Cf. Acts 13:28.
22. This sermon is about the envy of the older brother in Christ's parable of the prodigal son (cf. Lk 15:25–32), which Chrysologus perceptively connects with that of Cain.
23. Cf. Gn 4:1–16.

27 One feature of this vice, however, calls for our approval—the more vigorously it has been aroused, the more troublesome it is to the person afflicted. As arrows shot with great force come back upon the archer when they strike a hard and unyielding surface, so also do the movements of envy strike the envious person himself and they harm the object of his spite not at all. Who, by his feelings of annoyance, ever caused a neighbor's goods to be diminished? But the envious person himself is consumed and pines away with grief. **Basil of Caesarea, Concerning Envy, Homily 11 (FOTC 9)**

28 All things effortlessly slip into a circular pattern: when one moves on another takes its place, so that we may rather put our faith in the breezes of the air or in words written on water than in human happiness. Too, envy puts an end to prosperity as mercy does to misfortune, and that is a wise and wondrous thing in my estimation, in order that there may neither be adversity without consolation nor prosperity without restraint. **Gregory Nazianzen, Oration 17.4 (FOTC 107)**

29 Envy follows pride as her daughter and handmaid. Indeed, pride immediately begets her, and is never without this offspring and companion. By these two vices, that is, pride and envy, the Devil is the Devil. **Augustine of Hippo, Holy Virginity, 31.31 (FOTC 27)**

30 This courage, dearly beloved, is demanded of and instilled in us by nothing so much as these present days [leading up to the Paschal feast] in which, while we go through their special observance, we acquire the habits in which we are to persevere. It is well known to you that this is the time when throughout the world the Christian battle-line must combat the raging devil. If sloth holds any lukewarm or cares hold them occupied, now is the time to be equipped in spiritual arms and, aroused by the heavenly trumpet, to enter the battle, for that one "by whose envy death entered the world" burns especially at this time with jealousy and is at this time tortured by very great grief.[24] **Leo the Great, Sermon 39.2 (FOTC 93)**

---

24. Wis 2:24.

31 When jealousy blinds our senses and reduces the secrets of the mind to its sway, fear of God is scorned, the teaching of Christ is neglected, the day of judgment is not provided for. Pride inflates; cruelty embitters; faithlessness prevaricates; impatience agitates; discord infuriates; anger grows hot; nor can he who has become a subject of an alien power restrain or rule himself. Hence the bond of the Lord's peace is broken; hence fraternal charity is violated; hence truth is adulterated, unity is broken, there is a plunging into heresies and schisms, when priests are disparaged, when bishops are envied, when one complains that he himself rather has not been ordained or disdains to tolerate another who has been placed over him. Hence the proud man is recalcitrant and rebellious out of jealousy, perverse out of envy, out of animosity and jealousy an enemy not of the man but of the honor. **Cyprian of Carthage, Jealousy and Envy, 6 (FOTC 36)**

32 If anyone should look deeply into this, he will discover that nothing should be avoided more by a Christian, nothing provided for more cautiously than that one be not caught by envy and malice, that one, being entangled in the blind snares of a deceitful enemy, when brother by envy turns to hatred of brother, not himself unwittingly perish by his own sword. **Cyprian of Carthage, Jealousy and Envy, 3 (FOTC 36)**

Sadness[25]

33 A terrible thing indeed, a terrible thing is uncontrolled sadness, and it leads to spiritual death.[26] **John Chrysostom, Commentary on John, Homily 78 (FOTC 41)**

---

25. Sadness may not seem to correspond directly to envy. This section, however, seems best placed in this chapter more for organizational than thematic reasons, since the Fathers in the monastic tradition did not number envy among the eight (see the introduction above), but everyone included sadness. Certainly a thematic case could be made for including sadness in the treatment of sloth, which is Gregory the Great's approach. Even though envy and sadness are two different vices, the remedy to both is charity (treated below).

26. Cf. 2 Cor 7:10, Sir 38:17–19.

34 "He went away sad, for he had many possessions."[27] This is the sadness that leads to death.[28] The cause of his sadness is also recorded, that he had many possessions. There are the thorns and thistles that choked the Lord's seed.[29] **Jerome, *Commentary on Matthew*, III.19.22 (FOTC 117)**

35 From melancholy there arise malice, rancor, cowardice, despair, slothfulness in fulfilling the commands, and a wandering of the mind on unlawful objects. **Gregory the Great, *Morals on the Book of Job*, XXXI.45 (LF 31)**

36 [Sadness] does not allow the mind to say its prayers with its usual gladness of heart, nor permit it to rely on the comfort of reading the sacred writings, nor suffer it to be quiet and gentle with the brethren; it makes it impatient and rough in all the duties of work and devotion: and, as all wholesome counsel is lost, and steadfastness of heart destroyed, it makes the feelings almost mad and drunk, and crushes and overwhelms them with penal despair.... For "as the moth injures the garment, and the worm the wood, so dejection the heart of man."[30] **John Cassian, *Institutes* 9.1–2 (ACW 58)**

37 Against the soul that, due to the sadness that comes upon it, thinks that the Lord has not heard its groaning: "The children of Israel groaned because of their tasks, and cried, and their cry because of their tasks went up to God. And God heard their groanings."[31] **Evagrius of Pontus, *Antirrhetikos* 4.1 (CSS 229)**

38 Melancholy is also wont to exhort the conquered heart as if with reason, when it says, What ground hast thou to rejoice, when thou endurest so many wrongs from thy neighbors? Consider with what sorrow all must be looked upon, who are turned in such gall of bitterness against thee. **Gregory the Great, *Morals on the Book of Job*, XXXI.45 (LF 31)**

---

27. Mt 19:22.
28. Cf. 2 Cor 7:10; Origen, *Commentary on Matthew*, 15.19.
29. Cf. Mt 13:22.
30. Prv 25:20 (LXX).
31. Ex 2:23–24.

6. ENVY AND SADNESS

39 And so we must see that dejection is only useful to us in one case, when we yield to it either in penitence for sin, or through being inflamed with the desire of perfection, or the contemplation of future blessedness. And of this the blessed Apostle says: "For godly grief produces a repentance that leads to salvation and brings no regret, but worldly grief produces death."[32] **John Cassian, *Institutes* 9.10 (ACW 58)**

40 Cain, indeed, was saddened, but his was the sadness of this world.[33] Paul, also, was saddened, but his was sadness according to God.[34]
John Chrysostom, *Commentary on John*, Homily 75 (FOTC 41)

41 In a certain way, sadness is like dung. Dung, not consigned to its proper place, is filth; dung, not consigned to its proper place, makes a house unclean; but, in its place, it makes a field fertile. Notice the place provided for dung by the farmer. Now, the Apostle says: "And who can gladden me, save the very one who is grieved by me?"[35] And, in another passage, he says: "The sorrow that is according to God produces repentance that tends to salvation of which one does not repent."[36] He who is sad according to God is sad in penitence for his sins; sorrow because of one's own iniquity produces justice. **Augustine of Hippo, *Sermon* 254.2 (FOTC 38)**

42 Brother Andrew, may our kind and loving God not grant the enemy who hates good to sow his sadness and depression in you, so that he may not lead you to despair even about those things promised through the Holy Spirit to you, as the beloved one of the blessed God. Rather, may he open your heart to understand the Scriptures, just as he opened the heart of those around Cleopas.[37] ... Let us closely examine the sufferings of the Savior who became human, enduring with him the shame, the stigma, the humiliation, the contempt of the spitting, the

---

32. 2 Cor 7:10.
33. Cf. Gn 4:5–7. Here, Chrysostom speaks of envious sadness.
34. Cf. Rom 9:1–5.
35. 2 Cor 2:2, 7.
36. Cf. 2 Cor 7:10.
37. Cf. Lk 24:32.

insult of the cloak, the false glory of the crown of thorns, the vinegar of bitterness, the pain of the fixing of the nails, the piercing of the spear, and the water and the blood. In this way, you should take heart in your own pain. For he will not let your toil be in vain. Rather, in order that, at the time when you see the saints bearing the fruits of endurance and boasting of their afflictions, you may not feel that you have no share with them, he allows you to endure the labor for a while in order that you may partake with them and with Jesus, having boldness before him in company with the holy ones. Therefore, do not be sad. For God has not forgotten you, but cares for you as his true son, not as an illegitimate one. You shall be in good standing if you pay careful attention to yourself, so that you may not fall away from fear of and gratitude to God. **Barsanuphius and John, Letter 106 (FOTC 113)**

43 The grieving monk does not know spiritual pleasure. Grief is dejection of soul, and comes alongside thoughts of wrath. For anger is the desire for revenge, and the failure of revenge gives birth to grief. Grief is a lion's mouth, and quite easily devours the one who grieves. **Evagrius of Pontus, Eight Evil Thoughts, chap. 11**[38]

44 Melancholy also arises from anger, because the more extravagantly the agitated mind strikes itself, the more it confounds itself by condemnation; and when it has lost the sweetness of tranquility, nothing supports it but the grief resulting from agitation. Melancholy also runs down into avarice; because, when the disturbed heart has lost the satisfaction of joy within, it seeks for sources of consolation without, and is more anxious to possess external goods, the more it has no joy on which to fall back within. But after these, there remain behind two carnal vices, gluttony and lust. **Gregory the Great, Morals on the Book of Job, XXXI.45 (LF 31)**

45 There is, too, another still more objectionable sort of dejection, which produces in the guilty soul no amendment of life or correction

---

38. Editor's translation. PG 79:1156B–C. This work is also attributed to Nilus of Ancyra. See the introduction above.

of faults, but the most destructive despair: which did not make Cain repent after the murder of his brother, or Judas, after the betrayal, hasten to relieve himself by making amends, but drove him to hang himself in despair. **John Cassian, *Institutes* 9.9 (ACW 58)**

46 As I have said before, a suitable place for dung helps to produce fruit, but an unsuitable place leads to uncleanness. Someone or other is sad; I have come upon this sad person; I see the dung; I examine the place. Tell me, my friend, why are you sad? He says: "I have lost my money." The place is unclean; there is no fruit. Let him hear the Apostle: "The sorrow that is according to the world produces death."[39] Not only is there no fruit, but there is great danger. The outcome is the same of other things pertaining to worldly joys, things which it would take too long to mention. I see another person sorrowing, moaning, and weeping; I see much dung and there I examine the place. Although I have seen him sad and weeping, I have also seen him praying. Some good impression or other had brought to my attention this man who was sad, moaning, weeping, and praying; but still I examine the place. For, what if that man who is praying and groaning is also with much weeping imploring death for his enemies? Moreover it is thus, even thus that he now asks; he now begs; he now prays. The place is unclean; there is no fruit. What we find in Scripture goes further: the man begs that his enemy may die and he falls under the curse of Judas: "May his prayer be turned to sin."[40] I have looked at still another person groaning, weeping, and praying; I recognize the dung and I examine the place. Moreover, I have directed my ear to this man's prayer, and I have heard him say: "O Lord, be thou merciful to me: heal my soul, for I have sinned against thee."[41] He laments his sin; I recognize the field; I look for fruit. Thanks be to God! **Augustine of Hippo, *Sermon* 254.4 (FOTC 38)**

---

39. 2 Cor 7:10.
40. Ps 108:7.
41. Ps 40:5.

47 The man who flees from all worldly pleasures is an impregnable tower before the assaults of the demon of sadness. **Evagrius of Pontus, Praktikos 19 (CSS 4)**

48 Wicked spirits often appeared to Abbot Moses, saying: "You have conquered us and we can do nothing to you; for whenever we wish to humble you with despair, you are exalted; and when you exalt yourself, you are so humble that none of us can approach you." **Paschasius of Dumium, Questions and Answers of the Greek Fathers, 11.4 (FOTC 62)**

49 But, what was the use of the Lord Jesus Himself saying: "Then shall the just shine as the sun in the kingdom of their Father,"[42] which is to happen after the end of the world, and even exclaiming: "Woe to the world because of scandals"[43]—if it was not to keep us from flattering ourselves that we can attain the abodes of everlasting bliss in any other way than by standing firm when we are tried by temporal evils? What was the use of His saying: "Because iniquity hath abounded the charity of many shall grow cold,"[44] if it was not that those, of whom he speaks when He adds at once: "He that shall persevere to the end, he shall be saved,"[45] should not be disturbed, should not be frightened, when they see this charity growing cold with the prevalence of iniquity, should not fall into sadness as at things unanticipated and unexpected? But, seeing those things that were predicted happen before the end, should they not persevere patiently to the end so as to deserve, after the end of time, to reign without care in that life which has no end? **Augustine of Hippo, Letter 78 to the church of Hippo (FOTC 12)**

50 The tyranny exercised over us by despondency is a strong one. We need great courage if we are to persevere in resisting this emotion; and if, after deriving from it what profit we can, we are to refrain from indulging in it to excess—for, actually, it does have some usefulness. When we or other men commit sin, only then is it salutary to give in

42. Mt 13:43.
43. Mt 18:7.
44. Mt 24:12.
45. Mt 24:3.

to sadness. But when we meet with misfortune in human affairs, then sadness has no efficacy. **John Chrysostom, *Commentary on John*, Homily 78 (FOTC 41)**

51 Theatrical shows, filled with depictions of my miseries and with tinder for my own fire, completely carried me away. What is it that makes a man want to become sad in beholding mournful and tragic events which he himself would not willingly undergo? Yet, as he watches, he wishes to suffer their sorrow; this sorrow is his own pleasure. What is this but a wretched weakness of mind? **Augustine of Hippo, *Confessions*, 3.2.2 (FOTC 21)**

52 When we give way to anger, yield to detraction, surrender to a sadness that leads to death, entertain thoughts of the flesh, do we think that the Holy Spirit is abiding in us? Do we suppose that we may hate a brother with the Holy Spirit dwelling in us? That we may call to mind and dwell upon anything evil? **Jerome, *Homily* 75 on the beginning of Mark (FOTC 57)**

53 Abbot Pimenius used to say of Abbot Isidore that only he understood himself. For when his thought would say to him: "You are great," he would answer himself: "As great as Antony, or even Abbot Piamon, or the rest of the brothers who pleased God?" Whenever he had these thoughts, he would be at ease. When the devil, to torment him, threatened despair and punishment, saying: "After all of this you are going to go to tortures," he answered: "Although I may be sent to tortures, still I shall find you beneath me." **Paschasius of Dumium, *Questions and Answers of the Greek Fathers*, 11.3 (FOTC 62)**

54 We must not like the unbelievers have any sadness concerning the faithful departed and, to speak more precisely, our people who have fallen asleep. There must remain in our heart a distinction between a salutary and a harmful sadness by which it comes about that a spirit, given over to eternal things, does not collapse because of the loss of temporal solace and assumes a salutary sadness concerning these

things in which it considers that it did either something less or differently than it should have.... Therefore, do not have an undifferentiated sadness over the death of your husband beyond the way of the Christian faith. You should not think of him as lost but as sent on ahead of you. You should not think of his youth as prematurely cut off but rather see him confirmed in an endless eternity. To the faithful souls it is said: "Your youth shall be renewed like the eagle's."[46] **Fulgentius, *Letter* 2 to the Widow Galla (FOTC 95)**

55 "Blessed are they who mourn, for they shall be comforted."[47] My brethren, mourning is a sorrowful thing, for it is the sob of one who is sorry. Does anyone mourn, except for one who is dead? But, every sinner ought to mourn for himself, since there is nothing else so dead as a man in sin. Yet, how marvelous! If he mourns for himself, he comes to life again. Let him mourn through repentance, and he shall be comforted through forgiveness.[48] **Augustine of Hippo, *Sermon* 11.8 on the Sermon on the Mount (FOTC 11)**

56 I am trying to reconcile these words of Yours with the words You previously spoke, namely: "I have power to lay down my life, and I have power to take it up again."[49] Why is it that I hear: "My soul is sad, even unto death"?[50] Why are You sad, since no one can take away Your life from You? Since You have power to lay down Your life, why do You say: "Father, if it be possible, let this chalice pass from me"?[51] If we ask Him that question, He gives us this answer: "You are a man, but I assumed your flesh. Did I not therefore assume your voice as well? I, the Creator, am proclaiming Myself when I say: 'I have power to lay down My life,

---

46. Ps 103:5.
47. Mt 5:4.
48. Mourning for sins is a virtuous sadness in the tradition. Some Christians give the impression that one must be constantly happy. Christ, however, encourages a certain type of mourning and sorrow. Augustine here gives a glimpse at righteous sadness, which is different from the capital vice so closely connected with the passions. Virtuous sadness aligns with repentance for one's own sins, on the one hand, and penance for the sins of others, on the other. Augustine knew this intimately in the tears of his own mother, Monica (cf. *Confessions*, III.11.19, below).
49. Jn 10:18.
50. Mt 26:38; Mk 14:34.
51. Mt 26:39; cf. Mk 14:36; Lk 22:42.

and I have power to take it up again.' But I, the creature, am proclaiming Myself when I say: 'My soul is sad, even unto death.' Rejoice that I am one with you, and acknowledge that you are one with Me. Behold Me as your refuge and strength when I say: 'I have power to lay down My life.' Recognize Me as a mirror in which to behold yourself when I say: 'My soul is sad, even unto death.'" **Augustine of Hippo, *Sermon* 5.3, Life from Death (FOTC 11)**

Charity

57 Love is a good disposition of the soul by which one prefers no being to the knowledge of God. It is impossible to reach the habit of this love if one has any attachment to earthly things. **Maximus the Confessor, *Centuries on Charity*, 1.1 (CWS)**

58 And Thou didst "put forth Thy Hand from on high"[52] and draw forth my soul[53] from this deep darkness of mind, while my mother, one of Thy faithful, wept for me before Thee, far more than do mothers who weep at bodily deaths. She saw my death in the spirit of faith and the spirit which she had received from Thee, and Thou didst hear her, O Lord. Thou didst hear her and didst not despise her tears, as they flowed forth and watered the ground beneath her eyes in every place of her prayer; Thou didst hear her. **Augustine of Hippo, *Confessions*, 3.11.19 (FOTC 21)**

59 Perfect love is the love of an enemy, and this perfect love is found in brotherly love. **Augustine of Hippo, *Tractates on the First Epistle of John*, 8.3 (FOTC 92)**

60 You should love all men, even your personal enemies, not because they are brothers but in order that they may be brothers, in order that you may always burn with brotherly love, whether for one already

---

52. Ps 143:7.
53. Cf. Ps 85:13.

become a brother or for an enemy so that by [your] loving he may become a brother. Whenever you love a brother, you love a friend. Now he is with you, now he has been joined to you also in catholic unity. If you live well, you love one [who has] become a brother from an enemy. But you love someone who has not yet believed in Christ, or if he has believed, believes as the demons do. You reprehend his empty folly. [But] you—love him and love him with brotherly love. He is not yet your brother, but you love precisely in order that he may be your brother. Therefore all our brotherly love is directed toward Christians, toward all his members. **Augustine of Hippo, *Tractates on the First Epistle of John*, 10.7 (FOTC 92)**

61 Some men exhaust their coffers, others their bodies for the Spirit and are mortified in Christ and withdraw completely from the world; others consecrate what they hold most dear to God. Indeed, you have no doubt heard of the sacrifice of Abraham, who, more eagerly than when he first received the child from God, gave God his only son, the one who had been promised to him and who bore in himself the promise.[54] None of these things do we ask of you. In their stead offer compassion alone. God takes more pleasure in this than in all the other things put together, a special gift, a faultless gift, a gift that invites God to lavish his favor upon us. Mingle severity with clemency; temper threat with promise. I know that kindness accomplishes a great deal by winning us over into responding in kind; when we reject coercion in favor of forgiveness, our good will wins over the beneficiary of our mercy. **Gregory Nazianzen, *Oration* 17.10 (FOTC 107)**

62 It is evident that [the Apostle John] has put the perfection of justice in brotherly love, for he in whom there is no scandal is surely perfect, and yet it seems that he has kept silent about the love of God. He would never have done so if he did not intend that God should be understood in brotherly love itself. For a little later on in the same Epistle he expresses this most plainly in the following words: "Beloved, let us love

---

54. Cf. Gn 22:2–19.

one another, because love is from God. And everyone who loves is born of God and knows God. He who does not love, does not know God, for God is love."[55] The context shows sufficiently and clearly that brotherly love itself (for brotherly love is that whereby we love one another) is taught by so eminent an authority, not only to be from God, but also to be God. **Augustine of Hippo, *The Trinity*, 8.8.12 (FOTC 45)**

63 Either let us fear the wrath which is to come or else let us love the grace we have—one or the other, so long as we are found in Jesus Christ unto true life. **Ignatius of Antioch, *Letter to the Ephesians*, 11.1 (FOTC 1)**

64 If you light a lamp or torch with no oil, it can smoke and give a bad odor, but it cannot produce light. Similarly, one who possesses riches without charity can burn with anger or smoke with pride or have the foul odor of avarice; without charity, it is utterly impossible to produce light. **Caesarius of Arles, *Sermon* 29.2 (FOTC 31)**

65 A certain brother asked an old man: "Why is it that men working in communities today do not receive grace as did people of old?" The old man answered: "Then, there was love, and each one lifted his neighbor up, but now, love has grown cold and each one drags his neighbors down. That is why they do not merit the grace of God." **Paschasius of Dumium, *Questions and Answers of the Greek Fathers*, 28.4 (FOTC 62)**

66 When the young man inquired of the Lord how to attain to eternal life, and heard that he must sell all his goods and distribute them to the poor, and have his treasure in heaven, why else did he go away sad, except that he had, as the Gospel says, great riches?[56] ... With how great and how wonderful joy does Christian charity behold the happy fulfillment in our times of the Lord's Gospel, which that rich young man heard with sadness from the Lord Himself! **Augustine of Hippo, *Letter* 31, to Paulinus and Therasia (FOTC 12)**

---

55. 1 Jn 4:7–8.
56. Cf. Mt 19:16–30; Mk 10:17–31; Lk 18:18–30.

67 Keep in mind from what [John] has added on, that envy cannot exist in love. You have it openly when love was being praised: "Love envies not."⁵⁷ **Augustine of Hippo, *Tractates on the First Epistle of John*, 5.8 (FOTC 92)**

68 Whether these two loves come to the fullness of perfection together, or whether the love of God arises first but the love of neighbor is the first to come to perfection, this I do not know. Perhaps divine love takes hold upon us more quickly in the beginning, but we come to perfection more readily in lower things. Whichever way it be, the main point is that no one, while despising his neighbor, can believe he will arrive at happiness and the God whom he loves. Would that it were as easy to do something for one's neighbor's good or to avoid injuring him as it is for the kind-hearted and well-instructed individual to love him. But here good will alone does not suffice, for it is a work demanding great understanding and prudence, which no one can exercise unless they be given to him by God, the fountain of all good. **Augustine of Hippo, *The Catholic and Manichaean Ways of Life*, I.26.51 (FOTC 56)**

69 Therefore, he receives an eternal share of the heavenly inheritance, who, preserving the unity of fraternal charity within the Catholic Church before he ends this present life, puts away the fatal hardness of an impenitent heart and does not despair that in the one and truly Catholic Church, the forgiveness of all sins is given through the Holy Spirit to those who are converted. Our Savior himself shows this. For, after he rose, breathing on his disciples and giving them the gift of his Holy Spirit, he gave them the power to forgive sins, saying, "Receive the Holy Spirit. Whose sins you forgive are forgiven them and whose sins you retain are retained."⁵⁸ **Fulgentius, *On the Forgiveness of Sins*, I.25.2 (FOTC 95)**

70 Charity is possessed only in the unity of the Church. **Augustine of Hippo, *Sermon* 265.9 on the Ascension (FOTC 38)**

---

57. Cf. 1 Cor 13:4.
58. Jn 20:22–23.

6. ENVY AND SADNESS

71 Perhaps that man has virginity; love him, and it is yours. Again, you may have greater patience; if he loves you, it is his. Another can keep long vigils; if you do not envy him, his zeal is yours. Perhaps you can fast more; if he loves you, your fasting is his. For this reason you possess certain qualities in another; you are not thus in your own right, but by charity. **Caesarius of Arles, *Sermon* 24.2 (FOTC 31)**

72 I do not give you orders as though I were a person of importance, for I have not yet been made perfect in Jesus Christ, even though I am a prisoner for His name. But, at last, I am beginning to be His disciple and speak to you as His disciples, too. For I have need of being trained by you in faith, counsel, endurance and long-suffering. Still, love will not let me be silent in your regard, and so I make bold to beg you to be in harmony with God's mind. For Jesus Christ, the life that cannot be taken from us, is the mind of the Father, and the bishops appointed to ends of the earth are of one mind with Jesus Christ. **Ignatius of Antioch, *Letter to the Ephesians*, 3.1–2 (FOTC 1)**

73 With God's help we shall give you charity as well as truth. Whoever has these two will never be guilty of folly or envy, two vices discussed at length at the beginning of your volume. Error must yield to truth, envy to charity. **Augustine of Hippo, *Against Julian*, 6.1.1 (FOTC 35)**

74 Indeed, neither fasts nor vigils nor prayers nor alms nor faith nor virginity can help a man without charity. **Caesarius of Arles, *Sermon* 23.4 (FOTC 31)**

75 Where there is no envy, variety is harmonious. **Augustine of Hippo, *Holy Virginity*, 29.29 (FOTC 27)**

76 The poison of charity is the hope of getting and holding onto temporal things. The nourishment of charity is the lessening of covetousness, the perfection of charity, the absence of covetousness. The lessening of fear is the sign of its progress, the absence of fear, the sign of its perfection. For "the root of all evils is covetousness,"⁵⁹ and, "love made perfect casts out fear."⁶⁰ Accordingly whoever wants to nourish charity in himself, let him pursue the lessening of covetous desires (covetousness being the love of getting and holding onto temporal things). **Augustine of Hippo, *Various Questions*, 36.1 (FOTC 70)**

77 A brother asked Abbot Pimenius: "What is the meaning of the Lord's words: 'Greater love than this no one has, that one lay down his life for his friends'?⁶¹ How does one do this?" The old man answered: "If one hears an ill word from one's neighbor, and, although he could reply in kind, yet fights in his heart to endure the toil and forces himself not to reply ill so as to sadden the other, such a man lays down his life for his friend." **Paschasius of Dumium, *Questions and Answers of the Greek Fathers*, 37.3 (FOTC 62)**

78 So let us now follow the Word; let us seek the repose on high; let us cast aside the opulence of this world; let us have recourse to only that portion of it that serves a good end; let us gain our lives by acts of charity; let us share what we have with the poor that we may be rich in the bounty of heaven.⁶² Give a portion of your soul too, not just your body; give a portion to God too, not just the world; take something from the belly, dedicate it to the Spirit; pluck something from the fire, place it far from the devouring flame below; rob from the tyrant, commit to the Lord. **Gregory Nazianzen, *Oration* 14.22 (FOTC 107)**

79 The one who loves God cannot help but love also every man as himself even though he is displeased by the passions of those who are not yet purified. Thus when he sees their conversion and amendment, he rejoices with an unbounded joy. **Maximus the Confessor, *Centuries on Charity*, 1.13 (CWS)**

---

59. 1 Tm 6:10.
60. 1 Jn 4:18.
61. Jn 15:13.
62. Cf. Lk 21:19.

80 This is the "pearl of great price": love, without which nothing at all, whatever you have, profits you; but if you have it, it is sufficient for you.[63] Now you see with faith, then you will see with direct sight. For if we love when we do not see, how we shall embrace when we have seen! But in what ought we to train ourselves? In brotherly love. You can say to me, "I have not seen God." Can you say to me, "I have not seen a man"? Love your brother. For if you love your brother whom you see, you will love God too at the same time; for you will see love itself, and God dwells within. **Augustine of Hippo, *Tractates on the First Epistle of John*, 5.7 (FOTC 92)**

81 However, this blessed one, who had been found worthy of gifts surpassing nature, did at the time of the Passion suffer the pangs which she had escaped at childbirth. For, when she saw Him put to the death as a criminal, whom she knew to be God when she gave birth to Him, her heart was torn from maternal compassion and she was rent by her thoughts as by a sword. This is the meaning of "And thy own soul a sword shall pierce."[64] But her grief gave way to the joy of the resurrection, the resurrection which proclaimed Him to be God who had died in the flesh. **John Damascene, *The Orthodox Faith*, 4.14 (FOTC 37)**

---

63. Cf. Mt 13:45–46.
64. Lk 2:35.

7

Vainglory and Pride

Vainglory

1 Vainglory is an irrational passion, and readily becomes entangled with every work of virtue. **Evagrius of Pontus, *Eight Evil Thoughts*, chap. 15**[1]

2 For vainglory is wont to exhort the conquered heart, as if with reason, when it says, Thou oughtest to aim at greater things, that, as thou hast been able to surpass many in power, thou mayest be able to benefit many also. **Gregory the Great, *Morals on the Book of Job*, XXXI.45 (LF 31)**

3 For our other faults and passions may be said to be simpler and of but one form: but this takes many forms and shapes, and changes about and assails the man who stands up against it from every quarter, and assaults its conqueror on all sides. For it tries to injure the soldier of Christ in his dress, in his manner, his walk, his voice, his work, his vigils, his fasts, his prayers, when he withdraws, when he reads, in his knowledge, his silence, his obedience, his humility, his patience; and like some most dangerous rock hidden by surging waves, it causes an unforeseen and miserable shipwreck to those who are sailing with a

---

[1]. Editor's translation. PG 79:1160D.

fair breeze, while they are not on the lookout for it or guarding against it. **John Cassian, *Institutes* 11.3 (ACW 58)**

4 For from vainglory there arise disobedience, boasting, hypocrisy, contentions, obstinacies, discords, and the presumptions of novelties. **Gregory the Great, *Morals on the Book of Job*, XXXI.45 (LF 31)**

5 Ambition, too, what does it seek but honors and glory, whereas Thou art alone to be honored beyond all things and glorious for eternity? **Augustine of Hippo, *Confessions*, 2.6.13 (FOTC 21)**

6 Truly, it is not possible for a man who is enslaved to the glory of the present time to secure that which comes from God. Wherefore He chided them, saying: "How can you believe who receive glory from one another, and do not seek the glory which is from God?"[2] Vainglory is a kind of deep intoxication and therefore this passion makes its victim hard to convert. **John Chrysostom, *Commentary on John*, Homily 3 (FOTC 33)**

7 Surely it is not the case that, when I see someone rejoicing over the acquisition of money or over the extent of his possessions or the greatness of secular honors, I ought to congratulate such individuals. For I know that sorrows and tears will follow joys of this sort. **Origen, *Commentary on Romans*, 9.15 (FOTC 104)**

8 The spirit of vainglory is most subtle and it readily grows up in the souls of those who practice virtue. It leads them to desire to make their struggles known publicly, to hunt after the praise of men. **Evagrius of Pontus, *Praktikos* 13 (CSS 4)**

9 That righteousness, however, which is hypocrisy is not righteousness: it is deceptive to the eye, it is false in appearance, it mocks those who see it, it lies to those who hear it, it seduces the crowds, it leads people astray, it sells its reputation, it buys applause, it is done for the world,

---

2. Jn 5:44.

7. VAINGLORY AND PRIDE 165

not for God; it grabs its recompense in the present, it does not look for any reward in the future; blind itself it blinds the eyes; without sight itself it desires to be seen.[3] **Peter Chrysologus, *Sermon* 9.2 (FOTC 109)**

10 As even Cicero points out, there are a good many people who write their own books about despising glory and yet attach their names to them out of a desire for glory![4] **Jerome, *Commentary on Galatians*, 5.26 (FOTC 121)**

11 Often, a man may become more vainglorious because of his very contempt for vainglory; thus, it is no longer because of contempt for glory that he glories, for, when he glories, he does not contemn it. **Augustine of Hippo, *Confessions*, 10.38.63 (FOTC 21)**

12 If almsgiving is done for the purpose of obtaining praise, it is empty glory, and the same goes for prolonged prayer and the pallor caused by fasting. These words are not mine but the Savior's, who thunderously proclaims them in the Gospel.[5] Chastity in marriage, widowhood, and virginity also often seeks human applause.[6] What I was just now afraid of saying needs to be said: If we undergo martyrdom with the intention of being marveled at and praised by our brothers, then blood has been shed in vain. **Jerome, *Commentary on Galatians*, 5.26 (FOTC 121)**

13 So if we want to know how to gain real wealth, and along with the wealth find pardon for sin as well, let us pour our possessions into the hands of the needy and thus send them ahead of us to heaven.... Only, let us not do it from vainglory but in response to the laws given us by him so as to win the praise, not of human beings but of the common Lord of all, and thus we may not suffer the expense and yet lose the

---

3. Here, Peter Chrysologus is contrasting true righteousness with the self-righteousness of vainglory. Earlier in the same sermon, he says. "'See to it that you do not perform your righteousness before human beings' (Mt 6:1).... Brothers, this heavenly precept means to remove boastfulness, take away ostentation, do away with vanity, uproot empty glory; and so it does not mean to conceal righteousness."
4. Cf. *Tusculanae Disputationes* 1.34.
5. Cf. Mt 6:1–6, 16–18.
6. Cf. Jerome, *Letter* 22.27.

profit. I mean, as the wealth that is deposited there by the hand of the poor is proof against all other schemes, so it is at risk only to vainglory; and as here on earth worm and moth cause the ruin of clothing, so vainglory has this effect on the wealth amassed from almsgiving. **John Chrysostom, *Homily* 42.32 on Genesis (FOTC 82)**

14 Vainglory, the desire to please men, and acting for display are strictly forbidden to Christians under all circumstances, because even a man who observes the precept but does it for the purpose of being seen and glorified by men loses the reward for that observance. All manner of vainglory, consequently, is especially to be avoided by those who have embraced every kind of humiliation for the sake of the Lord's command. **Basil of Caesarea, *The Long Rules*, q. 16 (FOTC 9)**

15 The cause of all evils, however, is vainglory and the desire to give one's own name to property, baths, houses. **John Chrysostom, *Homily* 22.21 on Genesis (FOTC 82)**

16 Against the thoughts that entice us to go out in the world in order to benefit those who see us: "The words of crafty persons are gentle, but they strike into the depths of the bowels."[7] **Evagrius of Pontus, *Antirrhetikos* 7.18 (CSS 229)**

17 The other vices, in truth, though they inflict much harm, at least bring some pleasure, even if it is ephemeral and short. I say this, because the miser, and the drunkard, and the lustful have, together with the moral injury, some enjoyment, also, even though short; but those who are afflicted with vainglory always live a thoroughly bitter life, completely bereft of pleasure. They do not attain to what they very much desire—I mean fame in the eyes of the crowd. They only seem to enjoy it; actually, they do not enjoy it, because this is not fame at all. Therefore, this passion is said to be, not glory, but a thing empty of glory; hence, all the ancients have aptly called it vainglory. **John Chrysostom, *Commentary on John*, Homily 3 (FOTC 33)**

---

7. Prv 26:22.

18 Vanity is pretense. Vain things are found out to be false, or deceiving, or both. One may recognize how great is the difference between vanity and truth. Even though all these visible things, considered in themselves, are marvelous and beautiful, having been created by God their Maker, still, in comparison with the unseen realities, they are as nothing. **Augustine of Hippo, *The Magnitude of the Soul*, 33.76 (FOTC 4)**

19 O you Christian, a pauper begs you for money, why do you refuse him in secret but give to him in public?[8] If you seek God as your witness, why do you look around for human eyes? Your almsgiving in the presence of the unsophisticated looks like real almsgiving, but in the presence of God it is a wrong; you are doing an injury to your brother, for you wish to show him up as a beggar in the presence of others. **Jerome, *Homily* 46 on Psalm 133 (134) (FOTC 48)**

20 Let your dress be plain, not serving for adornment, but for necessary covering. The purpose of clothes is not to minister to your vanity, but to keep warm in winter and cover your nakedness. Take care lest, under pretense of hiding your unseemliness, by your extravagant apparel, you fall into another sort of unseemliness. **Cyril of Jerusalem, *Catechetical Lectures*, 4.29 (FOTC 61)**

21 Having cut away from heaven the souls of its slaves, [vainglory] pins them to the earth and does not permit them to gaze on the true light, but persuades them to wallow continually in the mud, providing them with masters so powerful that they rule them without issuing orders to them. **John Chrysostom, *Commentary on John*, Homily 3 (FOTC 33)**

22 It is only with considerable difficulty that one can escape the thought of vainglory. For what you do to destroy it becomes the principle of some other form of vainglory. **Evagrius of Pontus, *Praktikos* 30 (CSS 4)**

23 While Abbot Nesteron was walking with other brothers in the desert, they saw a serpent and ran away. One of them said to him:

---

8. Cf. Mt. 6:2–4.

"Are you afraid too, father?" The old man replied: "I am not afraid, son, but I had to run away, for otherwise I should not have escaped vainglorious thoughts." **Paschasius of Dumium, *Questions and Answers of the Greek Fathers*, 12.3 (FOTC 62)**

24 Let us abandon the vanities of the crowd and their false teachings; let us return to the word which was delivered to us from the beginning. **Polycarp, *Letter to the Philippians*, 7.2 (FOTC 1)**

25 If you want to be redeemed from the passions of dishonor, then cut away from yourself the boldness toward all people, especially those toward whom you see your heart leaning with passionate desire; in this way, you will also be freed from vainglory. For vainglory is an associate of people-pleasing, while people-pleasing is an associate of boldness. And boldness is the mother of all passions.[9] **Barsanuphius and John, *Letter* 261 (FOTC 113)**

26 All boasting is forbidden because it is culpable and harmful, and as a result James writes about it all in general in his letter, "All such boasting is evil,"[10] because it involves shame and reproach, and hence Jeremiah speaks with severe censure to the conceited, "Be ashamed of your boasting and reproach"[11] all day long. To the person in the grip of such vanity and vainglory the word says, "Why do you boast of evil, mighty one, of lawlessness all day long?"[12] Now, the boasting of the house of David is exaggerated, as also the conceit of the inhabitants of Jerusalem against the Savior who springs from Judah. This occurs when those who seem to be members of the Church think they practice virtue by their own power and not by the grace of the one who says, "Learn of me that I am gentle and humble of heart."[13] **Didymus the Blind, *Commentary on Zechariah*, 12:6–7 (FOTC 111)**

---

9. It seems that boldness is synonymous with ambition here.
10. Jas 4:16.
11. Jer 12:13 (LXX).
12. Ps 52:1.
13. Mt 11:29.

27 The righteousness that hires itself out to human eyes cannot expect a divine recompense from the Father. It wanted to be seen, and it has been seen; it wanted to please human beings, and it has pleased them. It has the recompense that it wanted; it will not have the reward that it had no desire to have. **Peter Chrysologus, *Sermon* 9.2 (FOTC 109)**

28 Let vanity not be known among you; rather, let simplicity and harmony and a guileless attitude weld the group together. Let each persuade himself that he is not only inferior to the brother at his side, but to all men. If he knows this, he will truly be a disciple of Christ. For, as the Savior says: "Everyone who exalts himself shall be humbled and he who humbles himself shall be exalted."[14] And again: "If any man wishes to be first among you, he will be last of all";[15] and the servant of all: "for the Son of man has not come to be served but to serve and to give his life as a ransom for many."[16] And the apostle: "For we preach not ourselves, but Jesus Christ as Lord; and ourselves merely as your servants in Jesus."[17] **Gregory of Nyssa, *On the Christian Mode of Life* (FOTC 58)**

29 It is no task to castigate the vice [of vainglory] (for all men agree in that); the object to be sought is how to overcome it. How, then, do we overcome it? If we exchange true glory for vainglory. For, just as we scorn earthly wealth when we look to other riches, and despise this life when we fix our mind on that much better one, so also we shall be able to reject the glory here when we fix our mind on that glory which is holier by far than this; namely, real glory. In truth, the former is vain and foolish, with a name empty of substance, while the latter is true, and from heaven, and has as eulogists not men, but angels, and archangels, nay, rather, it has even men also, together with Him. **John Chrysostom, *Commentary on John*, Homily 29 (FOTC 33)**

---

14. Mt 23:12; Lk 14:11, 18:14.
15. Mk 9:34.
16. Mt 20:28; Mk 10:45.
17. 2 Cor 4:5.

30 This, you see, is the reason why it is called vain, because it is quite empty and has no substance or stable foundation: it proves only to be a deceiver of the eyes before it disappears and flies away. Or do we not often see the case of a person who today is escorted by attendants and surrounded by bodyguards, whereas tomorrow he is incarcerated and lodged with brigands? What is more deceptive than this vain and empty glory? Even if in this present life the change in circumstances does not affect the person, death will come upon him to abolish his property completely, the person today swaggering in the public eye, who confines people to prison, the person seated on the throne with great ideas of his own importance, regarding all people as dust under his feet—in a trice he is next found stretched out a lifeless corpse, giving off a stench, the butt of countless insults from those he had wronged and those he had not wronged out of sympathy with their wrong. **John Chrysostom, Homily 22.21 on Genesis (FOTC 82)**

31 Give your souls to God on high, having the one thought of pleasing the Lord and never straying from the awareness of heavenly things; do not accept the honors of this life; run in such a way as to conceal your struggles in behalf of virtue lest the devil, finding an opportunity to tempt you with worldly honors and having distracted you from leisure for good, lead you to vanity and error. **Gregory of Nyssa, On the Christian Mode of Life (FOTC 58)**

32 We know that, as far as is lawful and commanded, we should assist souls of our own kind who have gone astray and struggle in error, and this task is to be undertaken with the conviction that its successful issue is to be attributed to God acting through us. Let us not appropriate anything to ourselves, deceived by the desire for vainglory, for, by this one vice we are brought down from the heights and sunk in the lowest depths. **Augustine of Hippo, The Magnitude of the Soul, 34.78 (FOTC 4)**

33 Thus, in truth, we shall be able to receive our reward from Him who closely scrutinizes our affairs if we are satisfied with His gaze alone. Why, indeed, do we need the eyes of others, also, since He who will reward us always sees what is done by us? **John Chrysostom, *Commentary on John*, Homily 3 (FOTC 33)**

34 Vainglory should be corrected by imposing practices of humility. **Basil of Caesarea, *The Long Rules*, q. 51 (FOTC 9)**

Pride

35 A flash of lightning predicts an echo of thunder, and the presence of vainglory announces pride. **Evagrius of Pontus, *Eight Evil Thoughts*, chap. 17**[18]

36 When you overcome any of the dishonorable passions, such as gluttony, fornication, anger, or covetousness, suddenly the thought of vanity lights upon you. But when you overcome this, that of pride follows in short order.... ascribing our right actions to God removes pride. **Maximus the Confessor, *Centuries on Charity*, 3.59, 3.62 (CWS)**

37 Why do you fly off to heaven, earthling that you are? Why do you build a tower if you do not have enough to complete it?[19] Just why do you measure the waters in the hollow of your hand and mark off the heavens with a span, and enclose all the earth in a measure, those primal elements that can be measured only by him who created them?[20] **Gregory Nazianzen, *Oration* 32.27 (FOTC 107)**

38 Other vices harm only those who commit them; pride inflicts far more injury upon everyone. **Jerome, *Homily* 95 on obedience (FOTC 57)**

39 The demon of pride is the cause of the most damaging fall for the soul. For it induces the monk to consider that he himself is the cause of virtuous actions. **Evagrius of Pontus, *Praktikos* 14 (CSS 4)**

---

18. Editor's translation. PG 79:1161C.
19. Cf. Lk 14:28–30.
20. Cf. Is 40:12.

40 For pride is the root of all evil, of which it is said, as Scripture bears witness; Pride is the beginning of all sin.[21] But seven principal vices, as its first progeny, spring doubtless from this poisonous root, namely, vainglory, envy, anger, melancholy, avarice, gluttony, lust. For, because He grieved that we were held captive by these seven sins of pride, therefore our Redeemer came to the spiritual battle of our liberation, full of the spirit of sevenfold grace. **Gregory the Great, Morals on the Book of Job, XXXI.45 (LF 31)**

41 And of this pride there are two kinds: the one, that by which we said that the best of men and spiritually minded ones were troubled; the other, that which assaults even beginners and carnal persons. And though each kind of pride is excited with regard to both God and man by a dangerous elation, yet that first kind more particularly has to do with God; the second refers especially to men. **John Cassian, Institutes 12.2 (ACW 58)**

42 A certain brother asked Abbot Pimenius if it were better to live with the other brothers or apart from them. The old man replied: "If a man reproaches himself, he can exist anywhere; but if he exalts himself, he stands nowhere, as it is written: 'If anyone thinks himself to be something, whereas he is nothing, he deceives himself.'[22] For whatever a man does for another, he should not exult over it, as he will soon lose it." **Paschasius of Dumium, Questions and Answers of the Greek Fathers, 12.1 (FOTC 62)**

43 Many of those men who are somewhat inclined to heap up sin upon sin, and, abusing the mercy of God, to indulge in excessive negligence, utter such words as these: "There is no hell; there is no judgment; God forgives all our sins." To silence them a certain wise man has said: "Say not: 'The mercy of the Lord is great, he will have mercy on the multitude of my sins.'" For mercy and wrath quickly come from him: and his

---

21. Sir 10:1.
22. Gal 6:3.

wrath looketh upon sinners."²³ And again: "According as his mercy is, so his correction" is abundant.²⁴ **John Chrysostom, *Commentary on John*, Homily 28 (FOTC 33)**

44 Pride mimics loftiness, whereas Thou art the one God, lifted above all things. **Augustine of Hippo, *Confessions*, 2.6.13 (FOTC 21)**

45 An old man said to someone: "Do not set your heart against your brother, saying that you are more sober than he and more continent, but be subjected to the grace of God in the spirit of poverty and in love that is not pretended, lest in the spirit of exaltation you lose your reward." **Paschasius of Dumium, *Questions and Answers of the Greek Fathers*, 13.4 (FOTC 62)**

46 Take care not to spurn the ordinary or go hunting after novelty to impress the mass. Let Solomon's advice be your guide: "Better is a little with security than much with uncertainty" and, "Better is a poor man who walks in his integrity," another of his wise sayings; that is, the man poor in words and understanding, who uses simple expressions and clings to them as to a flimsy raft in his effort to survive, is better than the unctuous fool who in his ignorance takes pride in feats of logic and by his facility with words empties the cross of Christ of its power,²⁵ a marvel beyond word, and thereby through logic and its inadequacy degrades the truth. **Gregory Nazianzen, *Oration* 32.26 (FOTC 107)**

47 The devil is the prince of the proud. "Lest he be puffed up with pride," says Holy Writ, "and incur the condemnation passed on the devil,"²⁶ for everyone who glorifies himself in his heart is partner to the devil, who used to say: "By my own power I have done it, and by my wisdom, for I am shrewd. I have moved the boundaries of peoples."²⁷ **Jerome, *Homily* 71 on Psalm 93 (94) (FOTC 57)**

---

23. Sir 5:6–7.
24. Sir 16:13.
25. Quotations from Prv 15:16, 19:1 (28:6 LXX). Cf. 1 Cor 1:17.
26. 1 Tm 3:6.
27. Is 10:13.

48 It belonged to the justice and the goodness of the Creator that the devil should be overcome by the same rational creature which he prided himself in having overcome, and indeed by one coming from the race itself, the whole of which he held captive by the corruption of its origin through one. **Augustine of Hippo, *The Trinity*, 13.17.22 (FOTC 45)**

49 But when the devil became a lover of power through the vice of his own perversity, and the betrayer and attacker of justice, and since in this respect men also imitate him so much the more, in proportion as they set aside or even hate justice and strive after power, and as they either rejoice in acquiring power or are inflamed with the lust of it, it pleased God that for the sake of rescuing men from the power of the devil, the devil should be overcome not by power but by justice, and that men, too, by imitating Christ should seek to overcome the devil not by power but by justice. **Augustine of Hippo, *The Trinity*, 13.13.17 (FOTC 45)**

50 "They who hate you lift up their heads."[28] If you ever have anything against another, if a brother disparages you, and you are humble for the sake of Christ while your opponent is haughty for the sake of the devil, you are imitating Him who says: "Learn from me, for I am meek and humble of heart."[29] But the proud man who glorifies himself follows the example of him who says: "I will scale the heavens, above the stars I will set up my throne; I will be like the Most High!"[30] "And they who hate you lift up their heads." **Jerome, *Homily* 15 on Psalm 82 (83) (FOTC 48)**

51 But for the devil, who is not subject to the death of the flesh and on this account has become inordinately proud, another kind of death is prepared in the eternal fire of hell, by which not only the spirits with earthly bodies, but also those with aerial bodies can be tortured. **Augustine of Hippo, *The Trinity*, 4.13.18 (FOTC 45)**

---

28. Ps 83:2.
29. Mt 11:29.
30. Cf. Is 14:13, 14.

7. VAINGLORY AND PRIDE   175

52 But he takes thought, first, not to commit any evils, and secondly, not to do good things inconsiderately; and, after he has subdued wickednesses, he strives also to subject to himself his very virtues, lest they should be converted into the sin of pride, if they should get beyond the control of the mind. For since, as has before been said, evils frequently spring from good deeds, through the vice of negligence; he observes with watchful zeal how arrogance rises from learning, cruelty from justice, carelessness from tenderness, anger from zeal, sloth from gentleness. And, when he performs these good deeds, he observes that these enemies are by these means able to rise against him. **Gregory the Great, Morals on the Book of Job, XXXI.44 (LF 31)**

53 How great is the evil of pride, that it rightly has no angel, nor other virtues opposed to it, but God Himself as its adversary! **John Cassian, Institutes 12.7 (ACW 58)**

54 Woe to you if your name has not been written in heaven. Do I say woe to you if you have not raised the dead? Do I say woe to you if you have not walked on the sea? Do I say woe to you if you have not driven out demons? If you have received the means to do so, use them humbly, not proudly. For also concerning certain pseudoprophets the Lord said that they would perform signs and wonders.[31] Therefore, let there not be the ambition of this age. The ambition of this age is pride.[32] It wishes to boast of itself in honors: a man seems important to himself, whether from riches or from some power. **Augustine of Hippo, Tractates on the Gospel of John, 2.13 (FOTC 78)**

55 "Do not set your mind on high things, but be of a common mind with the lowly."[33] He is teaching that pride must be avoided in everything; for this is what he calls "setting one's mind on high things." And rightly must pride be shunned, seeing that the Scripture says, "For pride is the beginning of falling away from God."[34] He has admirably

---
31. Cf. Mt 24:24.
32. Cf. 1 Jn 2:16.
33. Rom 12:16.
34. Sir 10:12 (LXX).

set forth the principle of humility with a single phrase. For to be of a common mind with the lowly and to love the lowly and to come down to their level means to accustom oneself to imitate him who, "though he was in the form of God, took the form of a slave and humbled himself to the point of death."[35] **Origen, Commentary on Romans, 9.17 (FOTC 104)**

56 Those who seek God by those powers that rule the world, or parts of the world … prefer in their pride to be able to do what an angel can, rather than to be by their piety what an angel is. For no holy person rejoices in his own power, but in the power of Him from whom he has whatever power he can suitably have. He knows that it is a proof of greater power to be united with the omnipotent One by a pious will, rather than to be able to do things by his own power and will, at which those tremble who cannot do such things. **Augustine of Hippo, The Trinity, 8.7.11 (FOTC 45)**

57 But, I was striving toward Thee and was pushed back by Thee, so that I might taste death, for Thou resisteth the proud.[36] Now, what more proud than to claim with wondrous foolishness that I was that, by nature, which Thou art?[37] Since I was mutable, and that was evident to me in the fact that I certainly wished to be wise, so that I might become better from worse, I preferred even to consider Thee mutable rather than that I should not be what Thou art. **Augustine of Hippo, Confessions, 4.15.26 (FOTC 21)**

58 There is this about pride: to itself, it always passes for wisdom. If any one of the brethren should advise a proud man: "Brother, you must not act that way," he thinks it beneath his dignity to listen because he considers himself a much wiser man. What does he say in his heart? "I think I know better; do I not have to follow my own conscience? Do you think you are wiser that I?" **Jerome, Homily 95 on obedience (FOTC 57)**

---

35. Cf. Phil 2:6–8.
36. Cf. Jas 4:6, 1 Pt 5:5.
37. This was Augustine's thinking when he was a member of the Manichean sect, namely, that certain souls were "as of the very substance of God" (cf. Augustine, *De duabus anim.* 1.1).

59 You, therefore, who laid the foundation of rebellion, submit to the presbyters, and accept chastisement for repentance, bending the knees of your heart. Learn to be submissive, laying aside the boastful and proud self-confidence of your tongue, for it is better for you to be found "little ones," but honorable within the flock of Christ, than to seem to be pre-eminent, but to be cast out from His hope. **Clement of Rome, *First Letter*, 57.1–2 (FOTC 1)**

60 And if I, in a short time, have achieved such spiritual and not merely human communion with your bishop, all the more do I congratulate you who have become one with him, as the Church is one with Jesus Christ and as Jesus Christ is one with the Father, so that all things may be in harmony. Let no man be deceived. If a person is not inside the sanctuary he is deprived of the Bread [of God]. For if the prayer of one or two men has so much force, how much greater is that of the bishop and of the whole Church.[38] Any one, therefore, who fails to assemble with the others has already shown his pride and set himself apart. For it is written: "God resists the proud."[39] Let us be careful, therefore, not to oppose the bishop, so that we may be obedient to God. **Ignatius of Antioch, *Letter to the Ephesians*, 5.1 (FOTC 1)**

61 Refuse to make an accord with pride, and fear more to be raised up in glory than to be trampled on in humiliation.[40] **Leo the Great, *Sermon* 84b (FOTC 93)**

62 Accordingly, because pride is the beginning of an evil will which is not from God, it is perfectly clear that the destruction for persons resulting from evil works is not from God, but the destruction of retribution is payment from the just judge for the evil. **Fulgentius, *To Monimus*, I.19.1 (FOTC 95)**

---

38. Cf. Mt 18:18–20.
39. Cf. Prv 3:34 (LXX), Jas 4:6, 1 Pt 5:5.
40. Cf. Sir 24:11.

63 The just Lord has humbled the pride of sinners.[41] Understand what this means. The psalmist did not say the Lord has destroyed sinners; if he had said that, no one could be saved; we are all sinners. What does he say? "The just Lord has humbled the pride of sinners"; they who are both sinful and proud, for "God resists the proud, but gives grace to the humble."[42] Therefore, does He humble the pride of sinners to the ground. **Jerome, *Homily* 43 on Psalm 128 (129) (FOTC 48)**

64 Likewise, it is especially the work of the Word of God to pull down the diabolical structures that the Devil has built in the human soul. For, in every one of us, that one raised up towers of pride and walls of self-exaltation. The Word of God overthrows and undermines these, so that justly, according to the Apostle, we are made "the cultivation of God and the building of God,"[43] "set upon the foundation of the apostles and prophets with Christ Jesus himself the chief cornerstone, from whom the uniting of the edifice grows into a temple of God in the spirit."[44] **Origen, *Homilies on Joshua*, 13.4 (FOTC 105)**

65 The man who is proud, however, possesses in his pride the source of all other evils, and he does not do penance, for he thinks that he is in God's favor. Pride is contrary to God because it does not submit to Him; hence, the proud man considers himself just. He does not repent of his evil deeds, but glories in his sham good works. **Jerome, *Homily* 95 on obedience (FOTC 57)**

66 Again, when you read, "The rich and the poor meet together; the Lord is the maker of them both," do not suppose that his making one poor and the other rich justifies harsh treatment of the poor on your part.[45] There is no evidence that such a distinction originates with God. Both alike are God's creation, according to Scripture, despite their superficial disparities. Let this fact shame you into showing sympa-

---

41. Cf. Ps 129:4.
42. Jas 4:6.
43. 1 Cor 3:9.
44. Eph 2:20.
45. Prv 22:2.

thy and brotherhood, so that when your pride is puffed up by those externals, this realization may chasten you and make you grow more humble. **Gregory Nazianzen, Oration 14.36 (FOTC 107)**

67 "Do not be wise in your own estimation."[46] The one who seems to be wise in his own estimation is a fool with arrogance; he cannot know the true wisdom of God who reveres his own foolishness as if it were wisdom. **Origen, Commentary on Romans, 9.18 (FOTC 104)**

Humility

68 Humility is a fine thing; the examples are many and varied, but chief among them is the Savior and Lord of all who not only humbled himself to the point of taking the form of a servant[47] and submitted his face to the shame of spitting[48] and was numbered with the transgressors,[49] he who purges the world from sin,[50] but who also put on servant garb and washed his disciples' feet.[51] **Gregory Nazianzen, Oration 14.4 (FOTC 107)**

69 Again, one old man was asked: "How can the soul attain humility?" He replied: "If a man considers only his own sins." He used to say: "The perfection of man is humility." **Paschasius of Dumium, Questions and Answers of the Greek Fathers, 13.10 (FOTC 62)**

70 And so we can escape the snare of this most evil spirit, if in the case of every virtue in which we feel that we make progress, we say these words of the Apostle: "Not I, but the grace of God which is with me," and "by the grace of God I am what I am";[52] and "God is at work in you,

---

46. Rom 12:16.
47. Cf. Phil 2:7.
48. Cf. Is 50:6.
49. Cf. Is 53:12.
50. Cf. Jn 1:29; 1 Jn 1:7.
51. Cf. Jn 13:5.
52. 1 Cor 15:10.

both to will and to work for his good pleasure."[53] As the author of our salvation Himself also says: "He who abides in me, and I in him, he it is that bears much fruit, for apart from me you can do nothing."[54] And "Unless the Lord builds the house, those who build it labor in vain. Unless the Lord watches over the city, the watchman stays awake in vain." And "It is in vain that you rise up early."[55] For "it depends not upon man's will or exertion, but upon God's mercy."[56] **John Cassian, *Institutes* 12.9 (ACW 58)**

71 The pride of man, which more than anything else hinders him from cleaving to God, might be refuted and cured by such great humility on the part of God. For man also learns how far he has departed from God and what efficacy there is in pain to cure him when he returns through such a Mediator, who, as God, helps men by His divinity, and as man adapts Himself to them by His weakness. **Augustine of Hippo, *The Trinity*, 13.17.22 (FOTC 45)**

72 If [Simon] the Pharisee had the Pharisees' pride, how was our Lord to grant him humility, so long as the treasury of humility was not within his reach?[57] But since our Lord taught humility to everyone, He showed how his treasury was free of the symptoms of pride. This happened on our account, to teach us that the pride that intrudes upon treasures dissipates all of them with its own bragging. This is why "you should not let your left hand know what your right hand is doing."[58] **Ephrem the Syrian, *Homily on Our Lord*, 22.2 (FOTC 91)**

73 A brother asked an old man: "What is humility?" He answered: "If one returns good to one who does him evil, that is perfect humility." The brother said: "What if one cannot be successful in doing this?"

---

53. Phil 2:13.
54. Jn 15:5.
55. Ps 126 (127):1, 2.
56. Rom 9:16.
57. Here, Ephrem is speaking of the story from the Gospel of Luke of the Pharisee Simon at whose house Jesus dined. In his own thoughts, Simon had taken exception to the sinful woman who washed the feet of Jesus with her tears (cf. Lk 7:36–50).
58. Mt 6:3.

He replied: "He should run away and remain quiet." **Martin of Braga, Sayings of the Egyptian Fathers, 57 (FOTC 62)**

74 And so do not cease to pray for all other men, for there is hope of their conversion and of their finding God. Give them the chance to be instructed, at least by the way you behave. When they are angry with you, be meek; answer their words of pride by your humility, their blasphemies by your prayers, their error by your steadfastness in faith, their bullying by your gentleness. Let us not be in a hurry to give them tit for tat, but, by our sweet reasonableness, show that we are their brothers. **Ignatius of Antioch, Letter to the Ephesians, 10.1 (FOTC 1)**

75 So our Lord did not admonish [Simon the Pharisee] roughly, because His coming was (one of) goodness.[59] Yet He did not refrain from admonishing him, because His next coming would be (one of) retribution. He terrified them by coming in humility, because "it is a terrible thing to fall into his hands" when He comes with flaming fire.[60] **Ephrem the Syrian, Homily on Our Lord, 22.3 (FOTC 91)**

76 God does not find the humble to whom he gives grace humble before the grace was given; but, by giving the grace, he makes them humble. God gives this through grace, so that anyone who accepts it becomes humble. Wherefore the only-begotten teacher and giver of holy humility himself says, "Learn from me, for I am meek and humble of heart and you will find rest for yourselves."[61] **Fulgentius, To Monimus, I.18.4 (FOTC 95)**

77 Abbot Motois said: "Humility is never angry with itself and never allows others to be angry." He also said: "Humility is when, if a brother has sinned against you, you forgive him before he repents." **Paschasius of Dumium, Questions and Answers of the Greek Fathers, 13.11–12 (FOTC 62)**

---

59. Cf. Lk 7:36–50.
60. Heb 10:31.
61. Mt 11:19; cf. Jas 4:6.

78 Humility means not reckoning oneself as anything in every situation and cutting off one's own will in everything and calmly enduring whatever occurs externally. This is true humility, in which there is no room for vainglory. The person who feels humble does not need to seek to speak humbly; rather, it is enough for that person to say: "Forgive me, and pray for me." **Barsanuphius and John, Letter 278 (FOTC 113)**

79 If, on the other hand, we have any sense of our own salvation, let us, while we still have time, abandon evil ways, concern ourselves with virtue and despise vainglory. This, you see, is the reason why it is called vain, because it is quite empty and has no substance or stable foundation: it proves only to be a deceiver of the eyes before it disappears and flies away. **John Chrysostom, *Homily* 22.21 on Genesis (FOTC 82)**

80 A standard of humility is given to each one from the very measure of his greatness, to which pride is a menace, since it lays more cunning snares for those of superior station. **Augustine of Hippo, *Holy Virginity*, 31.31 (FOTC 27)**

81 With a sweet tongue, humility subdues even its enemies to do it honor. For it is not among its friends that humility puts its power to the test, but among those who hate it that it displays its trophies. **Ephrem the Syrian, *Homily on Our Lord*, 24.2 (FOTC 91)**

82 Saying something with humility means not speaking as a teacher, but as one who has learned from the abbot or the fathers. If it is beneficial to speak to your brother and the vainglory of pleasure tempts you, then pay attention to yourself because it may wish to prevent you from benefiting your brother; and if you listen to this vainglory, your brother will never benefit from you. Instead, reprimand this vainglory and despise it; moreover, after speaking, repent to God, saying: "Forgive me; for I have spoken in vainglory." **Barsanuphius and John, *Letter* 290 (FOTC 113)**

83 Pride threw down the archangel from heaven, and as lightning it made him fall upon the earth.[62] But humility leads a man up into heaven, and makes him dance with the angels. **Evagrius of Pontus, Eight Evil Thoughts, chap. 18**[63]

84 God so hates pride that against it alone the Almighty humbled Himself so much. Unless, perhaps, you will on this account so fear less and be more puffed up that you will love Him less who loved you so much that He gave Himself up for you, because He forgave you less; that is, since you have from childhood lived religiously, modestly, in holy chastity and inviolate virginity. As though you ought not in truth love Him all the more ardently who forgave all things whatsoever to the profligates who turned to Him, but who did not allow you to fall into them! **Augustine of Hippo, Holy Virginity, 40.41 (FOTC 27)**[64]

85 The humility of our Lord prevailed from the womb to the tomb. **Ephrem the Syrian, Homily on Our Lord, 34.1 (FOTC 91)**

86 Humility is so powerful that even the all-conquering God did not conquer without it. **Ephrem the Syrian, Homily on Our Lord, 41.1 (FOTC 91)**

---

62. I.e., Satan.
63. Editor's translation. PG 79:1164A.
64. Augustine here anticipates the thought of St. Thérèse of Lisieux, who relates this allegory that describes the special providence that is God's preservative salvation from particular sins:

Let us suppose that the son of a very clever doctor, stumbling over a stone on the road, falls and breaks his leg. His father hastens to him, lifts him lovingly, and binds up the fractured limb, putting forth all his skill. The son, when cured, displays the utmost gratitude, and he has excellent reason for doing so. But let us take another supposition.

The father, aware that a dangerous stone lies in his son's path, is beforehand with the danger and removes it, unseen by anyone. The son, thus tenderly cared for, not knowing of the mishap from which his father's hand has saved him, naturally will not show him any gratitude, and will love him less than if he had cured him of a grievous wound. But suppose he heard the whole truth, would he not in that case love him still more? Well now, I am this child, the object of the foreseeing love of a Father "Who did not send His Son to call the just, but sinners" (Lk 5:32). He wishes me to love Him, because He has forgiven me, not much, but everything. Without waiting for me to love Him much, as St. Mary Magdalen did, He has made me understand how He has loved me with an ineffable love and forethought, so that now my love may know no bounds.

Thérèse of Lisieux, *The Story of a Soul*, trans. T. N. Taylor (London: Burns and Oates, 1912), 64–65.

7. VAINGLORY AND PRIDE

87 I know that your bishop has been given his ministry for the common good, not by any effort of his own or of others nor out of vainglory, but through the love of God the Father and of the Lord Jesus Christ. I am full of admiration for the sweet reasonableness of a man who can do more by his silence than others by speaking. He has been attuned to the commandments like a harp with its strings. And so my soul blesses his determination which is fixed on God. I know how virtuous and perfect it is, how unperturbable and calm, how modeled his life is on the sweet reasonableness of God. **Ignatius of Antioch, *Letter to the Philadelphians*, 1.1–2 (FOTC 1)**

88 Now who of you is there, dearly beloved, whom drunkenness has not defiled, or ambition carried away, or jealously consumed, or lust inflamed, or avarice wounded? Therefore, I advise you, dearly beloved, according to what is written, that you "Humble yourselves under the exceedingly mighty hand of God."[65] Since no one is without sin, no one should be without penance; for by this very fact a man becomes guilty if he presumes that he is innocent. A man may be guilty of lesser sin, but no one is guiltless. **Caesarius of Arles, *Sermon* 144.4 (FOTC 47)**

89 The old man also said: "To the extent that a man lowers himself in humility, so far does he climb on high. Just as pride, if it climbs to heaven, is cast down to hell, so humility, if it descends to hell, will then be exalted to heaven." **Paschasius of Dumium, *Questions and Answers of the Greek Fathers*, 13.5 (FOTC 62)**

90 What humility of Mary's did the Lord look upon? The mother of the Savior was carrying the Son of God in her womb. What was humble and despised in her? What she says, "He looked upon the humility of his handmaid,"[66] is equivalent to saying, "He looked upon the justice of his handmaid," "looked upon her temperance," "looked upon her fortitude and her wisdom." **Origen, *On Luke*, Homily 8.4 (FOTC 94)**

---

65. Cf. 1 Pt 5:6.
66. Lk 1:48.

91 If pride created differences of tongues, Christ's humility has joined the differences of tongues together. Now what that tower had dispersed, the Church binds together. From one tongue came many; do not be amazed, pride did this. From many tongues comes one; do not be amazed, love did this. **Augustine of Hippo, *Tractates on the Gospel of John*, 6.10.2 (FOTC 78)**

92 He loved equally all mankind, so that, just as His death is our life and His humility is the curing of our pride, so our integrity was bought with His wounds, for He wished to be struck Himself, rather than to permit us to be struck by the "hammer of the whole earth."[67] "You have been bought with a price," says the Apostle; "do not become the slaves of men."[68] **Leander of Seville, *The Training of Nuns and the Contempt of the World*, introduction (FOTC 62)**

93 Thus three things took place at the same time: the assuming of the flesh, its coming into being, and its being made divine by the Word. Hence, the holy Virgin is understood to be Mother of God, and is so called not only because of the nature of the Word but also because of the deification of the humanity simultaneously with which the conception and the coming into being of the flesh were wondrously brought about—the conception of the Word, that is, and the existence of the flesh in the Word Himself. In this the Mother of God, in a manner surpassing the course of nature, made it possible for the Fashioner to be fashioned and for the God and Creator of the universe to become man and deify the human nature which He had assumed, while the union preserved the things united, just as they had been united, that is to say, not only the divinity of Christ but His humanity, also; that which surpassed us and that which was like us. **John Damascene, *The Orthodox Faith*, 3.12 (FOTC 37)**

---

67. Jer 50:23.
68. 1 Cor 7:23, 24.

94 Therefore, the Word, though being in the form and equality of God the Father,[69] humbled himself when, being made flesh as John says,[70] he was born of a woman,[71] and having a begetting from God the Father, he also endured to experience a birth like ours for our sake. **Cyril of Alexandria, *Letter* 1.26 (FOTC 76)**

95 He grafted together both natures in such a union that glorification should not overwhelm the lower nor humbling diminish the higher. **Leo the Great, *Sermon* 21.2 (FOTC 93)**

96 And just as God highly exalted Christ because he had humbled himself, having become obedient to death, even death on a cross, and he gave him the name that is above every name, so also God exalts with him in glory those who suffer together with Christ and who follow the example of his sufferings.[72] Indeed, this is the way Christ has disclosed to his coheirs, that they might be exalted not because of strength or wisdom, but through humility, that they might attain to the glory of the eternal inheritance through their perseverance out of afflictions.[73] **Origen, *Commentary on Romans*, 7.3.4 (FOTC 104)**

97 For God has "highly exalted" what was humble, and to what had been given a human name he "gave the name that is above every name";[74] what was under command and a slave he made lord and king: as Peter said, "God has made him both Lord and Christ."[75] (By "Christ" we understand "king.") And because of the intimate union between the flesh that was assumed and the Godhead that assumed, the names can be exchanged, so that the human can be called divine and the divine human. **Gregory of Nyssa, *To Theophilus, Against the Apollinarians* (FOTC 131)**

---

69. Cf. Phil 2:5–11.
70. Cf. Jn 1:14.
71. Gal 4:4.
72. Cf. Phil 2:8–9.
73. Cf. Heb 9:15.
74. Phil 2:9.
75. Acts 2:36.

98 For just as the proud devil led the proud man to death, so the humble Christ led the obedient man back to life; and as the former fell when he was exalted and dragged down him who consented to him, so the latter, when He was humbled, arose and raised up him who believed in Him. **Augustine of Hippo, *The Trinity*, 4.10.13 (FOTC 45)**

99 O proof of infinite humility! The true God become true man! The mighty God beaten with whips; the Most High hung from the Cross! He bore all this for our salvation, without taunting in return those who taunted Him, without becoming angry with those who were ungrateful, but rather, at the moment of the Cross, He prayed for those who crucified Him and said: "Father, forgive them, for they do not know what they are doing."[76] You, certainly, if you love your Bridegroom, must observe His death, must picture in your mind His humility, and must press solidly to your intellect as on a coin the virtues which He bore in the flesh after the manner of man. Do not fear to imitate Him because He is God; but remember that He is more to be imitated because He is man. **Leander of Seville, *The Training of Nuns and the Contempt of the World*, 11 (FOTC 62)**

---

76. Lk 23:34.

Conclusion

1 The one who has self-love has all the passions.¹ **Maximus the Confessor, *Centuries on Charity*, 3.8 (CWS)**

2 Reading, vigils and prayer—these are the things that lend stability to the wandering mind. Hunger, toil, and solitude are the means of extinguishing the flames of desire. Turbid anger is calmed by singing the Psalms, by patience and almsgiving. **Evagrius of Pontus, *Praktikos* 15 (CSS 4)**

3 Almsgiving heals the irascible part of the soul, fasting extinguishes the concupiscible part, and prayer purifies the mind and prepares it for the contemplation of reality. **Maximus the Confessor, *Centuries on Charity*, 1.79 (CWS)**

4 Simplicity gives way to obedience, obedience to faith, faith to hope, hope to justice, justice to service, service to humility. From this comes

---

1. It may be difficult for some contemporary readers to grasp that Maximus is identifying a problem here. For Maximus, love of self (*philautia*) was not "the greatest love of all" (*pace* Whitney Houston), but rather the greatest obstacle to growth in the spiritual life. Thus, the one unable to deny himself falls victim to the pull of the passions. This calls to mind the sixteenth-century *Allegory of Passion* painted by Hans Holbein the Younger, featuring a wild-eyed rider on a horse with neither saddle nor bit. Inscribed under them: *E cosi desio me mena* ("And so desire carries me along").

gentleness which leads to grace, grace to love, and love to prayer. And thus, attached and dependent on each other, they lead us to the peak of what is desired, just as the crown of wickedness leads its own friends in the opposite direction through its own categories to extreme evil. **Gregory of Nyssa, *On the Christian Mode of Life* (FOTC 58)**

5 For whoever is exalted with pride, whoever is tortured by the longings of covetousness, whoever is relaxed with the pleasures of lust, whoever is kindled by the burnings of unjust and immoderate anger, what else is he but a testicle of Antichrist? **Gregory the Great, *Morals on the Book of Job*, XXXII.16 (LF 31)**

6 O crooked ways! Woe to my rash soul, which has hoped that by departing from Thee it will obtain something better![2] **Augustine of Hippo, *Confessions*, 6.16.26 (FOTC 21)**

7 If we must describe this wretched chain, let us imagine someone weakened by any of the pleasures connected with vanity. The desire for more accompanies vanity, since it is not possible for anyone to become greedy unless vanity has led him to that condition. Next, the desire for more than one's share and to be first excites him to anger against anyone who has as much as he, or to arrogance towards anyone below him, or envy towards anyone excelling him. Envy leads to hypocrisy, hypocrisy to bitterness, bitterness to misanthropy, and the final result of all of these is a condemnation which ends up in hell and darkness and fire. Do you see the succession of evils; how one passion follows upon the heels of another? **Gregory of Nyssa, *On Virginity*, 4 (FOTC 58)**

8 We ought to hate, therefore, not the victims of vice, but vice; not sinners, but sin. Toward all men we ought to have the will to help, even those who have injured us, or wish to harm us, or wish that we be harmed. This is the true, perfect, and only religion by which it belongs to the magnitude of the soul, which we are studying now, to be recon-

---

2. Cf. Is 3:9.

ciled to God and by which it makes itself worthy of freedom. **Augustine of Hippo, *The Magnitude of the Soul*, 34.78 (FOTC 4)**

9 The cure of those afflicted by evil passions should be effected according to the method used by physicians. The superior, therefore, must not become angry with the sick, but he must wage war upon their malady by setting up a counter-irritant to the vice, curing the infirmity of the soul by drastic measures, if need be. For example, vainglory should be corrected by imposing practices of humility, idle talking, by silence, excessive sleep, by watching in prayer, sloth, by physical labor, intemperance at table, by fasting, murmuring, by segregation, so that none of the brethren may desire to work in partnership with the offender and that the work of the others may not be coupled with his, as was said above, unless, to be sure, he shows that he has been freed from his vice by doing penance without shame. In that event, the work which was done in a murmuring spirit should be accepted; yet, not even then should it be put to the service of the brethren but made use of in some other way. **Basil of Caesarea, *The Long Rules*, q. 51 (FOTC 9)**

10 When through God's grace the possession of our soul is again restored to the virtues, we will be seen to recover our own land, rather than seizing what belongs to another. If, with the Lord's help, our vices are overcome by the people, that is, by the virtues which struggle against them, then chastity will occupy the position which was held in our heart by the spirit of concupiscence or fornication. Patience will possess the man whom fury captivated; salutary joy, which is full of happiness, will keep the soul which had been attacked by a sadness which effects death. If a man was ruined by the lukewarmness of sloth or carelessness, fortitude will begin to inflame him. If pride crushed him, humility will honor him. The man whom avarice had made obscure will be restored to his former renown by mercy; one who had been struck by the poison of envy will be adorned with kind simplicity. Thus, as each vice is expelled, the contrary virtues will take their position in the passions. **Caesarius of Arles, *Sermon* 114.3 (FOTC 47)**

11 When the people are purified of this passion, then they cross through the foreign life. As the Law leads them along the royal highway, they deviate from it in no way at all.[3] It is easy for a traveler to turn aside. Suppose two precipices form a high narrow pass; from its middle the person crossing it veers at his peril in either direction (for the chasm on either side swallows the person who turns aside). In the same way the Law requires the person who keeps in step with it not to leave the way which is, as the Lord says, "narrow and hard," to the left or to the right.[4] This teaching lays down that virtue is discerned in the mean. Accordingly, all evil naturally operates in a deficiency of or an excess of virtue.[5] In the case of courage, cowardice is the lack of virtue and rashness is its excess. What is pure of each of these is seen to lie between these corresponding evils and is virtue. In the same way all other things which strive for the better also somehow take the middle road between the neighboring evils. **Gregory of Nyssa, *Life of Moses*, II.287–88 (CWS)**[6]

12 For it does not suffice for avarice to know and love gold, unless it also possesses it; nor does it suffice to know and love to eat and to lie together, unless these actions are also performed; nor does it suffice to know and love honors and power, unless they are obtained. But all of these things do not suffice, even when they are acquired. "For he who shall drink of this water," He said, "shall thirst again."[7] **Augustine of Hippo, *The Trinity*, 9.9.14 (FOTC 45)**

13 And all the while, the cruel tyranny of evil desire holds sway, disrupting the entire soul and life of man by various and conflicting surges of passion; here by fear, there by desire; here by anxiety, there by

---

3. Cf. Philo, *On the Giants*, XIV.64: "And being such a character as this, [Abraham] is assigned to the one only God, whose minister he becomes, and so makes the path of his whole life straight, using in real truth the royal road, the road of the only king who governs all things, turning aside and deviating neither to the left hand nor to the right."
4. Cf. Mt 7:14, Dt 28:14.
5. Cf. Aristotle, *Nicomachean Ethics* 1108b11–1109b7.
6. Gregory of Nyssa, *The Life of Moses*, trans. Abraham J. Malherbe and Everett Ferguson, CWS (New York: Paulist Press, 1978).
7. Jn 4:13.

empty and spurious delights; here by torment over the loss of a loved object, there by a burning desire to acquire something not possessed; here by pain for an injury received, there by the urge to revenge an injury. On every possible side, the mind is shriveled up by greed, wasted away by sensuality, a slave to ambition, is inflated by pride, tortured by envy, deadened by sloth, kept in turmoil by obstinacy, and distressed by its condition of subjection. And so with other countless impulses that surround and plague the rule of passion. How could we ever think that this is not a punishment when, as you see, it is something that all have to suffer who do not hold fast to wisdom? **Augustine of Hippo, *The Free Choice of the Will*, 1.11.22 (FOTC 59)**

14 The flesh, then, is crucified when our members are mortified on earth destroying fornication, uncleanness, intemperance, avarice, and other such vices, of which he says: "For if you live according to the flesh, you shall die, but if by the spirit you mortify the deeds of the flesh, you shall live."[8] **Augustine of Hippo, *Letter* 55, to Januarius (FOTC 12)**

15 For we did not receive the eyes for gratifying carnal appetite, the tongue for speaking evil, the ears for listening to slander, the gullet for indulging in the sin of gluttony, the belly to be the gullet's partner, the organs of sex for immodest excesses, the hands for committing acts of violence, and the feet to lead a roving life; nor was the spirit implanted in the body that it might become a workshop for contriving acts of treachery and fraud and injustice. **Tertullian, *On Spectacles*, 2.10 (FOTC 40)**

16 But someone may say: Are you then chastising elegance in dress and the honors that go with wealth? And if there are those who have quantities stored up of valuable things of the kind that are praised to the skies, will you criticize that too, and say that it is nothing? I would reply that the divinely inspired John says enough when he cries, "Do not love the world, nor what is in the world. For all that is in the world is the lust of

---

8. Rom 8:13.

the flesh and the lust of the eyes and the pride of life."[9] Observe now the supreme philosophical skill with which this sharer in the Holy Spirit limits the enjoyment of what is earthly to three things. For the lusts of the flesh are surfeits of the stomach, and the seasonings of delicacies, and the impurity that then always somehow follows. And the pleasures and delights of the eyes are the variegated spectacle of clothing, and the lovely color and brightness of the materials, which wealth loves. But the pride of life is the name he gives to the preeminence in dignities, and exaltation in honor and glory. **Cyril of Alexandria, *Festal Letters*, 27.2 (FOTC 127)**

17 One who was proud should be humble; the unbelieving, faithful; the dissolute, chaste; the robber, worthy; the drunkard, sober; the sleepy, vigilant; the avaricious, generous; the deceitful, kind in speech. The detractor or envious person should be upright and kind; one who sometimes came late to church should now hasten there more frequently. Let each one redeem himself with abundant almsgiving, for, "As water quencheth a fire, so alms resisteth sins."[10] Distribute among the churches and the poor every year tithes of all the fruits you gather. Love fasting; avoid gluttony and drunkenness. Feed the hungry, give drink to the thirsty, clothe the naked, visit the sick, and seek those who are in prison. Receive strangers in your homes, wash their feet, and dry them with linen, kiss them tenderly, and prepare beds for them. **Caesarius of Arles, *Sermon* 10.3 (FOTC 31)**

18 Offer up faith, that faithlessness may suffer punishment. Offer a fast, that gluttony may cease. Offer up chastity, that lust may die. Put on piety, that impiety may be put off. Invite mercy, that avarice may be blotted out. That folly may be brought to naught, it is always fitting to offer up holiness as a sacrificial gift. Thus your body will become a victim, if it has been wounded by no javelin of sin. **Peter Chrysologus, *Sermon* 108 (FOTC 17)**

---

9. 1 Jn 2:15–16.
10. Sir 3:33.

19 Let the person who partakes of food and is unable to fast give evidence of more generous almsgiving, fervent prayers, and a heightened enthusiasm for listening to the divine sayings; let such a person be reconciled with enemies and eradicate from the soul all vindictiveness. If that is the intention, then such a person has practiced real fasting, and the kind the Lord requires most of all. **John Chrysostom, *Homily* 10.3 on Genesis (FOTC 74)**

20 For if your spirit boils up and is disturbed, even if the deed is not done, nevertheless the disturbance itself is not suitable for one who fights under the leadership of Jesus. And this must be perceived in like manner concerning the vice of lust and of melancholy and of all the rest. The disciple of Jesus must live so that nothing at all of these draws a breath in his heart, lest perchance, should the practice or thought of any petty vice remain in his heart, it become strong as time goes on, gathering strength in secret little by little, and recalling us at last "to our vomit."[11] It turns out that "the last things are worse than the first" for the person to whom this happens.[12] **Origen, *Homilies on Joshua*, 15.3 (FOTC 105)**

21 To have overcome lust is the palm of continence. To have resisted wrath and injury is the crown of patience. Triumph over avarice is to spurn money. Praise of faith is to endure the adversities of the world by faith in the future. And he who is not proud in prosperity obtains the glory of humility. **Cyprian of Carthage, *Jealousy and Envy*, 16 (FOTC 36)**

22 This body is in need of daily food. So also is the soul; or, rather, much more so. And unless it is well nourished it becomes weaker and more sluggish. Let us not neglect it, as it is perishing and being strangled. It receives many wounds every day from lust, anger, sloth, profanity, revenge, envy. Well, then, we must apply remedies to it. Now, almsgiving is no trifling remedy, since it can be applied to every wound. Indeed, "Give alms," Scripture says, "and all things will be

---

11. Prv 26:11.
12. Lk 11:26.

clean to you."[13] ... It is the almsgiving which is free from all injustice that makes all things clean. It is better than fasting and sleeping on the ground. Even though those practices are more difficult and demand more exertion, almsgiving is more profitable: it enlightens the soul, enriches it, makes it noble and beautiful. **John Chrysostom, *Commentary on John*, Homily 81 (FOTC 41)**

23 Now, it is necessary for anyone desiring to be closely united with another to take on the ways of that person through imitation. Therefore, it is necessary for the one longing to be the bride of Christ to be like Christ in beauty through virtue as far as possible. For nothing can be united with light unless the light is shining upon it. **Gregory of Nyssa, *On the Christian Mode of Life* (FOTC 58)**

24 A little while longer and the world is a thing of the past and the stage dismantled. Let us take advantage of the time we have. Let us buy what abides with what does not. Each of us is subject to judgment; we creatures of clay carry many obligations. Let us pardon that we may be pardoned; forgive, that we may seek forgiveness. **Gregory Nazianzen, *Oration* 17.11 (FOTC 107)**

25 Just as those who, by means of fire, purify gold mixed with matter, not only melt the impure matter, but also melt the pure gold along with the counterfeit, and when the counterfeit portion is consumed, the pure gold remains; so, also, when evil is being consumed by purifying fire, it is entirely necessary for the soul immersed in the evil to be in the fire until the alien and earthly and counterfeit elements scattered through it are destroyed. **Macrina, *On the Soul and the Resurrection* (FOTC 58)**[14]

26 To all our persecutors we say: "You are our brothers; apprehend, rather, the truth of God." But when neither they nor you will listen to us, but you do all in your power to force us to deny Christ, we resist you and prefer to endure death, confident that God will give us all the bless-

---

13. Cf. Lk 11:41.
14. The sister of Gregory of Nyssa. This dialogue is from Gregory's hand.

ings which He promised us through Christ. Furthermore, we pray for you that you might experience the mercy of Christ; for He instructed us to pray even for our enemies, when He said: "Be kind and merciful, even as your Heavenly Father is merciful."[15] **Justin Martyr, *Dialogue with Trypho*, 96 (FOTC 6)**

27 And so Joachim took the noble and praiseworthy Anna in marriage.[16] Then, even as the earlier Anna, although barren, had through prayer and a vow given birth to Samuel, so did this Anna through supplication and a vow receive from God the Mother of God, so that not even in this should she be inferior to any of the illustrious mothers.[17] Thus, Grace, for such is the interpretation of Anna, brings forth the Lady, for that is the meaning of the name Mary. And Mary really did become Lady of all created things, since she was accounted Mother of the Creator. And she was born in the house of Joachim at the Probatica and was brought to the Temple. From then on she grew up in the house of God, nourished by the Spirit, and like a fruitful olive tree became and abode of every virtue with her mind removed from every worldly and carnal desire.[18] And thus, as was fitting for her who was to conceive God within herself, she kept her soul and body virginal, for He is holy and abides in holy ones. Thus, then, she sought holiness and was shown to be a holy and wondrous temple worthy of the most high God. **John Damascene, *The Orthodox Faith*, 4.14 (FOTC 37)**

28 Just as a youth at a party, who observes his pedagogue nearby exhorting him by look to drink, eat, speak, and laugh with proper decorum is prevented from overstepping measure and thus injuring his reputation, likewise as soon as one arrives at Daphne and sees the martyr's shrine from the entrance of the suburb, he is chastened and, becoming more pious by the sight and imagining the blessed one, immediately hastens to the coffin; and when he comes there, he is

---

15. Lk 6:36.
16. Cf. *Protoevangelium of James*, 1–2.
17. Cf. 1 Sm 1:11.
18. Cf. Ps 51:10.

affected with greater fear, renounces all cynicism, and departs on wings. **John Chrysostom, *Discourse on Blessed Babylas and Against the Greeks*, 70 (FOTC 73)**

29 Return to the Merciful One. Avail yourselves of the clemency of the Forgiving One. The cruelty of your wickedness has been changed into the cause of your salvation. He lives, the one you wanted to kill. Acknowledge the one who was denied, worship the one who was sold, so that you might benefit from the goodness of the one whom your ill will could not harm. **Leo the Great, *Sermon* 35.2 (FOTC 93)**

30 Realize, O Christian, your dignity.[19] Once made a "partaker in the divine nature," do not return to your former baseness by a life unworthy [of that dignity].[20] Remember whose head it is and whose body of which you constitute a "member."[21] Recall how you had been wrested "from the power of darkness and brought into the light and the kingdom" of God.[22] Through the Sacrament of Baptism you were made "a temple of the Holy Spirit."[23] Do not drive away such a dweller by your wicked actions and subject yourself again to servitude under the devil, because your "price" is the very blood of Christ, because he "will judge" you "in truth" who has redeemed you in mercy, Christ our Lord. Amen.[24] **Leo the Great, *Sermon* 21.3 (FOTC 93)**

---

19. This saying, which stands at the beginning of the third part of the *Catechism* on the moral life, seems a fitting conclusion to this book. Cf. CCC, no. 1691.
20. Cf. 2 Pt 1:4.
21. Cf. 1 Cor 6:15.
22. Cf. Col 1:13.
23. Cf. 1 Cor 6:19.
24. For "price," cf. 1 Cor 6:20, 7:23; for "in truth," cf. Ps 95(96):13.

BIBLIOGRAPHY

All titles in The Fathers of the Church (FOTC) series are published by the Catholic University of America Press, Washington, D.C.

Primary Sources

Ambrose of Milan. *Hexameron, Paradise, and Cain and Abel*. Translated by John J. Savage. FOTC 42. 1961.

———. *Letters*. Translated by Mary Melchior Beyenka. Edited by Roy J. Deferrari. FOTC 26. 1954.

———. *Seven Exegetical Works*. Translated by Michael P. McHugh. Edited by Bernard M. Peebles. FOTC 65. 1972.

———. *Theological and Dogmatic Works*. Translated by Roy J. Deferrari. Edited by Roy J. Deferrari. FOTC 44. 1963.

Andrew of Caesarea. *Commentary on the Apocalypse*. Translated by Eugenia Scarvelis Constantinou. Edited by David G. Hunter. FOTC 123. 2011.

Apostolic Fathers. *The Apostolic Fathers*. Translated by Francis X. Glimm, Joseph M.-F. Marique, and Gerald G. Walsh. FOTC 1. 1947.

Augustine of Hippo. *Against Julian*. Translated by Matthew A. Schumacher. Edited by Hermigild Dressler. FOTC 35. 1957.

———. *The Catholic and Manichaean Ways of Life*. Translated by Donald A. Gallagher and Idella J. Gallagher. Edited by Roy J. Deferrari. FOTC 56. 1966.

———. *Christian Instruction; Admonition and Grace; The Christian Combat; Faith, Hope and Charity*. Translated by John J. Gavigan, John Courtney Murray, Robert P. Russell, and Bernard M. Peebles. Edited by Roy J. Deferrari. Second edition in FOTC 2. 1950.

———. *The City of God, Books I–VII*. Translated by Demetrius B. Zema and Gerald G. Walsh. Edited by Hermigild Dressler. FOTC 8. 1950.

———. *The City of God, Books VIII–XVI*. Translated by Gerald G. Walsh and Grace Monahan. Edited by Hermigild Dressler. FOTC 14. 1952.

———. *The City of God, Books XVII–XXII*. Translated by Gerald G. Walsh and Daniel J. Honan. Edited by Hermigild Dressler. FOTC 24. 1954.

———. *Commentary on the Lord's Sermon on the Mount with Seventeen Related Sermons*. Translated by Denis J. Kavanagh. Edited by Hermigild Dressler. FOTC 11. 1951.

———. *Confessions*. Translated by Vernon J. Bourke. Edited by Roy J. Deferrari. FOTC 21. 1953.

———. *Eighty-Three Different Questions*. Translated by David L. Mosher. Edited by Hermigild Dressler. FOTC 70. 1982.

———. *Four Anti-Pelagian Writings*. Translated by John A. Mourant and William J. Collinge. Edited by Thomas P. Halton. FOTC 86. 1992.

———. *The Happy Life and Answer to Skeptics and Divine Providence and the Problem of Evil and Soliloquies*. Translated by Denis J. Kavanagh, Robert P. Russell, Thomas F. Gilligan, and Ludwig Schopp. Edited by Ludwig Schopp. FOTC 5. 1948.

———. *The Immortality of the Soul; The Magnitude of the Soul; On Music; The Advantage of Believing; On Faith in Things Unseen*. Translated by Ludwig Schopp, John J. McMahon, Robert Catesby Taliaferro, Luanne Meagher, Roy J. Deferrari, and Mary Francis McDonald. Edited by Hermigild Dressler. FOTC 4. 1947.

———. *Letters (1*–29*)*. Translated by Robert B. Eno. Edited by Thomas P. Halton. FOTC 81. 1989.

———. *Letters (1–82)*. Translated by Wilfrid Parsons. FOTC 12. 1951.

———. *Letters (83–130)*. Translated by Wilfrid Parsons. Edited by Roy J. Deferrari. FOTC 18. 1953.

———. *Letters (131–164)*. Translated by Wilfrid Parsons. Edited by Roy J. Deferrari. FOTC 20. 1953.

———. *Letters (165–203)*. Translated by Wilfrid Parsons. Edited by Hermigild Dressler. FOTC 30. 1955.

———. *Letters (204–270)*. Translated by Wilfrid Parsons. Edited by Hermigild Dressler. FOTC 32. 1956.

———. *On Genesis: Two Books on Genesis against the Manichees; And, on the Literal Interpretation of Genesis: An Unfinished Book*. Translated by Roland J. Teske. Edited by Thomas P. Halton. FOTC 84. 1991.

———. *The Retractations*. Translated by Mary Inez Bogan. Edited by Roy J. Deferrari. FOTC 60. 1968.

———. *Sermons on the Liturgical Seasons*. Translated by Mary Sarah Muldowney. Edited by Hermigild Dressler. FOTC 38. 1959.

———. *The Teacher; The Free Choice of the Will; Grace and Free Will*. Translated by Robert P. Russell. Edited by Roy J. Deferrari. FOTC 59. 1968.

———. *Tractates on the Gospel of John 1–10*. Translated by John W. Rettig. Edited by Thomas P. Halton. FOTC 78. 1988.

———. *Tractates on the Gospel of John 11–27*. Translated by John W. Rettig. Edited by Thomas P. Halton. FOTC 79. 1988.

———. *Tractates on the Gospel of John 28–54*. Translated by John W. Rettig. Edited by Thomas P. Halton. FOTC 88. 1993.

———. *Tractates on the Gospel of John 55–111*. Translated by John W. Rettig. Edited by Thomas P. Halton. FOTC 90. 1994.

———. *Tractates on the Gospel of John, 112–24; Tractates on the First Epistle of John*. Translated by John W. Rettig. Edited by Thomas P. Halton. FOTC 92. 1995.

———. *Treatises on Marriage and Other Subjects*. Translated by Charles T. Wilcox, Charles T. Huegelmeyer, John McQuade, Marie Liguori, Robert P. Russell, John A. Lacy, and Ruth Wentworth Brown. Edited by Roy J. Deferrari. FOTC 27. 1955.

———. *Treatises on Various Subjects*. Translated by Mary Sarah Muldowney, Harold B. Jaffee, Mary Francis McDonald, Luanne Meagher, M. Clement Eagan, and Mary E. DeFerrari. Edited by Roy J. Deferrari and Hermigild Dressler. FOTC 16. 1952.

———. *The Trinity*. Translated by Stephen McKenna. Edited by Hermigild Dressler. FOTC 45. 1963.

Barsanuphius and John. *Ascetical Works*. Translated by M. Monica Wagner. Edited by Roy J. Deferrari. FOTC 9. 1962.

———. *Barsanuphius and John: Letters*. Translated by John Chryssavgis. Edited by Thomas P. Halton. FOTC 113. 2006.

———. *Barsanuphius and John: Letters*. Translated by John Chryssavgis. Edited by Thomas P. Halton. FOTC 114. 2007.

———. *Letters (1–185)*. Translated by Agnes Clare Way. Edited by Hermigild Dressler. FOTC 13. 1951.

———. *Letters (186–368)*. Translated by Agnes Clare Way. Edited by Roy J. Deferrari. FOTC 28. 1955.

Basil of Caesarea. *Against Eunomius*. Translated by Mark DelCogliano and Andrew Radde-Gallwitz. FOTC 122. 2011.

———. *Exegetic Homilies*. Translated by Agnes Clare Way. FOTC 46. 1963.

Braulio of Saragossa and Fructuosus of Braga. *Iberian Fathers, vol. 2*. Translated by Claude W. Barlow. Edited by Roy J. Deferrari. FOTC 63. 1969.

Caesarius of Arles. *Sermons (1–80)*. Translated by Mary Magdeleine Mueller. Edited by Hermigild Dressler and Bernard M. Peebles. FOTC 31. 1956.

———. *Sermons (81–186)*. Translated by Mary Magdeleine Mueller. Edited by Hermigild Dressler and Bernard M. Peebles. FOTC 47. 1964.

———. *Sermons (187–238)*. Translated by Mary Magdeleine Mueller. Edited by Hermigild Dressler and Bernard M. Peebles. FOTC 66. 1973.

Clement of Alexandria. *Christ the Educator*. Translated by P. Simon Wood. FOTC 23. 1954.

———. *Stromateis, Books One to Three*. Translated by John Ferguson. Edited by Thomas P. Halton. FOTC 85. 1991.

Cyril of Alexandria. *Commentary on the Twelve Prophets*. Translated by Robert C. Hill. Edited by Thomas P. Halton. FOTC 115. 2007.

———. *Commentary on the Twelve Prophets*. Translated by Robert C. Hill. Edited by Thomas P. Halton. FOTC 116. 2008.

———. *Commentary on the Twelve Prophets*. Translated by Robert C. Hill. Edited by David G. Hunter. FOTC 124. 2012.

———. *Festal Letters, 1–12*. Translated by Philip R. Amidon. Edited by John J. O'Keefe. FOTC 118. 2009.

———. *Festal Letters, 13–30*. Translated by Philip R. Amidon. Edited by John J. O'Keefe and David G. Hunter. FOTC 127. 2013.

———. *Letters, 1–50*. Translated by John I. McEnerney. Edited by Thomas P. Halton. FOTC 76. 1987.

———. *Letters, 51–110*. Translated by John I. McEnerney. Edited by Thomas P. Halton. FOTC 77. 1987.

———. *Three Christological Treatises*. Translated by Daniel King. FOTC 129. 2014.

Cyril of Jerusalem. *The Works of Saint Cyril of Jerusalem, vol. 1*. Translated by Leo P. McCauley and Anthony A. Stephenson. Edited by Roy J. Deferrari. FOTC 61. 1969.

———. *The Works of Saint Cyril of Jerusalem, vol. 2*. Translated by Leo P. McCauley and Anthony A. Stephenson. Edited by Bernard M. Peebles. FOTC 64. 1970.

Cyprian of Carthage. *Letters (1–81)*. Translated by Rose Bernard Donna. Edited by Hermigild Dressler. FOTC 51. 1964.

———. *Treatises*. Edited and translated by Roy J. Deferrari. FOTC 36. 1958.

Didymus the Blind. *Commentary on Zechariah*. Translated by Robert C. Hill. Edited by Thomas P. Halton. FOTC 111. 2006.

Dionysius the Areopagite (Pseudo-Dionysius). *The Complete Works*. Translated by Colm Luibheid. CWS. New York: Paulist Press, 1987.

Ephrem the Syrian. *The Hymns on Faith*. Translated by Jeffrey T. Wickes. FOTC 130. 2015.

———. *Selected Prose Works*. Translated by Edward G. Mathews Jr. and Joseph P. Amar. Edited by Thomas P. Halton and Kathleen McVey. FOTC 91. 2004.

Epiphanius of Cyprus. *Ancoratus*. Translated by Young Richard Kim. FOTC 128. 2014.

Eugippius. *The Life of Saint Severin*. Translated by Ludwig Bieler and Ludmilla Krestan. Edited by Roy J. Deferrari. FOTC 55. 1965.

Eusebius of Caesarea. *Ecclesiastical History, Books 1–5*. Edited and translated by Roy J. Deferrari. FOTC 19. 1953.

———. *Ecclesiastical History, Books 6–10*. Translated by Roy J. Deferrari. FOTC 29. 1955.

Evagrius of Pontus. *The Greek Ascetic Corpus*. Translated by Robert E. Sinkewicz. Oxford Early Christian Texts. Oxford: Oxford University Press. 2003.

———. *The Praktikos and the Chapters on Prayer*. Translated by John Eudes Bamberger, OCSO. CSS 4. Collegeville, Minn.: Liturgical Press, 1972.

———. *Talking Back: A Monastic Handbook for Combating Demons (Antirrhetikos)*. Translated by David Brakke. CSS 229. Trappist, Ky.: Cistercian Publications. 2009.

Fulgentius. *Fulgentius: Selected Works*. Translated by Robert B. Eno. Edited by Thomas P. Halton. FOTC 95. 1997.

Fulgentius and Scythian Monks. *Fulgentius of Ruspe and the Scythian Monks: Correspondence on Christology and Grace*. Translated by Rob Roy McGregor and Donald Fairbairn. FOTC 126. 2013.

Gregory the Great. *Dialogues*. Translated by Odo John Zimmerman. Edited by Hermigild Dressler. FOTC 39. 1959.

———. *Morals on the Book of Job*. 3 volumes. Translated by John Henry Parker. LF 18, 21, 23, 31. Oxford: F. and J. Rivington, 1844–50. Latin and French available in SC 32b, 212, 221, 476, 525, 538. Paris: Les Éditions du Cerf, 1975–2010.

Gregory Nazianzen. *Select Orations*. Translated by Martha Vinson. Edited by Thomas P. Halton. FOTC 107. 2003.

———. *Three Poems: Concerning His Own Affairs, Concerning Himself and the Bishops, Concerning His Own Life*. Translated by Denis Molaise Meehan. Edited by Thomas P. Halton. FOTC 75. 1987.

Gregory Nazianzen and Ambrose of Milan. *Funeral Orations*. Translated by Leo P. McCauley, John J. Sullivan, Martin R. P. McGuire, and Roy J. Deferrari. FOTC 22. 1953.

Gregory of Nyssa. *Anti-Apollinarian Writings*. Translated by Robin Orton. Edited by David G. Hunter. FOTC 131. 2015.

———. *Ascetical Works*. Translated by Virginia Woods Callahan. FOTC 58. 1967.

———. *The Life of Moses*. Translated by Abraham J. Malherbe and Everett Ferguson. CWS. New York: Paulist Press, 1978.

Gregory Thaumaturgus. *Life and Works*. Translated by Michael Slusser. Edited by Thomas P. Halton. FOTC 98. 1998.

Hilary of Poitiers. *Commentary on Matthew*. Translated by D. H. Williams. Edited by David G. Hunter. FOTC 125. 2012.

———. *The Trinity*. Translated by Stephen McKenna. Edited by Roy J. Deferrari. FOTC 25. 1954.

Jerome. *Commentary on Galatians*. Translated by Andrew Cain. Edited by David G. Hunter. FOTC 121. 2010.

———. *Commentary on Matthew*. Translated by Thomas P. Scheck. Edited by Thomas P. Halton. FOTC 117. 2008.

———. *Dogmatic and Polemical Works*. Translated by John N. Hritzu. Edited by Hermigild Dressler. FOTC 53. 1965.

———. *The Homilies of Saint Jerome (1–59 on the Psalms), vol. 1*. Translated by Marie Liguori Ewald. Edited by Hermigild Dressler. FOTC 48. 1964.

———. *The Homilies of Saint Jerome (Homilies 60–96), vol. 2*. Translated by Marie Liguori Ewald. Edited by Roy J. Deferrari. FOTC 57. 1966.

———. *On Illustrious Men*. Edited and translated by Thomas P. Halton. FOTC 100. 1999.

John Cassian. *The Conferences*. Translated by Boniface Ramsey, OP. ACW 57. New York: Newman Press, 1997.

---. *The Institutes*. Translated by Boniface Ramsey, OP. ACW 58. New York: Newman Press, 2000.

John Chrysostom. *Apologist*. Translated by Margaret A. Schatkin and Paul W. Harkins. Edited by Thomas P. Halton. FOTC 73. 1985.

---. *Commentary on Saint John the Apostle and Evangelist: Homilies 1–47*. Translated by Thomas Aquinas Goggin. FOTC 33. 1957.

---. *Commentary on Saint John the Apostle and Evangelist: Homilies 48–88*. Translated by Thomas Aquinas Goggin. FOTC 41. 1959.

---. *Discourses against Judaizing Christians*. Translated by Paul W. Harkins. FOTC 68. 1979.

---. *Homilies on Genesis 1–17*. Translated by Robert C. Hill. Edited by Thomas P. Halton. FOTC 74. 1986.

---. *Homilies on Genesis 18–45*. Translated by Robert C. Hill. Edited by Thomas P. Halton. FOTC 82. 1990.

---. *Homilies on Genesis 46–67*. Translated by Robert C. Hill. Edited by Thomas P. Halton. FOTC 87. 1992.

---. *On Repentance and Almsgiving*. Translated by Gus George Christo. Edited by Thomas P. Halton. FOTC 96. 1998.

---. *On the Incomprehensible Nature of God*. Translated by Paul W. Harkins. Edited by Hermigild Dressler. FOTC 72. 1984.

---. *On Wealth and Poverty*. Translated by Catharine P. Roth. PPS 9. Crestwood, N.Y.: St Vladimir's Seminary Press, 1981.

John Damascene. *Writings*. Translated by Frederic H. Chase, Jr. Edited by Hermigild Dressler. FOTC 37. 1958.

Justin Martyr. *The First Apology, The Second Apology, Dialogue with Trypho, Exhortation to the Greeks, Discourse to the Greeks, The Monarchy or The Rule of God*. Translated by Thomas B. Falls. FOTC 6. 1948.

Lactantius. *The Divine Institutes, Books I–VII*. Translated by Mary Francis McDonald. Edited by Roy J. Deferrari. FOTC 49. 1964.

---. *The Minor Works*. Translated by Mary Francis McDonald. Edited by Roy J. Deferrari. FOTC 54. 1965.

Leo the Great. *Letters*. Translated by Edmund Hunt. Edited by Roy J. Deferrari. FOTC 34. 1957.

---. *Sermons*. Translated by Jane Patricia Freeland and Agnes Josephine Conway. Edited by Thomas P. Halton. FOTC 93. 1996.

Marius Victorinus. *Theological Treatises on the Trinity*. Translated by Mary T. Clark. Edited by Hermigild Dressler. FOTC 69. 1981.

Martin of Braga, Paschasius of Dumium, and Leander of Seville. *Iberian Fathers*, vol. 1. Translated by Claude W. Barlow. FOTC 62. 1969.

Maximus the Confessor. *Maximus Confessor: Selected Writings*. Translated by George C. Berthold. CWS. New York: Paulist Press, 1985.

Niceta of Remesiana, Sulpicius Severus, Vincent of Lerins, and Prosper of Aquitaine.

Writings; Commonitories; Grace and Free Will. Translated by Rudolph E. Morris. Edited by Bernard M. Peebles. FOTC 7. 1949.

Novatian. *The Trinity, The Spectacles, Jewish Foods, In Praise of Purity, Letters.* Translated by Russell J. DeSimone. Edited by Hermigild Dressler. FOTC 67. 1974.

Oecumenius. *Commentary on the Apocalypse.* Translated by John N. Suggit. FOTC 112. 2006.

Origen. *Commentary on the Epistle to the Romans, Books 1–5.* Translated by Thomas P. Scheck. Edited by Thomas P. Halton. FOTC 103. 2001.

———. *Commentary on the Epistle to the Romans, Books 6–10.* Translated by Thomas P. Scheck. Edited by Thomas P. Halton. FOTC 104. 2002.

———. *Commentary on the Gospel according to John, Books 1–10.* Translated by Ronald E. Heine. FOTC 80. 1989.

———. *Commentary on the Gospel according to John, Books 13–32.* Translated by Ronald E. Heine. Edited by Thomas P. Halton. FOTC 89. 1993.

———. *Homilies on Genesis and Exodus.* Translated by Ronald E. Heine. Edited by Hermigild Dressler. FOTC 71. 1982.

———. *Homilies on Jeremiah and Homily on 1 Kings 28.* Translated by John Clark Smith. Edited by Thomas P. Halton. FOTC 97. 1998.

———. *Homilies on Joshua.* Translated by Barbara J. Bruce. Edited by Thomas P. Halton and Cynthia White. FOTC 105. 2002.

———. *Homilies on Judges.* Translated by Elizabeth Ann Dively Lauro. Edited by Thomas P. Halton. FOTC 119. 2010.

———. *Homilies on Leviticus 1–16.* Translated by Gary Wayne Barkley. Edited by Thomas P. Halton. FOTC 83. 1990.

———. *Homilies on Luke and Fragments on Luke.* Translated by Joseph T. Lienhard. Edited by Thomas P. Halton. FOTC 94. 2009.

Orosius of Braga. *The Seven Books of History against the Pagans.* Translated by Roy J. Deferrari. Edited by Hermigild Dressler. FOTC 50. 1964.

Pacian of Barcelona and Orosius of Braga. *Iberian Fathers, vol. 3.* Translated by Craig L. Hanson. Edited by Thomas P. Halton. FOTC 99. 1999.

Pamphilus of Caesarea. *Apology for Origen: With the Letter of Rufinus on the Falsification of the Books of Origen.* Translated by Thomas P. Scheck. FOTC 120. 2010.

Peter Chrysologus. *Selected Sermons of Saint Peter Chrysologus.* Translated by William B. Palardy. Edited by Thomas P. Halton. FOTC 109. 2004.

———. *Selected Sermons of Saint Peter Chrysologus.* Translated by William B. Palardy. Edited by Thomas P. Halton. FOTC 110. 2005.

Peter Chrysologus and Valerian. *Selected Sermons of Saint Peter Chrysologus and Saint Valerian's Homilies.* Translated by George E. Ganss. Edited by Hermigild Dressler. FOTC 17. 1953.

Pontius, Paulinus, Possidius, Athanasius, Jerome, Ennodius, and Hilary. *Early Christian Biographies.* Translated by Roy J. Deferrari, John A. Lacy, Mary Magdeleine Müller, Mary Emily Keenan, Marie Liguori Ewald, and Genevieve Marie Cook. Edited by Hermigild Dressler and Roy J. Deferrari. FOTC 15. 1952.

Prudentius. *The Poems of Prudentius, Vol. 1.* Translated by M. Clement Eagan. Edited by Hermigild Dressler. FOTC 43. 1962.

———. *The Poems of Prudentius, Vol. 2.* Translated by M. Clement Eagan. Edited by Roy J. Deferrari. FOTC 52. 1965.

Salvian. *The Writings of Salvian, the Presbyter.* Translated by Jeremiah F. O'Sullivan. Edited by Ludwig Schopp. FOTC 3. 1947.

Tertullian. *Disciplinary, Moral, and Ascetical Works.* Translated by Rudolph Arbesmann, Emily Joseph Daly, and Edwin A. Quain. Edited by Hermigild Dressler. FOTC 40. 1959.

Tertullian and Minucius Felix. *Apologetical Works and Octavius.* Translated by Rudolph Arbesmann, Emily Joseph Daly, and Edwin A. Quain. Edited by Roy J. Deferrari. FOTC 10. 1950.

Theodore of Mopsuestia. *Commentary on the Twelve Prophets.* Translated by Robert C. Hill. Edited by Thomas P. Halton. FOTC 108. 2004.

Theodoret of Cyrus. *Commentary on the Psalms 1–72.* Translated by Robert C. Hill. FOTC 101. 2000.

———. *Commentary on the Psalms: Psalms 73–150.* Translated by Robert C. Hill. Edited by Thomas P. Halton. FOTC 102. 2001.

———. *Eranistes.* Translated by Gerard H. Ettlinger. FOTC 106. 2003.

Selected Secondary Sources

Anderson, Gary A. *Sin: A History.* New Haven, Conn.: Yale University Press, 2009.

———. *Charity: The Place of the Poor in the Biblical Tradition.* New Haven, Conn.: Yale University Press, 2013.

———. "You Will Have Treasure in Heaven." In *New Approaches to the Study of Biblical Interpretation in Judaism of the Second Temple Period and in Early Christianity,* edited by Gary Anderson, Ruth A. Clements, and David Satran, 107–32. Leiden: Brill, 2013.

Balthasar, Hans Urs von. *Cosmic Liturgy: The Universe According to Maximus the Confessor.* Translated by Brian E. Daley, SJ. San Francisco: Ignatius Press / Communio, 2003.

Bathrellos, Demetrios. "Passions, Ascesis, and the Virtues." In *Oxford Handbook of Maximus the Confessor,* edited by Pauline Allen and Bronwen Neil, 287–306. Oxford: Oxford University Press, 2014.

Bazyn, Ken. *The Seven Perennial Sins and Their Offspring.* New York: Continuum, 2002.

Bloomfield, Morton W. *The Seven Deadly Sins: An Introduction to the History of a Religious Concept, with Special Reference to Medieval English Literature.* East Lansing: Michigan State University Press, 1967.

Cavadini, John, ed. *Gregory the Great: A Symposium.* Notre Dame Studies in Theology 2. Notre Dame, Ind.: University of Notre Dame Press, 1995.

BIBLIOGRAPHY

Cessario, Romanus, OP. *The Moral Virtues and Theological Ethics*. Second edition. Notre Dame, Ind.: University of Notre Dame Press, 2009.
Chadwick, Owen. *John Cassian*. Second edition. London: Cambridge University Press, 1968.
Daley, Brian E., SJ. *Gregory of Nazianzus*. The Early Church Fathers. London: Routledge, 2006.
Demacopoulos, George E. *Gregory the Great: Ascetic, Pastor, and First Man of Rome*. Notre Dame, Ind.: University of Notre Dame Press, 2015.
DeYoung, Rebecca Konyndyk. *Vainglory: The Forgotten Vice*. Grand Rapids, Mich.: Eerdmans, 2014.
Fairlie, Henry. *The Seven Deadly Sins Today*. Washington, D.C.: New Republic Books, 1978.
Harrison, Nonna Verna, and David G. Hunter, eds. *Suffering and Evil in Early Christian Thought*. Holy Cross Studies in Patristic Theology and History. Grand Rapids, Mich.: Baker Academic, 2016.
Hofer, Andrew, OP. "The Stoning of Christ and Gregory of Nazianzus." In *Re-Reading Gregory of Nazianzus*, edited by Christopher A. Beeley, 143–58. Washington, D.C.: The Catholic University of America Press, 2012.
Holman, Susan R., ed. *Wealth and Poverty in Early Church and Society*. Holy Cross Studies in Patristic Theology and History. Grand Rapids, Mich.: Baker Academic, 2008.
Leemans, Johan, Brian J. Matz, and Johan Verstraeten, eds. *Reading Patristic Texts on Social Ethics: Issues and Challenges for Twenty-First-Century Christian Social Thought*. Studies in Early Christianity 3. Washington, D.C.: The Catholic University of America Press, 2011.
Mortimer, Raymond, et al. *The Seven Deadly Sins*. London: Sunday Times Publications, 1962.
Nault, Jean-Charles, OSB. *The Noonday Devil: Acedia, The Unnamed Evil of Our Times*. San Francisco: Ignatius Press, 2015.
Okholm, Dennis. *Dangerous Passions, Deadly Sins: Learning from the Psychology of Ancient Monks*. Grand Rapids, Mich.: Brazos Press, 2014.
Sheen, Fulton J. *The Seven Capital Sins*. New York: Alba House, 2001.
Sinkewicz, Robert E. *Evagrius of Pontus: The Greek Ascetic Corpus*. Oxford: Oxford University Press, 2003.
Snell, R. J. *Acedia and Its Discontents: Metaphysical Boredom in an Empire of Desire*. Kettering, Ohio: Angelico Press, 2015.
Stewart, Columba, OSB. *Cassian the Monk*. Oxford Studies in Historical Theology. Oxford: Oxford University Press, 1998.
Straw, Carole. "Gregory, Cassian, and the Cardinal Vices." In *In the Garden of Evil: The Vices and Culture in the Middle Ages*, edited by Richard Newhauser. Medieval Studies 18. Toronto: Pontifical Institute of Medieval Studies, 2005.
Tilby, Angela. *The Seven Deadly Sins: Their Origin in the Spiritual Teaching of Evagrius the Hermit*. London: Society for Promoting Christian Knowledge, 2009.

Thunberg, Lars. *Microcosm and Mediator: The Theological Anthropology of Maximus the Confessor.* Lund: C. W. K. Gleerup, 1965.

———. *Man and the Cosmos: The Vision of St. Maximus the Confessor.* Crestwood, N.Y.: St. Vladimir's Seminary Press, 1997.

Tsakiridis, George. *Evagrius Ponticus and Cognitive Science: A Look at Moral Evil and the Thoughts.* Eugene, Ore.: Wipf and Stock, 2010.

Wessel, Susan. "The Theology of *Agape* in Maximus the Confessor." *St. Vladimir's Theological Quarterly* 55, no. 3 (2011): 319–42.

Young, Robin Darling. "*Xeniteia* According to Evagrius of Pontus." In *Ascetic Culture: Essays in Honor of Philip Rousseau,* edited by Blake Leyerle and Robin Young, 229–52. Notre Dame, Ind.: University of Notre Dame Press, 2013.

SCRIPTURE INDEX

The numbers on the left-hand side of the comma indicate the scriptural chapter and verse; the numbers on the right-hand side of the comma indicate the patristic saying. For example, the first citation under Genesis is "2:7, 2.50." Thus, Genesis 2:7 is cited in the fiftieth saying of chapter 2. The concluding chapter is cited simply as "c.," e.g., "c. 1" refers to the first saying in the conclusion.

Old Testament

Genesis
2:7, 2.50
2:9, 5.31
2:16–17, 6.25
3:5, 6.16
3:6–11, 1.83
3:19, 4.42
4:1–16, 6.25; 6.26
4:5–7, 6.40
4:8, 6.23
6:3, 2.42
6:5–8:22, 6.25
8:7–11, 1.13
18:27, 4.42
19:24, 6.25
22:2–19, 6.61
27:35, 5.70
27:41, 6.24
37:17–28, 6.24
39:6–18, 2.54
39:11–12, 1.83; 2.55
42:1–2, 5.45

Exodus
2:23–24, 6.37
12:43–45, 3.30
21:16, 3.7
22:25, 3.22

Leviticus
11:4–47, 1.93
19:29, 2.29
25:35–37, 3.22

Numbers
11:18–20, 1.24
12:3, 4.48
12:10, 6.25
16:31–33, 6.25
25:6–13, 2.33

Deuteronomy
23:20, 3.22
28:14, c. 11
31:6, 1.20

1 Samuel
1:11, c. 27
7:6–11, 1.71
18:6–16, 6.24
18:28–29, 6.24
19:1–17, 6.24
24:1–15, 6.24
26:1–16, 6.24

2 Samuel
7:8–16, 2.35
11:1, 2.34; 2.35

1 Kings
11:1–5, 2.35; 6.25
17:8–24, 3.49; 4.92

2 Kings
9:7, 6.25

Tobit
4:11, 1.90; 4.79
12:9, 1.90

209

SCRIPTURE INDEX

4 Maccabees
1:33–35, 1.93

Job
1:9–11, 6.16
5:6, 5.10

Psalms
13:3 (LXX 12:4), 5.11
24:9, 5.51
26:14, 5.75
30:16 (LXX), 3.53
32:3, 2.23
33:7, 3.74
39:3, 2.45
40:5, 6.46
40(41):2, 3.55
45:10, 3.68
45:11, 5.8
51:10, c. 27
52:1, 7.26
68:5, 3.68
78:30–31, 1.24
83:2, 7.50
85:13, 6.58
93:18, 5.74
95(96):13, c. 30
103:5, 6.54
108:7, 6.46
109:7, 1.32
116:12–13, 3.78
126 (127):1–2, 7.70
129:4, 7.63
132:1 (LXX 131:1), 4.48
141:4, 5.22
143:7, 6.58
146:9, 3.68

Proverbs
1:6, 4.41
3:34 (LXX), 7.60
4:26–27, 3.17; 5.55
6:6, 5.71; 5.94
6:9–11, 5.94
11:16 (LXX), 5.68
11:25 (LXX), 4.42
13:25, 3.79

15:16, 7.46
15:18, 4.17
15:19, 5.30
15:30, 2.13
19:1 (28:6 LXX), 7.46
20:3, 4.29
22:2, 7.66
24:12, 5.60
24:34, 3.21
25:20 (LXX), 6.36
26:11, c. 20
26:22, 7.16

Wisdom
2:24, 6.14; 6.23; 6.30
8:8, 5.41
8:21, 1.26; 1.68

Sirach
3:30, 4.80; 4.81
3:33, c. 17
4:28, 4.27
5:6–7, 7.43
5:13, 5.9
10:1, 7.40
10:9, 4.42
10:12 (LXX), 7.55
16:13, 7.43
22:2 [D-R], 5.33
23:26, 5.41
24:11, 7.61
38:17–19, 6.33
38:25 [D-R], 5.93

Isaiah
2:3, 5.78
3:9, c. 6
10:13, 7.47
14:12, 6.25
14:13–14, 7.50
22:12–13, 1.28
40:10, 5.60
40:12, 7.37
42:2, 4.48
50:6, 7.68
53:7, 4.48
53:12, 7.68

62:11, 5.60
66:7, 2.72

Jeremiah
3:6, 2.24
3:8–9, 2.24
5:8, 2.22
12:13 (LXX), 7.26
31:10, 5.87
38:6–9, 3.63
38:26, 4.41
50:23, 7.92
52:13, 2.21

Ezekiel
14:14–16, 3.66
44:2, 2.73

Daniel
3:29 [LXX], 5.83
13:1, 2.54

Hosea
4:17–19, 5.49

Joel
2:15–17, 1.28

Micah
3:5, 5.46
7:18, 4.50

Nahum
2:1–2, 1.88

Haggai
1:9–11, 5.56
2:15–17, 5.53

Zechariah
6:12–15, 2.54
7:8–10, 3.68
12:6–7, 3.17
14:21, 2.36

Malachi
1:2–3, 3.53

New Testament

Matthew
2:16, 6.25
3:12, 1.29
4:1–11, 1.82
5:3–7, 1.50; 3.57; 3.74;
4.83; 6.55
5:22, 4.22; 4.23
5:26, 4.88
5:28, 2.44; 2.56
5:29, 2.13
5:39, 4.23; 4.77
5:44, 4.23; 4.77
6:1–6, 7.11; 7.12; 7.19; 7.72
6:12, 2.32
6:16–18, 7.12
6:24, 3.47
7:5, 5.26
7:7–8, 1.94; 5.12; 5.74; 5.77
7:14, c. 11
8:12, 2.19
9:9–13, 3.46
10:22, 5.21
10:42, 3.51
11:19, 7.76
11:29, 7.26; 7.50
12:19, 4.48
12:36, 4.34
12:43–45, 5.28
13:22, 3.36; 6.34
13:25, 5.11
13:39, 5.81
13:43, 6.49
13:45–46, 6.80
13:58, 5.44
18:7, 6.49
18:18–20, 1.32; 7.60
18:21–22, 4.77
19:16–30, 3.36; 3.37; 4.93;
6.34; 6.66
20:28, 7.28
22:13, 2.19
23:12, 7.28
24:3, 6.49
24:12, 6.49
24:24, 7.54
25:26, 5.71
25:30, 2.19
25:35–36, 4.90
25:37–46, 4.86
25:40, 3.38
26:14–16, 3.42; 3.43; 6.25
26:26, 1.82
26:38–39, 6.56
26:53, 4.48
27:3–5, 6.25

Mark
1:13, 5.3
7:15, 4.34
9:34, 7.28
10:17–31, 6.66
10:45, 7.28
12:41–44, 4.92
14:34, 6.56
14:36, 6.56

Luke
1:5, 2.54
1:48, 7.90
2:35, 6.81
2:36–38, 2.54
4:2–4, 5.3
5:32, 7.84
6:27–29, 4.23; 4.77
6:30, 3.57; 3.69; 4.77;
4.84; 4.88
6:36, c. 26
6:37, 4.45
6:38, 3.75
7:36–50, 1.56; 4.65; 7.72;
7.75
11:26, c. 20
11:41, c. 22
12:16–20, 3.45
12:48, 5.71
14:11, 7.28
14:28–30, 7.37
15:20–24, 2.37
15:25–32, 6.26
16:19–31, 1.50; 3.60; 3.62;
3.63; 4.92
18:14, 7.28
18:18–30, 6.66
21:1–4, 4.92
21:19, 4.67; 6.78
21:34, 1.39
22:42, 6.56
22:50–51, 4.48
23:34, 4.76; 7.99
23:39–43, 3.65
24:32, 6.42

John
1:14, 7.94
1:29, 7.68
4:13, c. 12
5:44, 7.6
6:27, 1.56
6:56, 1.51
7:1–8, 4.66
8:1–11, 2.18
8:12, 4.33
9:4, 5.29
10:18, 6.56
12:4–7, 3.41
12:24–25, 5.45
13:5, 7.68
15:5, 7.70
15:13, 2.69; 6.77
18:10–11, 4.48
20:19, 2.73
20:22–23, 6.69
20:26, 2.73

Acts
2:36, 7.97
2:44, 3.37
4:34–35, 3.47
7:58–60, 4.48; 4.77
10:28, 1.67
13:28, 6.25
14:22, 1.60
18:25, 5.11

Romans
1:29, 6.23
1:31–32, 3.57
2:5, 4.44
2.23, 2.21
7:15, 4.27
7:23–25, 4.33
8:9, 2.42; 2.44
8:13, 2.44; c. 14
8:17, 5.37
9:1–5, 6.40
9:16, 7.70
10:10, 1.51
11:17–25, 1.82
12:11, 5.11
12:16, 7.55; 7.67
12:19, 4.10
13:14, 1.88

1 Corinthians
1:17, 7.46
3:9, 7.64
3:17, 2.21
4:7, 3.75
4:11, 3.79
5:1–2, 2.36
6:9–11, 1.42; 2.19–21
6:15, c. 30
6:16–17, 2.42
6:19–20, c. 30
7:2, 2.65
7:15, 5.21
7:23–24, 7.92; c. 30
7:25–39, 2.48
9:24, 5.78
9:27, 1.82
11:30–31, 5.82
13:4, 1.68; 6.67
15:9, 5.83
15:10, 7.70

2 Corinthians
2:2–7, 6.41
4:5, 7.28
6:2, 5.73
7:10, 3.36; 6.33; 6.34; 6.39;
6.41; 6.46

8:9, 3.68
11:24–27, 3.79; 5.17

Galatians
2:20, 3.6
4:4, 7.94
5:17, 2.42; 2.43; 4.33
5:19–21, 1.22; 1.39; 4.4; 4.5
5:22–23, 1.68; 4.31; 4.69
6:2, 4.83
6:3, 7.42
6:8, 1.6

Ephesians
1:7, 3.30
2:20, 7.64
5:18, 1.39

Philippians
2:5–11, 3.31; 7.55; 7.68;
7.94; 7.96; 7.97
2:13, 7.70
3:19, 2.19
3:20, 1.7
4:10, 1.84

Colossians
1:13, c. 30
2:21–22, 1.7

1 Thessalonians
3:5, 5.81
5:23, 2.42

2 Thessalonians
3:10–11, 1.21

1 Timothy
1:5, 3.58
1:15, 5.83
2:6, 3.30
3:6, 7.47
5:6, 1.45
5:8, 3.32
6:10, 2.14; 3.27; 3.28; 6.76
6:18, 3.39; 3.57
6:20, 2.19

2 Timothy
3:1–3, 2.46
3:12, 5.54

Titus
1:15, 2.19
1:16, 3.32
3:1, 5.60

Hebrews
4:1, 5.17
9:15, 7.96
10:31, 7.75
11:26, 3.63

James
1:19–20, 4.15; 4.23
4:6, 7.57; 7.60; 7.63; 7.76
4:16, 7.26
5:11, 5.17
5:16, 5.81

1 Peter
1:19, 3.30
3:9, 2.69
4:8, 1.68
5:5, 7.57; 7.60
5:6, 7.88

2 Peter
1:4, c. 30
2:15, 2.37

1 John
1:7, 5.80; 7.68
2:15–16, 7.54; c. 16
3:15, 4.21
3:16, 2.69
4:7–8, 6.62
4:18, 6.76

Revelation
3:2, 5.59
3:15–16, 5.50
9:17–19, 2.23
20:12–15, 2.19
21:27, 2.19
22:10–12, 4.72; 5.60

SUBJECT INDEX

Numeric references with decimal points refer to the patristic saying rather than the page number: for example, "2.50" refers to the fiftieth saying in chapter 2. The concluding chapter is cited simply as "c.," where "c. 1" refers to the first saying in the conclusion.

Abel, 3.9; 5.40; 5.42; 6.21; 6.22
Abiram, 6.25
Abraham, 3.60; 3.61; 3.65; 6.61
acedia (see sloth)
Adam, 1.83; 2.72; 6.25
adultery, 1.42; 1.83; 2.2; 2.13–15; 2.19; 2.21; 2.24; 2.28; 2.29; 2.44; 2.47; 2.55; 2.66; 3.9; 6.12
Agatho, Abbot, 3.69
alms, giving of, 1.74; 1.90; 3.32; 3.50; 3.59; 4.78–96; 6.74; 7.12; 7.13; 7.19; c. 2; c. 3; c. 17; c. 19; c. 22
Ambrose of Milan, 1.7; 1.38; 1.44; 1.47; 1.83; 1.93; 2.14; 2.33; 2.55; 3.9; 3.22; 3.27; 3.29; 3.40; 3.42; 4.17; 5.38; 5.40–42; 5.45; 5.70
Anacreon, 2.20
Andrew of Caesarea, 2.23; 5.59
anger, 1.40; 3.41; 4.1–96; 5.75; 6.21; 6.31; 6.43; 6.44; 6.52; 6.64; 7.36; 7.40; 7.52; 7.74; 7.77; c. 2; c. 5; c. 7; c. 9; c. 22
Anonymous texts:
    Didache of the Twelve Apostles, 1.61; 2.2; 4.1; 4.54; 4.88
    Letter to Diognetus, 4.18
    The Shepherd of Hermas, 4.6; 4.25; 4.58; 4.63
Antony, Abbot, 6.53
Aristotle, 3–4; c. 11

asceticism, 9–13; 2.58
attachment, 3.19; 3.53; 6.57
Augustine of Hippo, 13–15; 1.16; 1.26; 1.48; 1.52; 1.53; 1.84; 2.1; 2.9; 2.11; 2.15; 2.16; 2.18; 2.27; 2.28; 2.31; 2.32; 2.39; 2.41; 2.43; 2.45; 2.47; 2.53; 2.60; 2.62; 2.63; 2.66; 2.67; 2.69; 3.10; 3.15; 3.18; 3.19; 3.23; 3.33; 3.59; 3.71; 4.10; 4.20; 4.33; 4.36; 4.40; 4.47; 4.49; 4.51; 4.56; 4.67; 4.71; 4.73; 4.74; 4.90; 4.93; 4.94; 5.4; 5.7; 5.13–15; 5.58; 5.61; 5.64; 5.88; 5.90; 5.93; 5.96; 6.7; 6.21; 6.29; 6.41; 6.46; 6.49; 6.51; 6.55; 6.56; 6.58–60; 6.62; 6.66–68; 6.70; 6.73; 6.75; 6.76; 6.80; 7.5; 7.11; 7.18; 7.32; 7.44; 7.48; 7.49; 7.51; 7.54; 7.56; 7.57; 7.71; 7.80; 7.84; 7.91; 7.98; c. 6; c. 8; c. 12–14
avarice. *See* greed

baptism, 1.44; 2.19; 4.80; 4.81; 5.28; c. 30
Barnabas, Epistle of, 4.57
Barsanuphius and John, 1.9; 1.20; 2.37; 4.68; 5.17; 5.21; 5.24; 5.26; 5.29; 5.81; 5.87; 6.42; 7.25; 7.78; 7.82
Basil of Caesarea (Basil the Great), 1.30; 1.70; 1.81; 2.30; 2.35; 2.40; 2.46; 2.49; 2.59; 3.21; 3.57; 3.70; 3.74; 4.28; 5.71; 5.73; 6.1; 6.11; 6.19; 6.23; 6.27; 7.14; 7.34; c. 9

SUBJECT INDEX

Benedict XVI, Pope, 2.72
Bosch, Hieronymus, 1

Caesarius of Arles, 1.37; 1.74; 1.89; 2.61; 3.14;
  3.38; 5.9; 5.28; 5.50; 5.66; 5.74; 6.9; 6.64;
  6.71; 6.74; 7.88; c. 10; c. 17
Cain, 3.9; 5.40; 5.42; 6.21–23; 6.25; 6.26;
  6.40; 6.45
charity, 1.77; 1.90; 2.11; 2.39; 3.32; 3.58; 4.74;
  4.84; 4.86; 5.50; 6.31; 6.49; 6.57–81
Cicero, 4–5; 7.10
Clement of Alexandria, 9; 1.12; 1.58; 1.73; 1.78;
  1.94; 2.6; 2.13; 2.19; 2.20; 2.26; 2.29; 2.68;
  3.13; 4.24; 4.35; 4.39; 4.53; 4.86; 5.18; 5.77;
  5.82
Clement of Rome, 1.69; 4.55; 5.6; 5.60; 6.2;
  7.59
covetousness, 1.42; 3.5; 3.14; 3.27; 3.48; 6.12;
  6.76; 7.36; c. 5
Cyprian of Carthage, 4.77; 5.80; 5.86; 6.8;
  6.10; 6.14; 6.24; 6.31; 6.32; c. 21
Cyril of Alexandria, 1.6; 1.11; 1.21; 1.28; 1.33;
  1.76; 1.88; 2.58; 3.30; 3.31; 3.45; 3.53; 3.56;
  3.78; 5.34; 5.46; 5.49; 5.53; 5.56; 5.57; 5.63;
  5.68; 5.78; 7.94; c. 16
Cyril of Jerusalem, 1.95; 2.64; 5.8; 5.65; 7.20

Daniel, 3.66; 5.83
Dante, 1–2
Dathan, 6.25
David, 1.32; 1.44; 1.83; 2.34; 2.35; 4.48; 6.24;
  7.26
death, 1.50; 2.29; 2.45; 2.49; 3.36; 3.40; 4.27;
  4.33; 4.78; 4.95; 5.11; 6.14; 6.15; 6.18; 6.33;
  6.34; 6.39; 6.46; 6.52; 6.54; 6.56; 6.58;
  6.81; 7.30; 7.51; 7.55; 7.92; 7.96; 7.98; 7.99;
  c. 10; c. 26
De Koninck, Charles, 2.76
demons, 2.23; 2.69; 3.30; 3.72; 5.81; 6.60; 7.54
detachment, 10–12; 1.80; 3.52; 3.53
detraction, 4.29; 6.3; 6.52; c. 17
devil, the. *See* Satan
Didache. See anonymous texts
Didymus the Blind, 2.36; 2.54; 3.17; 3.68; 7.26
Diognetus, Letter to. See anonymous texts
dissipation, 1.37; 1.39; 2.7
drunkenness. *See* intoxication

envy, 2.69; 3.8; 3.9; 5.94; 6.1–32; 6.67; 6.71;
  6.73; 6.75; 7.40; c. 7; c. 10; c. 13; c. 22
Ephrem the Syrian, 1.56; 4.7; 4.65; 7.72; 7.75;
  7.81; 7.85; 7.86
Esau, 1.19; 5.70; 6.24
eucharist, 1.45; 3.79; 7.60
Evagrius of Pontus, 9–11; 1.23; 1.60; 2.8; 3.7;
  4.15; 4.38; 4.79; 5.2; 6.37; 6.43; 6.47; 7.1;
  7.8; 7.16; 7.22; 7.35; 7.39; 7.83; c. 2
Eve, 2.72

fasting, 1.11; 1.27; 1.31; 1.35; 1.51; 1.52; 1.61–64;
  1.71; 1.80; 1.82; 1.83; 1.86; 1.87; 1.89–92;
  2.4; 2.63; 3.79; 5.23; 5.92; 6.71; 6.74; 7.3;
  7.12; c. 3; c. 9; c. 17–19; c. 22
flood, the, 1.13; 6.25
food, 1.4–12; 1.24; 1.28; 1.45–47; 1.51; 1.56;
  1.64; 1.67; 1.70; 1.71; 1.79; 1.80; 1.83; 1.89;
  1.92; 1.93; 3.39; 3.49; 3.62; 3.79; 4.40; 4.90;
  5.45; 5.65; 5.67; 5.70; c. 19; c. 22
forgiveness, 2.32; 4.45; 4.51; 4.65; 4.76; 4.77;
  4.90; 5.89; 6.55; 6.61; 6.69; 7.43; 7.77; 7.78;
  7.82; 7.99; c. 24
Francis, Pope, 21
Fulgentius, 1.45; 1.68; 1.77; 3.58; 5.36; 6.54;
  6.69; 7.62; 7.76

gentleness, 4.55; 4.69; 4.77; 7.52; 7.74;
  c. 4
God: anger of, 1.24; 1.28; 2.33; 3.12; 4.41; 4.47;
  4.50; 7.43; 7.99; the Father, 4.41; 4.55; 4.74;
  4.88; 5.52; 6.72; 7.27; 7.60; 7.87; 7.94; 7.96;
  the Holy Spirit, 1.81; 3.28; 3.58; 4.58; 4.74;
  5.9; 6.42; 6.52; 6.69; 7.40; c. 16; c. 30;
  mercy of, 1.26; 2.37; 4.50; 4.51; 5.36; 7.43;
  7.70; c. 26; c. 29; c. 30; patience of, 4.47;
  4.51; 4.74; 4.77; the Son, 2.72; 2.73; 3.79;
  5.52; 5.77; 6.72; 7.26; 7.60; 7.64; 7.87; 7.90;
  7.93–99
gossip, 1.42; 2.69; 4.37; 7.87; c. 9; c. 15; c. 17.
  See also slander
grace, 1.51; 1.94; 2.49; 2.70; 4.33; 5.8; 5.25;
  5.36; 5.43; 5.45; 6.14; 6.65; 7.26; 7.40; 7.45;
  7.63; 7.70; 7.76; c. 4, c. 10; c. 27
greed, 1.15; 1.24; 1.40; 1.42; 2.12; 3.1–48; c.
  7; c. 13
Gregory the Great, 17–18, 1.2; 1.4; 2.3; 2.5; 3.2;

SUBJECT INDEX 215

3.4; 4.2; 4.3; 5.10; 5.33; 6.3; 6.4; 6.35; 6.38;
6.44; 7.2; 7.4; 7.40; 7.52; c. 5
Gregory of Nazianzus, 1.29; 1.34; 1.82; 2.48;
2.52; 3.52; 3.80; 4.48; 4.52; 4.60; 5.11; 6.13;
6.25; 6.28; 6.61; 6.78; 7.37; 7.46; 7.66;
7.68; c. 24
Gregory of Nyssa, 1.59; 1.66; 1.79; 4.13; 4.21;
4.43; 4.62; 4.76; 5.30; 5.84; 7.28; 7.31; 7.97;
c. 4; c. 11; c. 23
Gregory Thaumaturgus, 1.72; 2.7
gluttony, 1.1–95; 2.12; 3.13; 5.63; 6.12; 6.44;
7.36; 7.40; c. 15; c. 17; c. 18

hatred, 2.3; 3.8; 4.18; 4.19; 4.21; 4.22; 4.24;
4.27; 4.30; 4.35; 4.36; 4.39; 4.43; 4.62; 4.70;
5.19; 6.1; 6.3; 6.10; 6.24; 6.32; 6.42; 6.52;
7.49; 7.50; 7.84; c. 8
heaven, 1.7; 1.84; 2.12; 2.50; 2.57; 2.69; 2.71;
3.9; 3.32; 3.34; 3.35; 3.37–39; 3.48; 3.71; 3.77;
3.79; 4.74; 4.93; 5.20; 5.37; 5.75; 5.91; 5.95;
6.9; 6.15; 6.20; 6.30; 6.66; 6.69; 6.78; 7.13;
7.21; 7.29; 7.31; 7.37; 7.50; 7.54; 7.83; 7.89
hell, 1.89; 2.12; 2.18; 4.80; 7.43; 7.51; 7.89;
c. 7
heresy, 5.13; 6.31
Herod, 6.25
Hilary of Poitiers, 3.37; 5.67; 5.76
homosexuality, 1.42; 2.19; 2.21
Horace, 5
humility, 1.7; 1.25; 2.4; 4.55; 5.30; 6.48; 7.3;
7.26; 7.28; 7.34; 7.50; 7.55; 7.63; 7.66;
7.68–99; c. 4; c. 9; c. 10; c. 21

Ignatius of Antioch, 5.84; 6.63; 6.72; 7.60;
7.74; 7.87
impurity, 2.8; 2.25; 2.30; 6.12; c. 16
indecency, 2.20; 2.69
indulgence (in food or drink), 1.6; 1.8; 1.11;
1.12; 1.14; 1.17; 1.28–34; 1.45; 1.49; 1.51; 1.55;
1.65; 1.82; 1.88; c. 15
intemperance, 1.10; 1.43; 1.50; 2.13; 5.31; c. 9;
c. 14
intoxication, 1.5; 1.27; 1.35; 1.37–43; 1.48; 1.49;
1.72; 1.85; 2.19; 2.31; 2.69; 3.8; 6.12; 6.36;
7.6; 7.17; 7.88; c. 17
Isaiah, 5.14; 5.83
Isidore, Abbot, 6.53

Israel, the people of, 1.24; 1.28; 1.71; 1.82; 2.24;
5.34; 5.46; 6.25; 6.37

Jacob, 1.93; 4.79; 5.44; 5.45; 5.78; 6.24
jealousy, 4.1; 4.47; 6.2; 6.8; 6.10; 6.14; 6.23;
6.24; 6.26; 6.30–32; 7.88. *See also* envy
Jeremiah, 2.21; 2.24; 3.63; 4.41; 5.83; 6.18; 7.26
Jerome, 1.22; 1.39; 2.51; 3.16; 3.36; 3.41; 3.43;
3.51; 3.63; 3.65; 4.4; 4.5; 4.11; 4.23; 4.29;
4.31; 4.37; 4.44; 4.61; 4.69; 4.80; 4.83;
5.22; 5.44; 5.72; 6.6; 6.34; 6.52; 7.10; 7.12;
7.19; 7.38; 7.47; 7.50; 7.58; 7.63; 7.65
Jesus Christ, 7, 1.25; 1.32; 1.39; 1.47; 1.50; 1.56;
1.57; 1.67; 1.80; 1.82; 1.88; 2.13; 2.18; 2.48;
2.49; 2.56; 2.72; 3.6; 3.30; 3.37–39; 3.43;
3.46; 3.63; 3.65; 3.68; 3.71; 3.73; 3.74; 3.77;
3.78; 4.22; 4.33; 4.43; 4.48; 4.52; 4.65–67;
4.86; 5.1; 5.3; 5.12; 5.36; 5.54; 5.61; 5.71;
5.79; 5.83; 6.20; 6.31; 6.42; 6.49; 6.56;
6.66; 6.69; 6.72; 6.77; 7.12–14; 7.26; 7.28;
7.49; 7.60; 7.64; 7.68; 7.72; 7.75; 7.85–87;
7.90–99; c. 20; c. 23; c. 30
Job, 1.2; 1.4; 1.44; 1.83; 2.3; 2.5; 3.2; 3.4; 3.66;
4.2; 4.3; 5.10; 5.17; 5.33; 6.3; 6.4; 6.16; 6.35;
6.38; 6.44; 7.2; 7.4; 7.40; 7.52; c. 5
John Cassian, 16–17; 1.1; 2.4; 2.17; 3.5; 6.36;
6.39; 6.45; 7.3; 7.41; 7.53; 7.70
John Chrysostom, 1.1; 1.5; 1.14; 1.15; 1.17; 1.19;
1.25; 1.32; 1.35; 1.40; 1.41; 1.43; 1.49; 1.80;
1.86; 1.92; 2.12; 2.22; 2.56; 3.3; 3.8; 3.12;
3.26; 3.32; 3.35; 3.44; 3.49; 3.50; 3.54; 3.61;
3.62; 3.64; 3.76; 4.8; 4.12; 4.14; 4.16; 4.30;
4.32; 4.42; 4.45; 4.46; 4.59; 4.66; 4.75;
4.81; 4.82; 4.84; 4.85; 4.87; 4.89; 4.91;
4.92; 4.95; 4.96; 5.5; 5.19; 5.20; 5.25; 5.31;
5.32; 5.35; 5.39; 5.47; 5.48; 5.85; 5.89; 6.15;
6.22; 6.33; 6.40; 6.50; 7.6; 7.13; 7.15; 7.17;
7.21; 7.29; 7.30; 7.33; 7.43; 7.79; c. 19; c.
22; c. 28
John of Damascus, 1.8; 1.55; 2.65; 2.72; 2.73;
4.9; 6.5; 6.17; 6.81; 7.93; c. 27
John the Baptist, 2.54
Joseph, husband of Mary, 2.51
Joseph, the patriarch, 1.83; 2.54; 2.55; 6.24
Judas Iscariot, 3.41–43; 4.44; 6.25; 6.45;
6.46
Justin Martyr, c. 26

216 SUBJECT INDEX

Lactantius, 1.57
Lazarus, 1.50; 3.54; 3.60–65; 4.84
laziness, 1.15; 1.21; 2.30; 3.33; 3.35; 3.38; 5.6; 5.12; 5.14; 5.16; 5.17; 5.20–22; 5.26; 5.27; 5.32; 5.37; 5.59; 5.63; 5.70; 5.76; 5.78; 5.85; 5.93; 5.94
Leander of Seville, 1.10; 1.31; 1.42; 2.71; 7.92; 7.99
Leo the Great, 1.46; 1.54; 1.63; 1.65; 1.71; 1.87; 3.11; 3.20; 3.24; 3.25; 3.39; 3.55; 3.75; 4.26; 5.15; 5.37; 5.43; 5.52; 5.54; 5.62; 5.92; 6.30; 7.61; 7.95; c. 29; c. 30
licentiousness, 1.15; 1.33; 1.64; 2.7; 2.12; 2.19; 2.21; 2.22; 2.30; 2.36; 3.8
long-suffering, 4.46–77; 5.30; 6.72
love: love of God, 6.15; 6.62; 6.68; 7.87; love of money (*see* greed); love of neighbor, 6.59; 6.68; love of self, 1.6; 2.3; c. 1
Lucifer. *See* Satan
lust, 1.16; 1.37; 1.39; 1.64; 1.95; 2.1–38; 2.42–44; 2.47; 2.55; 2.56; 2.59; 2.61; 3.9; 4.33; 4.74; 6.44; 7.17; 7.40; 7.49; 7.88; c. 5; c. 16; c. 18; c. 20–22

Macarius, Abbot, 3.72
Macrina, c. 25
Martin of Braga, 1.85; 2.10; 3.66; 3.72; 7.73
Matthew, 3.41; 3.46
Mary, the mother of God, 2.50; 2.51; 2.70–73; 6.20; 7.90; 7.93; 7.94; c. 27
Maximus the Confessor, 11–13; 3.1; 5.1; 6.57; 6.79; 7.36; c. 1; c. 3
meekness, 4.34; 4.48; 4.76; 5.51; 7.50; 7.74; 7.76
Minucius Felix, 3.67
Miriam, 6.25
money, 3.5; 3.7; 3.8; 3.14; 3.17; 3.23; 3.25–28; 3.30; 3.32; 3.34; 3.40; 3.43; 3.47; 3.50; 3.70; 3.73; 3.75; 4.85; 4.94; 5.22; 6.46; 7.7; 7.19; c. 21
mortification, 1.14; 1.81; 1.82; 2.56; 5.73; 5.94; 6.61; 7.65; 7.88; c. 9; c. 14
Moses, 1.29; 3.63; 4.48; 6.25; c. 11
Moses, Abbot, 3.66; 6.48
Motois, Abbot, 7.77

nature, 1.72; 1.85; 2.6; 2.70; 2.72; 3.31; 3.39; 4.13; 4.19; 4.39; 4.41; 4.47; 5.57; 5.76; 6.14; 6.23; 6.26; 6.81; 7.57; 7.93; 7.95; c. 30
Nebuchadnezzar, 2.21
Nesteron, Abbot, 7.23
Niceta of Remesiana, 5.94
Noah, 3.66
Novatian, 1.50

obedience, 7.3; 7.60; 7.96; 7.98; c. 4
Oecumenius, 5.27; 6.20
Origen, 1.18; 1.62; 1.67; 2.21; 2.24; 2.38; 2.42; 2.44; 3.6; 3.34; 3.79; 4.27; 4.41; 5.3; 5.12; 6.18; 7.7; 7.55; 7.64; 7.67; 7.90; 7.96; c. 20

pain, 1.14; 1.32; 1.50; 1.71; 1.72; 3.65; 6.5; 6.6; 6.42; 7.71; c. 13
Pamphilus of Caesarea, 5.12
Paschasius of Dumium, 1.36; 3.60; 3.69; 5.69; 6.48; 6.53; 6.65; 6.77; 7.23; 7.42; 7.45; 7.69; 7.77; 7.89
passions, 1.40; 1.52; 1.76; 1.88; 1.93; 2.19; 2.27; 2.31; 2.33; 3.8; 3.13; 3.30; 4.31; 5.1; 6.79; 7.3; 7.25; 7.36; c. 1; c. 9; c. 10
patience, 1.70; 3.10; 3.66; 4.3; 4.27; 4.44; 4.46–77; 5.1; 5.17; 5.75; 6.24; 6.49; 6.71; 7.3; c. 2; c. 10; c. 21
Paul (the Apostle), 7–8; 1.7; 1.39; 1.68; 1.82; 1.84; 2.36; 2.42; 2.44; 2.46; 2.48; 3.14; 3.28; 3.32; 3.68; 3.79; 4.84; 5.17; 5.37; 5.73; 5.78; 5.83; 6.23; 6.40; 6.41; 6.46; 7.28; 7.64; 7.70; 7.92
peace, 1.13; 3.20; 3.65; 4.25; 4.31; 4.43; 4.54; 4.55; 4.62; 5.46; 5.54; 6.31
penance. *See* mortification
Peter Chrysologus, 1.27; 1.91; 2.50; 2.70; 3.46; 3.48; 3.77; 5.16; 5.75; 5.79; 5.95; 6.26; 7.9; 7.27; c. 18
Pimenius, Abbot, 6.53; 6.77; 7.42
Pius XII, Pope, 21
Plato, 3; 3.8; 4.9; 5.18
pleasure, 1.1; 1.5; 1.8; 1.9; 1.22; 1.27; 1.29; 1.33; 1.34; 1.44–46; 1.49; 1.50; 1.55; 1.59; 1.76; 1.85; 1.88; 1.93; 2.5; 2.19; 2.26; 2.29; 2.30; 2.32; 2.37; 2.45; 2.72; 3.8; 3.17; 4.18; 4.91; 5.57; 5.67; 5.83; 6.43; 6.47; 6.51; 6.61; 7.17; 7.70; 7.82; c. 5; c. 7; c. 16
Polycarp, 1.75; 4.78; 7.24
Pontius Pilate, 6.25

SUBJECT INDEX   217

prayer, 1.21; 1.82; 2.4; 2.16; 2.32; 2.65; 3.56; 4.37; 5.34; 5.63; 5.74–96; 6.36; 6.46; 6.58; 6.74; 7.3; 7.12; 7.60; 7.74; c. 2–4; c. 9; c. 19; c. 26; c. 27
presumption, 2.60; 7.4; 7.88
pride, 2.36; 2.53; 5.50; 5.51; 6.12; 6.25; 6.29; 6.31; 6.64; 7.35–67; 7.71; 7.72; 7.74; 7.80; 7.83; 7.84; 7.89; 7.91; 7.92; c. 5; c. 10; c. 13; c. 16
Prudentius, 1.13; 1.51; 1.57; 1.64; 1.90
purity, 2.4; 2.17; 2.41; 2.48; 2.50; 2.54; 2.70; 4.57

quarreling, 4.1; 4.5; 4.17; 4.29–31; 4.33; 4.69; 4.70; 6.2; 6.7

resentment, 4.12; 4.26; 4.28; 4.34; 4.36–38; 4.64; 4.79
restlessness, 1.89; 3.2; 3.55; 5.9; 5.13; 5.40; 5.79; 5.96

sadness, 3.34; 3.36; 5.79; 6.33–56; 6.66; c. 10. *See also* death
Salvian, 2.25; 4.22
Satan, 1.27; 1.37; 1.82; 1.89; 2.9; 2.37; 3.66; 4.12; 4.57; 5.3; 5.11; 5.27; 5.47; 5.50; 5.92; 6.14–20; 6.25; 6.29; 6.30; 6.42; 6.53; 7.31; 7.47–51; 7.64; 7.98; c. 30
self-denial. *See* mortification
self-love, 2.3; c. 1
self-mastery, 1.12; 1.18; 1.19; 1.56–95; 2.19; 2.68; 4.57; 7.59
Shepherd of Hermas, The. See anonymous texts
silence, 7.3; 7.87
slander, 2.46; 3.8; 4.25; c. 15. *See also* gossip

sleep, excessive, 1.64; 5.3; 5.11; 5.13; 5.23; 5.37; 5.59; 5.70; 5.79; 5.94; c. 9
sloth, 1.15; 1.64; 2.56; 3.71; 4.40; 5.1–57; 5.62; 5.65; 5.66; 5.68; 5.69; 5.71–74; 5.79; 5.80; 5.83; 5.85; 5.86; 5.88; 5.93; 6.30; 6.35; 7.52; c. 9; c. 10; c. 13; c. 22
Solomon, 2.35; 3.79; 5.55; 5.71; 5.94; 6.25; 7.46
Stephen, 4.48; 4.77

temperance, 1.11; 1.46; 1.93; 1.39–73; 4.17; 7.90
Tertullian, 3.28; 3.47; 3.73; 4.19; 4.34; 4.64; c. 15
Theodore of Mopsuestia, 4.50
Theodoret of Cyrus, 1.24; 2.34; 5.83; 6.16
Thomas Aquinas, 2; 15; 17–19
treasure, 3.9; 3.38; 3.48; 3.61; 3.63; 3.71; 3.74; 4.44; 4.93; 5.24; 5.47; 6.66; 7.72

usury, 3.22; 3.23; 3.25; 3.46; 3.75

vainglory, 1.40; 7.1–35; 7.40; 7.78; 7.79; 7.82; 7.87; c. 9
Valerian, 4.70; 5.23; 5.91; 6.12
vanity, 3.13; 5.30; 7.18; 7.20; 7.26; 7.28; 7.31; 7.36; c. 7
vengeance, 4.4; 4.9–11; 4.26; 4.28; 4.72; 4.76; 4.77; 6.23; 6.43; c. 13; c. 22
vigils, 1.82; 5.23; 5.93; 5.94; 6.71; 6.74; 7.3; c. 2

work, 1.21; 1.32; 1.45; 1.68; 1.76; 2.4; 3.26; 3.60; 3.75; 5.6; 5.10; 5.34; 5.44; 5.48–73; 5.81; 5.87; 5.90; 5.91; 5.95; 6.36; 6.42; 6.65; 7.3; 7.64; 7.70; c. 9; c. 15
wrath. *See* anger